AA007123

First Workshop on Natural Language Processing for Indo-Aryan and Dravidian Languages (IndoNLP2025)

Abu Dhabi, United Arab Emirates
20 January 2025

ISBN: 979-8-3313-1369-2

Printed from e-media with permission by:

Curran Associates, Inc.
57 Morehouse Lane
Red Hook, NY 12571

CURRAN ASSOCIATES INC. proceedings.com

Some format issues inherent in the e-media version may also appear in this print version.

Copyright© (2025) by the Association for Computational Linguistics
All rights reserved.

Printed with permission by Curran Associates, Inc. (2026)

For permission requests, please contact the Association for Computational Linguistics
at the address below.

Association for Computational Linguistics
209 N. Eighth Street
Stroudsburg, Pennsylvania 18360

Phone: 1-570-476-8006
Fax: 1-570-476-0860

acl@aclweb.org

Additional copies of this publication are available from:

Curran Associates, Inc.
57 Morehouse Lane
Red Hook, NY 12571 USA
Phone: 845-758-0400
Fax: 845-758-2633
Email: curran@proceedings.com
Web: www.proceedings.com

IndoNLP 2025

Proceedings of the First Workshop on Natural Language Processing for Indo-Aryan and Dravidian Languages (IndoNLP2025)

Proceedings of the Workshop

January 20, 2025

©2025 The Association for Computational Linguistics

Order copies of this and other ACL proceedings from:

Association for Computational Linguistics (ACL)
209 N. Eighth Street
Stroudsburg, PA 18360
USA
Tel: +1-570-476-8006
Fax: +1-570-476-0860
acl@aclweb.org

The workshop is supported in part by the Informatics Institute of Technology, Colombo, Sri Lanka

Preface

The rapid advancement of Natural Language Processing (NLP) and Large Language Models (LLMs) has transformed the landscape of computational linguistics. However, Indo-Aryan and Dravidian Languages (IADL), which represent a significant portion of South Asia's linguistic heritage, remain under-resourced and under-researched in these technological developments. This workshop aims to bridge this gap by bringing together researchers, linguists, and technologists to focus on the unique challenges and opportunities. Participants will explore innovative methods for creating and annotating digital corpora, develop speech and language technologies suited to IADL, and promote interdisciplinary collaborations. By leveraging LLMs, we seek to address the complexities of syntax, morphology, and semantics in these languages to enhance the performance of NLP applications. Furthermore, the workshop will provide a platform for sharing best practices, tools, and resources, enhancing the digital infrastructure necessary for language preservation. Through collaborative efforts, we aim to build a research community to advance NLP for IADL, contributing to linguistic diversity and cultural preservation in the digital age.

In parallel with the workshop, we have also organised a shared task to address key challenges in transliteration for Indian languages. The primary objectives of the shared task are to develop a real-time transliterator, effectively manage linguistic variations, and improve typing accuracy. A significant focus of the task is on enabling the transliterator to handle ad-hoc transliterations, which involve short typing scripts and diverse typing patterns, with or without vowel combinations. This initiative aims to create a robust transliteration system that accommodates the dynamic and complex nature of typing practices in Indian languages.

We received 27 submissions for the workshop and shared task. Following the review process, we accepted 15 papers and 4 shared task submissions to appear in the workshop proceedings.

The success of IndoNLP 2025 would not have been possible without the contributions of several exceptional individuals who supported this initiative. First and foremost, we extend our heartfelt gratitude to the authors who submitted their work to the workshop, driving forward research in low-resource languages across diverse areas of study. We are equally thankful to the program committee members, whose dedicated efforts were instrumental to the success of this workshop. Their timely engagement in the review process and constructive feedback not only enhanced the quality of the submissions but also ensured that the papers met the highest academic standards. Moreover we would like to thank to Prof. Pushpak Bhattacharyya for accepting our invitation to be as the keynote speaker in the workshop. Finally, we would like to express our sincere gratitude to the Informatics Institute of Technology, Colombo, for their generous sponsorship of the workshop. We are truly thankful to everyone who contributed to the success of IndoNLP 2025 through their invaluable support and encouragement.

Organizing Committee

Ruvan Weerasinghe,Informatics Institute of Technology, Sri Lanka
Isuri Anuradha, Lancaster University, UK
Deshan Sumanathilaka, Swansea University, UK
Mo El-Haj, Lancaster University, UK
Chamila Liyanage, University of Colombo School of Computing, Sri Lanka
Fahad Khan, Istituto di Linguistica Computazionale in CNR, Italy
Andrew Hardie, Lancaster University, UK
Asim Abbas, Birmingham University, UK
Ruslan Mitkov Lancaster University, UK
Paul Rayson, Lancaster University, UK
Julian Hough, Swansea University, UK
Nicholas Micallef, Swansea University, UK
Naomi Krishnarajah, Informatics Institute of Technology, Sri Lanka

Program Committee

Abdullah Alzahrani, Swansea University, Wales, UK
Abdul Nazeer, National Institute of Technology, Calicut, India
Arka Majhi, Indian Institute of Technology, Bombay, India
Anand Kumar, National Institute of Technology, Karnataka, India
Asanka Wasala, Dell Technologies, Ireland
Arjumand Younus, University College Dublin, Ireland
Ayush Agarwal, Walmart, USA
Dulip Herath, Queensland University, Australia
Daisy Lal, Lancaster University, UK
Damith Premasiri, Lancaster University, UK
Gayanath Chandrasena, University of Helsinki, Finland
Girish Nath Jha, School for Sanskrit and Indic Studies, JNU, India
Jiby Mariya Jose, Indian Institute of Information Technology, India
Kishorjit Nongmeikapam, Indian Institute of Information Technology (IIIT) Manipur, India
Kengatharaiyer Sarveswaran, University of Jaffna, Sri Lanka
Kaza Sri Sai Swaroop, IBM, India
Lochandaka Ranathunga, University of Moratuwa, Sri Lanka
Nishantha Medagoda, Auckland University of Technology, New Zealand
Pabitra Mitra, Indian Institute of Technology, Kharagpur, India
Prasan Yapa, Kyoto University of Advance Science, Japan
Pumudu Fernando,Informatics Institute of Technology, Sri Lanka
Randil Pushpanandha, University of Colombo, Sri Lanka
Saman Galgodage, Swansea University, UK
Sinnathamby Mahesan, University of Jaffna, Sri Lanka
Torin Wirasinghe,Informatics Institute of Technology, Sri Lanka
Tanmoy Chakraborty, Indian Institute of Technology, Delhi, India
Tirthankar Dasgupta, Indian Institute of Technology, Kharagpur, India
Venkatesh Raju, Stealth Mode AI Startup, India

Table of Contents

Conference Program

8.45–9.00 **Opening Remark**

9.00–10.00 **Keynote Speech**

Theme: Language Processing and Evaluation

10.00–10.15 *Crossing Language Boundaries: Evaluation of Large Language Models on Urdu-English Question Answering*
Samreen kazi, Maria Rahim and Shakeel Ahmed Khoja

10.15–10.30 *Hindi Reading Comprehension: Do Large Language Models Exhibit Semantic Understanding?*
Daisy Monika Lal, Paul Rayson and Mo El-Haj

Coffee Break

11.00–11.15 *Machine Translation and Transliteration for Indo-Aryan Languages: A Systematic Review*
Sandun Sameera Perera and Deshan Koshala Sumanathilaka

11.15–11.30 *Investigating the Effect of Backtranslation for Indic Languages*
Sudhansu Bala Das, Samujjal Choudhury, Dr Tapas Kumar Mishra and Dr Bidyut Kr Patra

11.30–11.45 *BERTopic for Topic Modeling of Hindi Short Texts: A Comparative Study*
Atharva Mutsaddi, Anvi Jamkhande, Aryan Shirish Thakre and Yashodhara Haribhakta

11.45–12.00 *Evaluating Structural and Linguistic Quality in Urdu DRS Parsing and Generation through Bidirectional Evaluation*
Muhammad Saad Amin, Luca Anselma and Alessandro Mazzei

12.00–12.15 *Studying the Effect of Hindi Tokenizer Performance on Downstream Tasks*
Rashi Goel and Fatiha Sadat

12.15–12.30 *Adapting Multilingual LLMs to Low-Resource Languages using Continued Pre-training and Synthetic Corpus: A Case Study for Hindi LLMs*
Raviraj Joshi, Kanishk Singla, Anusha Kamath, Raunak Kalani, Rakesh Paul, Utkarsh Vaidya, Sanjay Singh Chauhan, Niranjan Wartikar and Eileen Long

12.30–12.45 *OVQA: A Dataset for Visual Question Answering and Multimodal Research in Odia Language*
Shantipriya Parida, Shashikanta Sahoo, Sambit Sekhar, Kalyanamalini Sahoo, Ketan Kotwal, Sonal Khosla, Satya Ranjan Dash, Aneesh Bose, Guneet Singh Kohli, Smruti Smita Lenka and Ondřej Bojar

12.45–13.00 *Advancing Multilingual Speaker Identification and Verification for Indo-Aryan and Dravidian Languages*
Braveenan Sritharan and Uthayasanker Thayasivam

13.00–14.00 Lunch Break

Theme: Applications and Societal Impact: Applying NLP to Real-World Problems and Societal Challenges

14.00–14.15 *Sentiment Analysis of Sinhala News Comments Using Transformers*
Isuru Bandaranayake and Hakim Usoof

14.15–14.30 *ExMute: A Context-Enriched Multimodal Dataset for Hateful Memes*
Riddhiman Swanan Debnath, Nahian Beente Firuj, Abdul Wadud Shakib, Sadia Sultana and Md Saiful Islam

14.30–14.45 *Studying the capabilities of Large Language Models in solving Combinatorics Problems posed in Hindi*
Yash Kumar and Subhajit Roy

14.45–15.00 *From Scarcity to Capability: Empowering Fake News Detection in Low-Resource Languages with LLMs*
Hrithik Majumdar Shibu, Shrestha Datta, Md. Sumon Miah, Nasrullah Sami, Mahruba Sharmin Chowdhury and Md Saiful Islam

15.00–15.15 *Enhancing Participatory Development Research in South Asia through LLM Agents System: An Empirically-Grounded Methodological Initiative from Field Evidence in Sri Lankan*
Xinjie Zhao, Hao Wang, Shyaman Maduranga Sriwarnasinghe, Jiacheng Tang, Shiyun Wang, Sayaka Sugiyama and So Morikawa

15.15–15.30 *Identifying Aggression and Offensive Language in Code-Mixed Tweets: A Multi-Task Transfer Learning Approach*
Bharath Kancharla, Prabhjot Singh, Lohith Bhagavan Kancharla, Yashita Chama and Raksha Sharma

15.30–16.00 Coffee Break

Shared Task Discussion

Team IndiDataMiner at IndoNLP 2025: Hindi Back Transliteration - Roman to Devanagari using LLaMa
Saurabh Kumar, Dhruvkumar Babubhai Kakadiya and Sanasam Ranbir Singh

IndoNLP 2025 Shared Task: Romanized Sinhala to Sinhala Reverse Transliteration Using BERT
Sandun Sameera Perera, Lahiru Prabhath Jayakodi, Deshan Koshala Sumanathilaka and Isuri Anuradha

Sinhala Transliteration: A Comparative Analysis Between Rule-based and Seq2Seq Approaches
Widanalage Mario Yomal De Mel, Kasun Imesha Wickramasinghe, Nisansa de Silva and Surangika Dayani Ranathunga

Romanized to Native Malayalam Script Transliteration Using an Encoder-Decoder Framework
Bajiyo Baiju, Kavya Manohar, Leena G. Pillai and Elizabeth Sherly

Final Remark

Hindi Reading Comprehension: Do Large Language Models Exhibit Semantic Understanding?

Daisy Monika Lal[1], Paul Rayson[1], Mo El-Haj[1]
[1]School of Computing and Communications, Lancaster University, UK.
Correspondence: d.m.lal@lancaster.ac.uk

Abstract

In this study, we explore the performance of four advanced Generative AI models—GPT-3.5, GPT-4, Llama3, and HindiGPT, for the Hindi reading comprehension task. Using a zero-shot, instruction-based prompting strategy, we assess model responses through a comprehensive triple evaluation framework using the HindiRC dataset. Our framework combines (1) automatic evaluation using ROUGE, BLEU, BLEURT, METEOR, and Cosine Similarity; (2) rating-based assessments focussing on correctness, comprehension depth, and informativeness; and (3) preference-based selection to identify the best responses[1]. Human ratings indicate that GPT-4 outperforms the other LLMs on all parameters, followed by HindiGPT, GPT-3.5, and then Llama3. Preference-based evaluation similarly placed GPT-4 (80%) as the best model, followed by HindiGPT(74%). However, automatic evaluation showed GPT-4 to be the lowest performer on n-gram metrics, yet the best performer on semantic metrics, suggesting it captures deeper meaning and semantic alignment over direct lexical overlap, which aligns with its strong human evaluation scores. This study also highlights that even though the models mostly address literal factual recall questions with high precision, they still face the challenge of specificity and interpretive bias at times.

1 Introduction

Machine reading comprehension (MRC) in Natural Language Processing (NLP) is the task of making machines retrieve or generate precise and contextually relevant answers from a specific question and a body of text(Chen, 2018; Liu et al., 2019; Baradaran et al., 2022). It has numerous real-world applications, ranging from search engines to educational tools and domain-specific conversational agents or chatbots (Qiu et al., 2019; Baradaran et al., 2022; Kazi et al., 2023). MRC involves understanding the underlying context and is extremely challenging as it requires complex cognitive capabilities like summarising, sequencing, inferencing, and comparing and contrasting facts presented in the given text (Khashabi et al., 2018; Gardner et al., 2019; Sun, 2021). While NLP has seen significant advancements for widely spoken languages, much of the research has left low-resource languages like Hindi underexplored, especially for complex tasks such as MRC. (Jing and Xiong, 2020; Nguyen et al., 2022; Lal et al., 2022).

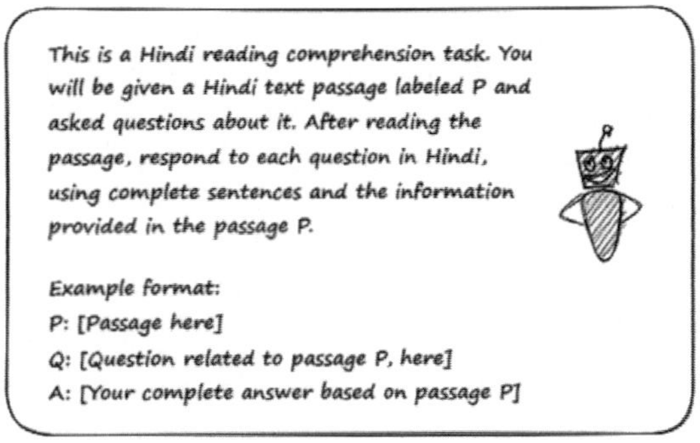

Figure 1: Instruction-Based Prompting Strategy for Hindi MRC.

Hindi, the fourth most-spoken language globally (Yadav, 2023), has witnessed major breakthroughs in NLP technologies in recent years. Nevertheless, as large language models (LLMs) emerge as the cornerstone of NLP research, it is essential to ask: How well do these models understand Hindi? While LLMs perform admirably on surface-level tasks like text generation, text classification, and machine translation (Parida et al., 2024) that do not always require in-depth analysis of comprehension; MRC, that involves nuanced understanding of context, factual information, and reasoning, can serve as a benchmark for assess-

[1]Human annotations available at `https://github.com/dml2611/HindiMRC`.

Proceedings of the First Workshop on Natural Language Processing for Indo-Aryan and Dravidian Languages (IndoNLP2025), pages 1–10
January 20, 2025. ©2025 Association for Computational Linguistics

ing the comprehension abilities of these models for Hindi texts.

In this study, we investigate the performance of four prominent LLMs—GPT-3.5 (Winata et al., 2021), GPT-4 (Ai et al., 2023), HindiGPT[2], and Llama3 (Dubey et al., 2024)—to uncover how well these models perform on Hindi reading comprehension tasks—not just in terms of accurate answers, but the limits of their comprehension and informativeness. To assess the performance of each model, we conducted both automatic and human evaluations (rating-based and preference-based), as shown in Figure 2. The automatic evaluations provide a quantitative assessment of the models, while the human evaluations enable a qualitative assessment of each model's responses. This extensive study allows us to investigate and emphasize where these models thrive and where they fall short, as well as where they need to catch up to human comprehension.

The rest of the paper is organized as follows. Section 2 presents prior Related Work; Section 3 outlines the Methodology; Section 4 states the results, followed by the conclusions and limitations in Sections 5 and 5.

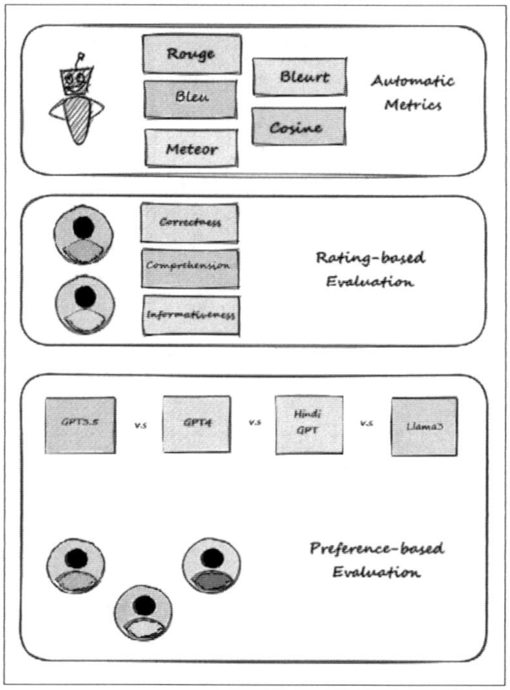

Figure 2: Triple evaluation framework for assessing Hindi reading comprehension in LLMs using automatic and human evaluation methods.

2 Related Work

Researchers in the field of NLP consistently highlight the resource limitations that hinder the development of effective question-answering (QA) systems for low-resource languages such as Hindi (Maddu and Sanapala, 2024; Kumari and Shivhare, 2023; Chaudhari et al., 2024). The scarcity of high-quality, annotated datasets and linguistic tools specifically tailored for Hindi is a significant barrier. State-of-the-art QA models, like BERT and GPT, rely on extensive gold-standard corpora to produce accurate and robust results. However, for Hindi, the availability of such resources remains limited, creating a gap in model performance (Nanda et al., 2016; GUPTA and KHADE, 2020; Khurana et al., 2024). Existing models and datasets are primarily designed for tasks involving short answer spans or multiple-choice responses, which restricts their flexibility.

Another significant challenge is the constrained context length used during model training, primarily due to computational costs associated with handling large amounts of text (Kumar et al., 2022). As a result, the models struggle to grasp the linguistic subtleties of Hindi, such as syntax and morphology, which can reduce overall performance (Ray et al., 2018; Anuranjana, 2021). The complexity of Hindi is further increased by distinct syntactic structures, numerous semantic variants, and prevalent code-mixing (Hindi-English hybrids) in written and spoken forms, add further barriers to QA development (Viswanathan et al., 2019). However, LLMs have shown significant potential in handling diverse languages and can flexibly adapt to code-mixed texts (Brown, 2020; Conneau, 2019; Raffel et al., 2020; Chung et al., 2024), making them potentially valuable tools to address Hindi NLP challenges, like reading comprehension.

3 Methods

In order to examine the comprehension abilities of GPT-3.5, GPT-4, HindiGPT, and Llama3 for Hindi texts, the LLMs were directed to complete the Hindi MRC task using instruction-based prompting on the HindiRC[3] dataset, as described in Sections 3.1 and 3.2, respectively. We evaluated the

[2] *HindiGPT* available at `https://chatgpt.com/g/g-oKGVbNtmC-hindi-gpt`

[3] *HindiRC* available at `https://github.com/erzaliator/HindiRC-Data`

Table 1: LLM responses to Hindi reading comprehension highlighting the challenge of Literal vs. Interpretive Bias.

Passage: जब वह बहुत छोटा था, तभी उसने संयोग(coincidence) से किले का गुप्त(hidden) द्वार(entrance) खोज(found) लिया था। लेकिन न उसने किसी को बताया था और न ही इसके बारे में किसी और को पता था। बस, वह जब चाहे गुप्त(hidden) मार्ग(path) से किले में जा पहुँचता और खेल–कूदकर उसी रास्ते से वापस आ जाता। इस गुप्त(hidden) मार्ग(path) की जानकारी के बिना इस किले पर चढ़ाई करना अत्यंत कठिन था। बालू समझ गया था कि शिवाजी ने इसीलिए इसे अपना गढ़ बनाया, क्योंकि वह इस तरह बना हुआ था कि कोई भी शत्रु इसपर अचानक आक्रमण नहीं कर सकता था। When he was very young, he accidentally discovered the secret entrance of the fort. However, he didn't tell anyone, and no one else knew about it either. So, whenever he wanted, he would go to the fort through the secret route, play around, and return the same way. Without knowledge of this secret path, climbing this fort was extremely difficult. Balu understood that Shivaji had chosen it as his stronghold for this reason, as it was built in such a way that no enemy could launch a sudden attack on it.		
Question	बालू ने क्या रहस्य जान लिया था ? What secret did Balu know??	
GPT-3.5	बालू ने रहस्य जान लिया था कि शिवाजी ने इस किले को इस तरह बनाया था कि कोई भी शत्रु इसपर अचानक आक्रमण नहीं कर सकता था। Balu discovered the secret that Shivaji had built this fort in such a way that no enemy could launch a sudden attack on it.	$\mathcal{C}_o = 1.5$ $\mathcal{C}_h = 1.5$ $\mathcal{I}_f = 1.5$
GPT-4	बालू ने यह रहस्य जान लिया था कि शिवाजी ने किले को अपना गढ़ इसलिए बनाया था क्योंकि इसकी संरचना ऐसी थी कि कोई भी शत्रु इसपर अचानक आक्रमण नहीं कर सकता था। Balu discovered the secret that Shivaji had made the fort his stronghold because its structure was such that no enemy could launch a sudden attack on it.	$\mathcal{C}_o = 1.5$ $\mathcal{C}_h = 1.5$ $\mathcal{I}_f = 1.5$
HindiGPT	बालू ने किले का गुप्त द्वार खोजने का रहस्य जान लिया था। Balu discovered the secret of finding the fort's secret entrance.	$\mathcal{C}_o = 4.0$ $\mathcal{C}_h = 4.0$ $\mathcal{I}_f = 4.0$
Llama3	बालू ने किले का गुप्त द्वार खोज लिया था। Balu discovered the secret entrance of the fort.	$\mathcal{C}_o = 5.0$ $\mathcal{C}_h = 5.0$ $\mathcal{I}_f = 5.0$

performances of the LLMs using both automatic and human assessments, as described in Section 3.3.

3.1 Prompting Strategy

We adopted the zero-shot, instruction-based prompting strategy to evaluate the generalization abilities of the LLMs on the Hindi MRC challenge in a zero-shot setting. All four LLMs were given the same prompt, as shown in Figure 1. This strategy taps into the pre-trained knowledge of the LLM without requiring any task-specific fine-tuning. The structured guidance through explicit instructions directs the LLM on how to carry out a task, even if it hasn't seen it before (Schick and Schütze, 2021; Liu et al., 2023; Chen et al., 2024). Moreover, the instruction template (Passage P, Question Q, Answer A) helps to standardize responses across all LLMs (see Tables 1, 6), enabling direct comparison of performance.

3.2 Dataset

The HindiRC dataset (Anuranjana et al., 2019) is a collection of 24 Hindi reading comprehension passages assembled from two educational websites, Sandeep Barouli[4] and 2classnotes[5]. It comprises 127 questions with corresponding single-sentence answers, manually selected from the passage by the annotator.

[4] *Sandeep Barouli* available at https://sandeepbarouli.com/

[5] *2classnotes* available at https://www.2classnotes.com/

Table 2: The Rating Scale for Human Evaluation. This rating scale grades LLM responses on three criteria: correctness, comprehension depth, and informativeness, with grades ranging from 1 to 5.

Correctness (Factual and Logical Accuracy)	
5 - Entirely correct	no factual errors or inconsistencies.
4 - Mostly correct	minor inaccuracies that don't significantly affect meaning.
3 - Partially correct	contains few inaccuracies that slightly affect meaning.
2 - Mostly incorrect	significant factual or logical errors that compromise accuracy.
1 - Incorrect	fails to address the question with any factual or logical accuracy.
Comprehension (Depth of Understanding)	
5 - Deep understanding	captures nuances and underlying meanings.
4 - Good understanding	covers key concepts though minor details may be missed.
3 - Basic understanding	general answer, missing some deeper context or meaning.
2 - Limited understanding	simplistic or surface-level answer, with key misinterpretations.
1 - No understanding	fails to grasp the main idea or gives an irrelevant answer.
Informativeness (Coverage of Essential Points)	
5 - Fully informative	includes all essential points and relevant details.
4 - Mostly informative	covers most key points, with minor oversights.
3 - Moderately informative	includes some key points but misses several important details.
2 - Minimally informative	misses many important details.
1 - Not informative	fails to include any essential points or details.

Table 3: This table illustrates the scores for automatic evaluation metrics, ROUGE, BLEU, BLEURT, METEOR, and Cosine Similarity (CoS). Here, R1 F1, R2 F1, and RL F1 refer to ROUGE-1 F1, ROUGE-2 F1, and ROUGE-L F1 Scores, respectively.

	Metric	GPT-3.5	GPT-4	HindiGPT	Llama3
n-gram matching	**R1 F1**	0.540	0.512	0.540	0.533
	R2 F1	0.405	0.401	0.404	0.433
	RL F1	0.510	0.494	0.515	0.516
	BLEU	0.348	0.317	0.358	0.373
semantic similarity	**BLEURT**	0.530	0.431	0.497	0.458
	METEOR	0.515	0.516	0.507	0.508
	CoS	0.922	0.924	0.924	0.914

3.3 Evaluation Strategy

The evaluation setup includes seven automatic metrics and three human evaluation rating scales. We also use preference-based human evaluation to gain additional insights into human preferences.

3.3.1 Automatic Assessment

The automatic assessment was carried out using five different metrics: 1) ROUGE (Lin, 2004) predominantly assesses recall by calculating overlapping n-grams (ROUGE-1), word pairs (ROUGE-2), and word sequences (ROUGE-L), between machine-generated and reference responses. 2) BLEU (Papineni et al., 2002) compares the n-grams in the machine-generated response to those in the reference response. Typically used in translation, but can also assess how effectively a machine-generated response captures the key terms. 3) BLEURT (Sellam et al., 2020) is a learned metric that addresses the shortcomings of conventional n-gram-based metrics like BLEU and ROUGE. It leverages a pre-trained transformer model to determine the semantic similarity between machine-generated and reference responses. 4) METEOR (Banerjee and Lavie, 2005) measures semantic similarity using synonyms, stemming, and partial matches, and has a high correlation with human judgment. 5) Cosine Similarity (CoS) (Rahutomo et al., 2012) compares model-generated responses to reference answers using word embeddings, judging similarity in sense rather than precise word

Table 4: Preference-based selection results for three annotators $\mathcal{H}_1$, $\mathcal{H}_2$, and $\mathcal{H}_3$.

	GPT-3.5	GPT-4	HindiGPT	Llama3
$\mathcal{H}_1$	75%	75%	73%	65%
$\mathcal{H}_2$	73%	83%	75%	68%
$\mathcal{H}_3$	68%	83%	73%	68%
Avg	**72%**	**80%**	**74%**	**67%**

match. We employed FastText Hindi[6] embeddings to compute CoS.

3.3.2 Human Evaluation

Two human evaluators rated responses based on correctness, comprehension depth, and informativeness. Another set of three evaluators determined the best responses based on overall preferences. All evaluations were conducted on a randomly selected set of 40 questions from eight distinct passages.

a) Rating-based Evaluation or (Likert-rating) involves grading each response individually based on predefined criteria, such as correctness, comprehension, and informativeness (described in Table 2). This strategy allows evaluators to express the extent to which each criterion is met. Correctness ensures factual and logical accuracy, which is fundamental to comprehension quality. Comprehension measures the depth of understanding, indicating whether the LLM genuinely understands the underlying context rather than providing shallow responses. Informativeness evaluates the information coverage, ensuring that important facts and nuances are not overlooked.

b) Preference-based Selection (or Best-Answer Selection) This approach requires assessors to select the answers they find most satisfactory among the provided options. This method offers a more precise indication of which models consistently generate higher-quality responses, allowing for a direct assessment of performance based on the overall quality of response.

4 Results

The overall results of human and automatic evaluations, along with the inter-rater reliability, are covered in Sections 4.1, 4.2, and 4.3, respectively.

4.1 Automatic Assessment

The results of the automatic assessment (Table 3) demonstrate that GPT-3.5 (BLEURT = 0.530, CoS = 0.922) and GPT-4 (BLEURT = 0.431, CoS = 0.924) score better on semantic metrics, suggesting that they prioritize meaning over exact wording and structure. This indicates that for tasks seeking nuanced interpretation and linguistic mobility, these LLMs might be a preferable choice. HindiGPT consistently performs well across ROUGE (R1 F1 = 0.540, R2 F1 = 0.404, and RL F1 = 0.515), BLEU (0.358), and cosine similarity (0.924), demonstrating that it successfully captures meaning. This makes it suitable for tasks where semantic comprehension is essential. Llama3 exhibits notable word sequence and phrase-matching abilities, which could signify higher proficiency and coherence at the phrase-level. It also scores well in BLEU (0.373) and ROUGE metrics (R1 F1 = 0.533, R2 F1 = 0.433, and RL F1 = 0.516), suggesting that tasks where exact match is preferred to subtle understanding may be its ideal fit.

4.2 Human Assessment

The rating-based evaluation sheds light on how well each LLM performed for each metric, based on both annotators' ratings and the confidence intervals (CIs) around these ratings (see Table 5).

Correctness ($\mathcal{C}_o$): GPT-4 ($\mathcal{A}_1 = 4.725 \pm 0.029$ and $\mathcal{A}_2 = 4.700 \pm 0.035$) has the highest mean scores for both annotators, with very narrow CIs, signifying high precision and annotator confidence in ratings. HindiGPT scores ($\mathcal{A}_1 = 4.650 \pm 0.026$ and $\mathcal{A}_2 = 4.600 \pm 0.026$) fall closely behind GPT-4, implying good precision but slightly lower than GPT-4. GPT-3.5 ($\mathcal{A}_1 = 4.625 \pm 0.039$ and $\mathcal{A}_2 = 4.550 \pm 0.038$) and Llama3 ($\mathcal{A}_1 = 4.575 \pm 0.039$ and $\mathcal{A}_2 = 4.550 \pm 0.029$) have comparatively lower mean scores than GPT-4 and HindiGPT. Llama3 exhibited a wider CI, implying greater variation in the perception of

[6] *fasttext-hi-vectors* available at https://huggingface.co/facebook/fasttext-hi-vectors

Table 5: Human evaluation results for LLM performance across metrics (correctness ($\mathcal{C}_o$), comprehension ($\mathcal{C}_h$), and informativeness ($\mathcal{I}_f$)) with Mean Scores and Confidence Intervals for each model, alongside the Cohen's Kappa (κ) statistic for inter-annotator agreement between annotators $\mathcal{A}_1$ and $\mathcal{A}_2$.

		GPT-3.5	**GPT-4**	**HindiGPT**	**Llama3**
$\mathcal{A}_1$	$\mathcal{C}_o$	4.625 ± 0.039	4.725 ± 0.029	4.650 ± 0.026	4.575 ± 0.039
	$\mathcal{C}_h$	4.620 ± 0.039	4.775 ± 0.034	4.650 ± 0.027	4.600 ± 0.039
	$\mathcal{I}_f$	4.525 ± 0.041	4.750 ± 0.028	4.650 ± 0.028	4.550 ± 0.041
$\mathcal{A}_2$	$\mathcal{C}_o$	4.550 ± 0.038	4.700 ± 0.035	4.600 ± 0.026	4.550 ± 0.029
	$\mathcal{C}_h$	4.625 ± 0.036	4.850 ± 0.032	4.675 ± 0.027	4.450 ± 0.036
	$\mathcal{I}_f$	4.575 ± 0.033	4.750 ± 0.034	4.600 ± 0.028	4.450 ± 0.036
κ	$\mathcal{C}_o$	0.634	0.808	0.695	0.520
	$\mathcal{C}_h$	0.508	0.696	0.840	0.675
	$\mathcal{I}_f$	0.709	0.712	0.694	0.682

correctness.

Comprehension ($\mathcal{C}_h$): GPT-4 receives the highest scores for this measure, particularly from $\mathcal{A}_2 = 4.850 \pm 0.032$ ($\mathcal{A}_1 = 4.775 \pm 0.034$), signifying GPT-4's strong comprehension abilities, particularly with a low CI, suggesting annotators found its answers consistently comprehensive. HindiGPT performs well too, scoring $\mathcal{A}_1 = 4.650 \pm 0.027$ and $\mathcal{A}_2 = 4.675 \pm 0.027$, with consistently high comprehension scores, although slightly lower than GPT-4. GPT-3.5 ($\mathcal{A}_1 = 4.620 \pm 0.039$ a and $\mathcal{A}_2 = 4.625 \pm 0.036$) and Llama3 ($\mathcal{A}_1 = 4.600 \pm 0.039$ and $\mathcal{A}_2 = 4.450 \pm 0.036$) yield slightly lower scores. Llama3 has a lower comprehension score, demonstrating some variation in perceived comprehension quality.

Informativeness ($\mathcal{C}_o$): GPT-4 obtains the highest scores ($\mathcal{A}_1 = 4.750 \pm 0.028$ and $\mathcal{A}_2 = 4.750 \pm 0.034$), suggesting strong information coverage in responses. HindiGPT ($\mathcal{A}_1 = 4.650 \pm 0.028$ and $\mathcal{A}_2 = 4.600 \pm 0.028$) follows GPT-4, exhibiting adequate but slightly less information coverage. GPT-3.5 ($\mathcal{A}_1 = 4.525 \pm 0.041$ and $\mathcal{A}_2 = 4.575 \pm 0.033$) has slightly lower scores than HindiGPT, indicating that it may overlook a few crucial details. Llama3 scores the lowest, implying having the least information coverage and some fluctuation in perceived quality.

Preference-based evaluation (see Table 4) revealed that GPT-4 was consistently favoured by the three annotators, with an average score of 80%. Its high preference indicates that, in terms of human judgment, GPT-4's answers were relevant, demonstrating an excellent ability to provide accurate and consistent responses to questions. With an average score of 72%, GPT-3.5 was slightly lower than GPT-4 but still obtained significant preference, indicating that it might have occasionally fallen short of GPT-4. With a 74% average, HindiGPT performed in the competitive range of GPT-4 and around GPT-3.5. Its consistent ranking indicates that it offered replies that were linguistically and semantically appropriate. Llama3 received the lowest preference from the annotators, with an average of 67%.

4.3 Inter-Annotator Agreement

We apply Cohen's Kappa coefficient (κ) to gauge the inter-annotator agreement for rating-based evaluation (McHugh, 2012). We compute κ per metric for all question-answer pairs in the HindiRC evaluation set. Finally, we assess the reliability for each LLM separately to determine agreement per metric between evaluators (see Table 5).

Correctness ($\mathcal{C}_o$): GPT-4 (0.808) had the highest κ for correctness, while Llama3 (0.520) had the lowest. This suggests that GPT-4 responses were more reliable and easier for annotators to agree on. Annotators were relatively in agreement on the correctness of this GPT-3.5 (0.634) and HindiGPT (0.695) responses.

Comprehension ($\mathcal{C}_h$): HindiGPT (0.840) obtained the highest κ for comprehension, suggesting that the responses were generated with in-depth understanding of the context that leads to accurate answers. In contrast, GPT-3.5 (0.508)

Table 6: LLM responses to Hindi reading comprehension highlighting the challenge of fact recall and specificity in responses.

Passage: अमीर खुसरो न केवल साधारण जन के लिए कविताएँ लिखते थे, बल्कि उस समय के बादशाहों की प्रशंसा में भी शायरी लिखते थे। वे युद्ध में भी भाग लेते थे और रण क्षेत्र में अपनी बहादुरी का जौहर भी दिखलाते थे। उनकी कविता और वीरता से प्रभावित होकर अनेक बादशाहों ने उन्हें अपने दरबार में रखा। इस प्रकार प्रजा से लेकर राजा तक अर्थात्झों पड़ी से लेकर महल तक अमीर खुसरो की प्रसिद्धि फैल गई। उनकी प्रसिद्धि का एक कारण उनका संगीतकार होना था। वे संगीत के ज्ञाता(expert in music) थे। उन्हें राग–रागिनियों का अच्छा ज्ञान(knowledge) था और उन्होंने कई राग–रागिनियों की रचना भी की। Amir Khusro not only wrote poems for the common people but also composed poetry in praise of the kings of his time. He participated in wars and displayed his bravery on the battlefield as well. Impressed by his poetry and valor, many kings kept him in their courts. Thus, Amir Khusro's fame spread from the common folk to royalty, from humble huts to grand palaces. One reason for his fame was his talent as a musician. He was a knowledgeable musician. He had a good knowledge of Raga-Raginis. He also composed many Raga-Raginis.		
Question	अमीर खुसरो किसके ज्ञानी माने जाते थे ? Amir Khusro was considered knowledgeable in what?	
GPT-3.5	अमीर खुसरो संगीत के ज्ञाता माने जाते थे। Amir Khusro was considered knowledgeable in music.	$\mathcal{C}_o = 5.0$ $\mathcal{C}_h = 4.5$ $\mathcal{I}_f = 4.0$
GPT-4	अमीर खुसरो संगीत के ज्ञानी माने जाते थे, उन्हें राग–रागिनियों का अच्छा ज्ञान था और उन्होंने कई राग–रागिनियों की रचना भी की। Amir Khusro was considered knowledgeable in music; he had a deep understanding of Raga-Raginis and also composed many Raga-Raginis.	$\mathcal{C}_o = 5.0$ $\mathcal{C}_h = 5.0$ $\mathcal{I}_f = 5.0$
HindiGPT	अमीर खुसरो राग–रागिनियों के ज्ञानी माने जाते थे। Amir Khusro was considered knowledgeable in Raga-Raginis.	$\mathcal{C}_o = 3.0$ $\mathcal{C}_h = 3.0$ $\mathcal{I}_f = 3.0$
Llama3	अमीर खुसरो संगीत के ज्ञानी माने जाते थे, उन्हें राग–रागिनियों का अच्छा ज्ञान था। Amir Khusro was considered knowledgeable in music; he had a good understanding of Raga-Raginis.	$\mathcal{C}_o = 5.0$ $\mathcal{C}_h = 5.0$ $\mathcal{I}_f = 5.0$

showed moderate agreement, indicating a degree of variability in perceived comprehension quality. GPT-4 (0.696) and Llama3 (0.675) showed substantial agreement, indicating that annotators were generally aligned.

Informativeness ($\mathcal{I}_f$): All models exhibited relatively similar kappa scores for informativeness, with substantial agreement across GPT-3.5 (0.709), GPT-4 (0.712), HindiGPT (0.694), and Llama3 (0.682). This consistency indicates that informativeness was relatively straightforward to assess, resulting in consistent alignment amongst annotators.

5 Conclusion

In this study, we use a novel triple assessment framework to compare the performance profiles of LLMs, GPT-3.5, GPT-4, Llama3, and HindiGPT for Hindi reading comprehension. The ability of GPT-4 to generate contextually relevant and meaningful responses is demonstrated by its preference rating of 80%, which consistently outperformed competing models across all human-evaluated metrics—correctness, comprehension depth, and informativeness. With competitive scores, particularly in correctness and comprehension, HindiGPT and GPT-3.5 trailed closely behind. GPT-3.5 was somewhat preferred above HindiGPT for perceived understanding and precise responses.

The results of automatic evaluations presented a contrasting picture, indicating fewer exact matches with reference texts, particularly for GPT-4 with lower n-gram metric scores (ROUGE and BLEU). The high human evaluation scores of GPT-4 are consistent with its superior alignment with the underlying meaning as measured by semantic metrics (BLEURT and Cosine Similarity), which show a greater grasp of the text than surface-level similarity. This comparison of automatic and human evaluations highlights the significance of semantic-based metrics and human evaluations for precisely assessing the level of a LLM's comprehension, particularly in non-English languages like Hindi.

Limitations

Our research reveals limitations in some of the metrics which do not align well with human assessment. As well as limitations of the domains or topics expressed within the dataset, our results are tied to the current versions of the four specific LLMs that we have used in our experiments. In future work, we will test other open-source models. In some cases, we find that models have a tendency to overinform in their answers, and we will investigate further techniques to reduce this.

Literal vs. Interpretive Responses: In Table 1, the question "*What secret did Balu discover?*" seeks a factual answer about the "गुप्त द्वार""(*secret entrance*)." HindiGPT and Llama3 are more literal in answering the question, providing answers that adher to exact phrases from the passage. However, GPT-3.5 and GPT-4 misinterpret the question's focus and provide an interpretative response about the strategic purpose of the fort's design, showing an interpretive bias (Sheng et al., 2019; Bender et al., 2021). This disparity between question focus and model response arises because of the models' tendency to prioritize interpretations and contextual meaning over literal facts. The likelihood of LLMs adding extraneous information is a common issue with models in open-ended tasks (Koul, 2023).

Fact Recall and Specificity in Responses: In Table 6, in response to the question "*Amir Khusro was considered knowledgeable in what?*", the factual answer is संगीत(*music*), as the passage makes it abundantly evident that Khusro was an expert in music and that his knowledge of Raga-Raginis was a core reason for his fame. Yet, the models provided responses with varying degrees of specificity highlighting a gap in fact recall (Petroni et al., 2019). GPT-3.5 states that Amir Khusro was knowledgeable in music, but it omits the details of Raga-Raginis, giving a less comprehensive response. GPT-4 correctly mentions Amir Khusro's expertise of music and Raga-Raginis, and it also adds that he composed many of them. HindiGPT generates a partially correct response. It focuses on "Raga-Raginis" but omits the broader aspect of Amir Khusro's music knowledge, missing the broader context of his musical knowledge and his composition of them. Is informative but lacks the extra detail about his compositions. Llama3's provides a good amount of detail, mentioning both music and Raga-Raginis, but omits the fact that Amir Khusro composed them.

References

Lets Build Your Ai, Corporate Ai, and Restaurant Ai. 2023. Gpt-4 technical report. *arXiv preprint arXiv:2303.08774*.

Kaveri Anuranjana. 2021. *Towards building Question Answering Resources for Hindi*. Ph.D. thesis, International Institute of Information Technology Hyderabad.

Kaveri Anuranjana, Vijjini Rao, and Radhika Mamidi. 2019. Hindirc: a dataset for reading comprehension in hindi. In *0th International Conference on Computational Linguistics and Intelligent Text*.

Satanjeev Banerjee and Alon Lavie. 2005. Meteor: An automatic metric for mt evaluation with improved correlation with human judgments. In *Proceedings of the acl workshop on intrinsic and extrinsic evaluation measures for machine translation and/or summarization*, pages 65–72.

Razieh Baradaran, Razieh Ghiasi, and Hossein Amirkhani. 2022. A survey on machine reading comprehension systems. *Natural Language Engineering*, 28(6):683–732.

Emily M Bender, Timnit Gebru, Angelina McMillan-Major, and Shmargaret Shmitchell. 2021. On the dangers of stochastic parrots: Can language models be too big?□□. In *Proceedings of the 2021 ACM conference on fairness, accountability, and transparency*, pages 610–623.

Tom B Brown. 2020. Language models are few-shot learners. *arXiv preprint arXiv:2005.14165*.

Deepti A Chaudhari, Rahul Shrivastava, and Sanjeevkumar Angadi. 2024. A survey on conversational ai question answering system for low resource language. *Journal of Electrical Systems*, 20(6s):2531–2540.

Danqi Chen. 2018. *Neural reading comprehension and beyond*. Stanford University.

Jin Chen, Zheng Liu, Xu Huang, Chenwang Wu, Qi Liu, Gangwei Jiang, Yuanhao Pu, Yuxuan Lei, Xiaolong Chen, Xingmei Wang, et al. 2024. When large language models meet personalization: Perspectives of challenges and opportunities. *World Wide Web*, 27(4):42.

Hyung Won Chung, Le Hou, Shayne Longpre, Barret Zoph, Yi Tay, William Fedus, Yunxuan Li, Xuezhi Wang, Mostafa Dehghani, Siddhartha Brahma, et al. 2024. Scaling instruction-finetuned language models. *Journal of Machine Learning Research*, 25(70):1–53.

A Conneau. 2019. Unsupervised cross-lingual representation learning at scale. *arXiv preprint arXiv:1911.02116*.

Abhimanyu Dubey, Abhinav Jauhri, Abhinav Pandey, Abhishek Kadian, Ahmad Al-Dahle, Aiesha Letman, Akhil Mathur, Alan Schelten, Amy Yang, Angela Fan, et al. 2024. The llama 3 herd of models. *arXiv preprint arXiv:2407.21783*.

Matt Gardner, Jonathan Berant, Hannaneh Hajishirzi, Alon Talmor, and Sewon Min. 2019. On making reading comprehension more comprehensive. In *Proceedings of the 2nd Workshop on Machine Reading for Question Answering*, pages 105–112.

SOMIL GUPTA and NILESH KHADE. 2020. Bert based multilingual machine comprehension in english and hindi. *ACM Trans. Asian Low-Resour. Lang. Inf. Process*, 19(1).

Yimin Jing and Deyi Xiong. 2020. Effective strategies for low-resource reading comprehension. In *2020 International Conference on Asian Language Processing (IALP)*, pages 153–157. IEEE.

Samreen Kazi, Shakeel Khoja, and Ali Daud. 2023. A survey of deep learning techniques for machine reading comprehension. *Artificial Intelligence Review*, 56(Suppl 2):2509–2569.

Daniel Khashabi, Snigdha Chaturvedi, Michael Roth, Shyam Upadhyay, and Dan Roth. 2018. Looking beyond the surface: A challenge set for reading comprehension over multiple sentences. In *Proceedings of the 2018 Conference of the North American Chapter of the Association for Computational Linguistics: Human Language Technologies, Volume 1 (Long Papers)*, pages 252–262.

Khushboo Khurana, Rachita Bharambe, Hardik Dharmik, Krishna Rathi, and Mayur Rawte. 2024. A textual question answering and handwritten answer evaluation system for hindi language. *International Journal of Knowledge-based and Intelligent Engineering Systems*, 28(3):435–455.

Nimrita Koul. 2023. *Prompt Engineering for Large Language Models*. Nimrita Koul.

Shailender Kumar et al. 2022. Bert-based models' impact on machine reading comprehension in hindi and tamil. In *2022 4th International Conference on Advances in Computing, Communication Control and Networking (ICAC3N)*, pages 1458–1462. IEEE.

Pooja Kumari and Rakesh Shivhare. 2023. Study of various approaches used for machine reading comprehension in question answering systems. *International Journal of Technology Research and Management*.

Bechoo Lal, G Shivakanth, Arun Bhaskar, M Bhaskar, Ashish, and Deepak Kumar Panda. 2022. Critical review on machine reading comprehension (mrc) developments: From high resource to low resource languages. In *International Advanced Computing Conference*, pages 341–352. Springer.

Chin-Yew Lin. 2004. Rouge: A package for automatic evaluation of summaries. In *Text summarization branches out*, pages 74–81.

Pengfei Liu, Weizhe Yuan, Jinlan Fu, Zhengbao Jiang, Hiroaki Hayashi, and Graham Neubig. 2023. Pre-train, prompt, and predict: A systematic survey of prompting methods in natural language processing. *ACM Computing Surveys*, 55(9):1–35.

Shanshan Liu, Xin Zhang, Sheng Zhang, Hui Wang, and Weiming Zhang. 2019. Neural machine reading comprehension: Methods and trends. *Applied Sciences*, 9(18):3698.

Sandeep Maddu and Vizianandа Row Sanapala. 2024. A survey on nlp tasks, resources and techniques for low-resource telugu-english code-mixed text. *ACM Transactions on Asian and Low-Resource Language Information Processing*.

Mary L McHugh. 2012. Interrater reliability: the kappa statistic. *Biochemia medica*, 22(3):276–282.

Garima Nanda, Mohit Dua, and Krishma Singla. 2016. A hindi question answering system using machine learning approach. In *2016 international conference on computational techniques in information and communication technologies (ICCTICT)*, pages 311–314. IEEE.

Bach Hoang Tien Nguyen, Dung Manh Nguyen, and Trang Thi Thu Nguyen. 2022. Machine reading comprehension model for low-resource languages and experimenting on vietnamese. In *International Conference on Industrial, Engineering and Other Applications of Applied Intelligent Systems*, pages 370–381. Springer.

Kishore Papineni, Salim Roukos, Todd Ward, and Wei-Jing Zhu. 2002. Bleu: a method for automatic evaluation of machine translation. In *Proceedings of the 40th annual meeting of the Association for Computational Linguistics*, pages 311–318.

Shantipriya Parida, Shakshi Panwar, Kusum Lata, Sanskruti Mishra, and Sambit Sekhar. 2024. Building pre-train llm dataset for the indic languages: a case study on hindi. *arXiv preprint arXiv:2407.09855.*

Fabio Petroni, Tim Rocktäschel, Sebastian Riedel, Patrick Lewis, Anton Bakhtin, Yuxiang Wu, and Alexander Miller. 2019. Language models as knowledge bases? In *Proceedings of the 2019 Conference on Empirical Methods in Natural Language Processing and the 9th International Joint Conference on Natural Language Processing (EMNLP-IJCNLP)*. Association for Computational Linguistics.

Boyu Qiu, Xu Chen, Jungang Xu, and Yingfei Sun. 2019. A survey on neural machine reading comprehension. *arXiv e-prints*, pages arXiv–1906.

Colin Raffel, Noam Shazeer, Adam Roberts, Katherine Lee, Sharan Narang, Michael Matena, Yanqi Zhou, Wei Li, and Peter J Liu. 2020. Exploring the limits of transfer learning with a unified text-to-text transformer. *Journal of machine learning research*, 21(140):1–67.

Faisal Rahutomo, Teruaki Kitasuka, Masayoshi Aritsugi, et al. 2012. Semantic cosine similarity. In *The 7th international student conference on advanced science and technology ICAST*, volume 4, page 1. University of Seoul South Korea.

Santosh Kumar Ray, Amir Ahmad, and Khaled Shaalan. 2018. A review of the state of the art in hindi question answering systems. *Intelligent Natural Language Processing: Trends and Applications*, pages 265–292.

Timo Schick and Hinrich Schütze. 2021. Exploiting cloze-questions for few-shot text classification and natural language inference. In *Proceedings of the 16th Conference of the European Chapter of the Association for Computational Linguistics: Main Volume*, pages 255–269.

Thibault Sellam, Dipanjan Das, and Ankur Parikh. 2020. Bleurt: Learning robust metrics for text generation. In *Proceedings of the 58th Annual Meeting of the Association for Computational Linguistics*, pages 7881–7892.

Emily Sheng, Kai-Wei Chang, Prem Natarajan, and Nanyun Peng. 2019. The woman worked as a babysitter: On biases in language generation. In *Proceedings of the 2019 Conference on Empirical Methods in Natural Language Processing and the 9th International Joint Conference on Natural Language Processing (EMNLP-IJCNLP)*, pages 3407–3412.

Kai Sun. 2021. *Machine reading comprehension: challenges and approaches*. Cornell University.

Sujith Viswanathan, M Anand Kumar, and KP Soman. 2019. A comparative analysis of machine comprehension using deep learning models in code-mixed hindi language. *Recent Advances in Computational Intelligence*, pages 315–339.

Genta Indra Winata, Andrea Madotto, Zhaojiang Lin, Rosanne Liu, Jason Yosinski, and Pascale Fung. 2021. Language models are few-shot multilingual learners. In *Proceedings of the 1st Workshop on Multilingual Representation Learning*, pages 1–15.

Vinod Kumar Yadav. 2023. Impact of globalization on english and hindi languages: An analysis. *Anand Bihari*, page 230.

Machine Translation and Transliteration for Indo-Aryan Languages: A Systematic Review

Sameera Perera
Informatics Institute of Technology
Colombo 006
Sri Lanka
sameeraperera827@gmail.com

T.G.D.K. Sumanathilaka
Swansea University
Wales
United Kingdom
deshankoshala@gmail.com

Abstract

With the advent of Web 2.0, digital platforms have become increasingly multilingual. Non-English speakers are rapidly adopting their native languages on social media, highlighting the need for robust translation and transliteration models to facilitate effective communication. This systematic review paper provides an overview of recent machine translation and transliteration developments for Indo-Aryan languages spoken by a large South Asian population. The paper examines advancements in translation and transliteration systems for a few language pairs that have appeared in recently published papers in the last half a decade. The review summarizes the current state of these technologies, providing a worthwhile resource for anyone who is doing research in these fields to understand and find existing systems and techniques for translation and transliteration. The current challenges and limitations in the current systems are identified, and possible directions are suggested.

1 Introduction

The Indo-Aryan languages constitute a main branch of the Indo-European language family, predominantly spoken in Central and North India as well as in neighbouring countries such as Sri Lanka, Pakistan, Nepal, Maldives, Bangladesh and Bhutan (Pal and Zampieri, 2020). The large linguistic varieties within the Indo-Aryan language family make it challenging to communicate both outside and within the region. Machine translation and transliteration systems help to bridge language barrier,s enabling effective communication between different linguistic societies.

The goal of this review paper is to provide an overview of the current state of machine translation and transliteration techniques for Indo-Aryan languages. The review discusses diverse techniques used in the recently published translation and transliteration systems which handle the various scripts and linguistic features of Indo-Aryan languages.

The contribution of this study can be summarized as performing a systematic review of existing translation and transliteration techniques related to Indo-Aryan languages, highlighting the significant contributions and developments made by researchers in this constantly developing field. Going forward, the review is structured to clearly look into the recent developments in machine translation and transliteration for Indo-Aryan languages. Starting with the methodology explains how studies were selected based on their relevance. The following sections dive into various translation and transliteration approaches and outline the challenges faced in the field.

2 Methodology

A systematic approach was adopted in this review to choose the relevant studies on machine translation and transliteration for Indo-Aryan languages. A comprehensive search was conducted across several major academic databases, including IEEE Xplore and Google Scholar. In addition to the academic database searches, several key papers were identified from references cited in already published research, ensuring a wide-ranging collection of studies relevant to the focus of the review. Keywords such as "machine translation", "transliteration" and "Romanized languages" were used to identify relevant literature. To avoid redundancy, duplicate publications across different databases were identified and removed.

This review focused on papers published from 2018 to the available 2024 publications to ensure that the recent advancements were included. Studies were chosen based on the relevance to machine translation and transliteration within the context of Indo-Aryan languages. This review also includes

Proceedings of the First Workshop on Natural Language Processing for Indo-Aryan and Dravidian Languages (IndoNLP2025), pages 11–21
January 20, 2025. ©2025 Association for Computational Linguistics

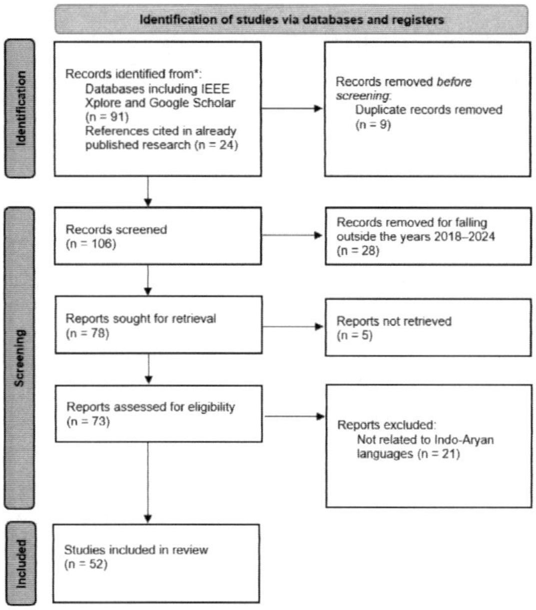

Figure 1: PRISMA Flow of the Paper Selection Process

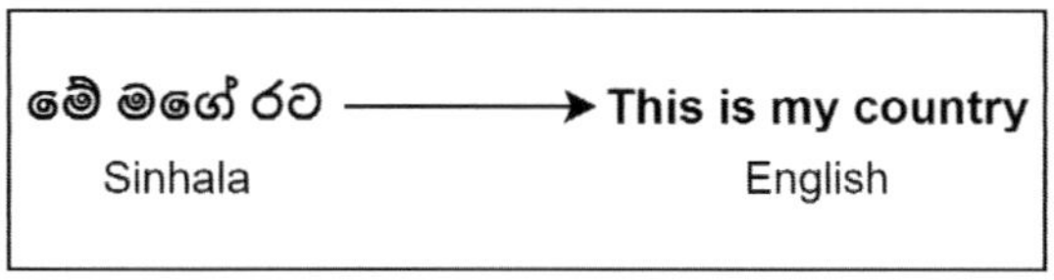

Figure 2: Sinhala to English Translation

papers that have proposed and utilized relevant techniques as part of their work while not directly focused on translation or transliteration. Specifically, the papers which proposed novel methodologies or made outstanding contributions to the field were prioritized. Figure 1 illustrates the systematic flow of the paper selection process.

3 Machine Translation (MT) and Transliteration

Machine Translation (MT) is the study of how to use machines to translate from a source language into another target language. This concept was first put forward by Warren Weaver in 1947 (Wang et al., 2022). From then on, MT has been one of the most challenging tasks in the natural language processing (NLP) field. Figure 2 is an example of machine translation between Sinhala and English.

Machine transliteration is the process of words transformation from one language into their phonetic equivalent of another. There are two types of machine transliteration: forward and backward transliteration. forward transliteration is the pro-

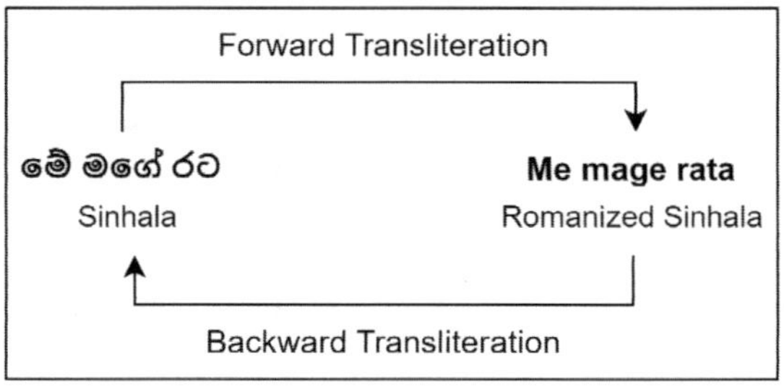

Figure 3: Forward and Backward Transliteration

cess of transliterating a word to a foreign language from the language from which it originated. On the other hand, when a word is converted back to the language of its origin from a foreign language, it is known as backward transliteration (Kaur and Garg, 2022). Figure 3 illustrates the difference between forward and backward transliteration using Romanized Sinhala.

4 Approaches in Machine translation and Transliteration

Many machine translation and transliteration systems have been implemented for Indo-Aryan languages. Since transliteration is considered a form of translation, both translation and transliteration systems have used similar approaches. The following section will discuss the various machine translation and transliteration approaches found in the literature. Here, the ISO 15919 standard[1] for the transliteration of Devanagari and related Indic scripts into Latin characters has not been the focus, but it may be relevant in rule-based approaches.

4.1 Rules-based Machine Translation (RBMT)

RBMT (Rules-Based Machine Translation) is a type of MT system which translates languages based on the rules which represent linguistic knowledge. Large number of linguistic terms can be applied to using the Rules-Based Machine Translation methodology in 3 stages: analyzing, transferring, and generating. Programmers and linguists who have already spent a significant amount of time to understand the principles and patterns between 2 languages have established rules. RBMT methods only produce good results only if the translation rules are applied correctly. Transfer-based machine translation and Interlingual machine translation are

[1] https://www.unige.ch/biblio_info/files/5116/3775/9122/ISO_15919_en.pdf

two main types of RBMT (Khepra et al., 2023).

Transfer-based machine translation: This MT type breaks down the process of translation into several subtasks, such as morphological analysis, syntactic parsing, and semantic analysis, and then translates the meaning of source input into the target languages. This approach is useful to handle complex grammatical structures and idiomatic expressions (Khepra et al., 2023).

Interlingual machine translation: This approach involves using an intermediary language to translate between the source and target languages and then translate it into the target language. One of the major advantages of this approach is that it can handle multiple languages at once, and it may bring down errors in the output (Khepra et al., 2023).

4.2 Corpus-based Machine Translation (CBMT)

Corpus-based machine translation (CBMT) relies on large amounts of parallel corpus (bilingual text) to train statistical models for translation. The models are trained to learn patterns in the data, then use those patterns to make translations. The study by Khepra et al. (2023) describes two types of CBMTs: Example-based machine translation and Statistical Machine Translation (SMT).

Example-based machine translation (EBMT): This type of MT uses a bilingual sentence pairs database to translate text. The system gets the most similar sentence pair from the database and use it to generate the target sentence. This approach is useful to handle less common language pairs or rare languages (Khepra et al., 2023).

Statistical Machine Translation (SMT): In Statistical Machine Translation, the model is developed completely from the information in corpora without user intervention. It was the dominant paradigm up until the beginning of 2010. A computer requires examples which provide information about the translation of the phrases (the bilingual word mappings) and the appropriate placements of the converted words in the targeted phrase (alignment) to learn how to translate (Khepra et al., 2023).

4.3 Knowledge-based Machine Translation (KBMT)

This kind of MT uses a predetermined set of grammatical and lexical rules to translate text. A different name for it is a rule-based machine translation. KBMT is especially advantageous in its capability to handle specific domains such as legal or technical texts where the text structure is well-defined (Khepra et al., 2023).

4.4 Neural Machine Translation (NMT)

Neural Machine Translation (NMT) uses deep learning techniques to train an MT model on large amounts of parallel data. Typically, NMT models are more accurate than rule-based or statistical models but also need more computational resources for the training process (Khepra et al., 2023).

4.5 Hybrid Machine Translation

This approach is one of the latest approaches in machine translation systems. This will be developed with the combination of more than one existing MT-based approach. Two or more approaches discussed in the above sections can be used in the Hybrid approach to produce accurate results (Sumanathilaka et al., 2023).

4.6 Discussion of MT Approaches

Each machine translation (MT) approach has different strengths and limitations according to their underlying mechanisms. To address some of the issues with these single approaches, researchers have used a combination of these approaches to overcome those issues. RBMT and KBMT approaches depend on predefined rules, making them effective for structured texts. However, those approaches struggle with unseen text which does not follow predefined rules. CBMT approaches, including SMT and EBMT, utilize large parallel corpora, offering more adaptability, but these approaches require substantial data. NMT can be identified as the most commonly used approach recently. Both NMT and CBMT face the challenge of data scarcity for low-resource languages. When corpus size is small, SMT performs better than the NMT according to results obtained by Tennage et al. (2017). Recently, there has been an outstanding trend to use transformers (Vaswani et al., 2017), which is one of the latest NMT approaches.

5 Current State of Machine Translation for Indo-Aryan Languages

This section provides an overview of the current state of MT approaches developed for diverse Indo-Aryan language pairs.

5.1 Hindi-English Translation

Recently, NMT has been broadly explored for this language pair. Singh et al. (2019) proposed LSTM

(Long Short-Term Memory) based NMT system for English-Hindi translation showing promising results, especially for shorter sentences. Further advancements include the study by Tiwari et al. (2020), who suggested 2 other NMT approaches, which are ConvS2S and LSTM Seq2Seq, with the ConvS2S model outperforming the proposed LSTM model. Similarly, Gogineni et al. (2020) proposed an NMT model based on Bidirectional LSTM (BiLSTM), outperforming the traditional SMT approaches in terms of BLEU scores. Attention mechanisms have also been a major focus in enhancing the performance of NMT systems. Laskar et al. (2019) studied the comparison between two NMT approaches, one based on the modern transformer model, which is based on a recently introduced self-attention mechanism and the other on the LSTM. The results demonstrated that the transformer-based model outperformed the LSTM-based model. Rose et al. (2023) showed that incorporating an attention mechanism into an Encoder-Decoder-based LSTM model significantly improved the translation. The use of a guided transformer model proposed by Bisht et al. (2023) further increased the translation performance by integrating dependency parsing into the encoder. For addressing challenges in long sentence translation, Sarode et al. (2023) explored the Recurrent Neural Networks (RNN) and Gated Recurrent Units (GRU) usage in a Seq2Seq architecture with an attention mechanism. Lastly, Watve and Bhalekar (2023) implemented a transformer-based English-to-Hindi translator, contributing to the improvement of work in this area.

5.2 Sinhala-English Translation

To improve the accuracy of Sinhala to English translation, Nugaliyadde et al. (2019) proposed a novel approach using an Evolutionary Algorithm (EA). This method iteratively refines the translation ensuring that the final output is meaningful and grammatically correct. According to their paper, this is one of the early efforts to apply EA in MT for Sinhala-English language pairs. Fonseka et al. (2020) introduced a transformer-based translation system particularly developed for translating official government documents between English and Sinhala. To address one of the common issues in MT, which is the out-of-vocabulary (OOV) issue, they implemented Byte Pair Encoding (BPE). Further advancements were made by researchers who explored the document alignment in Sinhala and English. For example, research extended the Si-Ta (Ranathunga et al., 2018) system (Will be discussed in the next section) to include SMT techniques improving the alignment process between Sinhala and English texts (C et al., 2020). To enable Sinhala speakers to search English web content effectively, Hisan et al. (2020) focused on a cross-language information retrieval system using word embeddings to enhance the translation of Sinhala queries into English. Additionally, Sandaruwan et al. (2021) addressed the challenge of translating Romanized Sinhala into English. They built a Seq2Seq NMT model with an attention mechanism that effectively handled the various spelling variations in Singlish. In this system, a deep multi-layer RNN, which consists of bidirectional LSTMs, is considered recurrent units.

5.3 Sinhala-Tamil Translation

The first dedicated MT system for Sinhala and Tamil official documents was Si-Ta which is proposed by Ranathunga et al. (2018). Nissanka et al. (2020) further explored Neural Machine Translation for this pair of languages using Byte Pair Encoding (BPE) to address the OOV problem as described above in the study by Fonseka et al. (2020). In their approach, they combined monolingual and parallel corpus data utilizing transformer architecture to improve translation accuracy. In a study comparing different translation models done by Pramodya et al. (2020), they found that the introduction of the Incrementally Filtered Back-Translation technique, which was proposed by Arukgoda et al. (2019), enabled NMT models to surpass SMT models, especially in low-resource conditions. They compared different translation models, including RNNs, SMT and Transformer models for Tamil to Sinhala translation. Thillainathan et al. (2021) extended this line of research by fine-tuning modern pre-trained large language models such as mBART for extremely low-resource translation tasks. They showed that fine-tuning these models significantly enhanced the quality of translation for Sinhala-Tamil, especially in domain-specific contexts (such as official government documents) compared to traditional Transformer-based NMT models.

5.4 Punjabi-English Translation

SMT-based system for Punjabi-English language pair using the Moses toolkit has been studied by Jindal et al. (2018). That involved creating a 20,000-

sentence parallel corpus encompassing diverse domains and utilizing GIZA++ for word alignment.

5.5 Bengali-English Translation

Research on Bengali-English translation has been focused on both NMT and SMT approaches. Rahman et al. (2018) proposed an MT system which uses a corpus-based method with an N-gram language model. The results of this system have been shown to outperform Google Translate in terms of computational efficiency and accuracy. More recently, Paul et al. (2023) evaluated four different Seq2Seq models, which are LSTM, GRU, BiLSTM and Bidirectional GRU (BiGRU), concluding that the BiLSTM model performed well achieving high BLEU scores.

5.6 Sanskrit-Hindi Translation

For the Sanskrit-Hindi language pair, a Corpus-Based Machine Translation (CBMT) system using deep neural networks to translate Vedic texts and other sacred writings was proposed by Singh et al. (2020). This system was able to handle phrasal and idiomatic expressions, achieving a BLEU score of 41.17. Lastly, Bhadwal et al. (2020) explored an RBMT model which utilizes a direct (dictionary-based) approach for translating text from Hindi to Sanskrit.

5.7 Sanskrit-Gujarati Translation

Raulji et al. (2022) introduced a novel framework to translate Sanskrit to Gujarati using a symbolic approach. They focused on keeping grammatical structures through a sequential process involving morphological and syntactic analysis, lexical transfer and grammatical transfer. This system achieved a BLEU score of 58.04 despite the challenge of scarcity of resources, which demonstrated the effectiveness of this system for low-resource languages.

5.8 Urdu-English Translation

A study proposed by Naeem et al. (2023) evaluated the performance of different neural network models (RNN, GRU, and LSTM) for translation between English and Urdu languages and the results showed that the GRU model outperformed the others.

5.9 Marathi-English Translation

Recent research on the Marathi-English translation has been relatively limited. For the Marathi-English translation, Gunjal et al. (2023) proposed a Seq2Seq transformer model, which was trained on a large dataset of parallel English-Marathi sentences and achieved a BLEU score of 41. 99.

5.10 Kashmiri-English Translation

Research on the Kashmiri-English language translation has also been relatively limited. A study (Giri et al., 2024) proposed an RNN-based MT system focusing on the tourism domain. This system is structured on an Encoder-Decoder model, indicating initial efforts for this pair of languages, especially in domain-specific contexts.

5.11 Other Multilingual Translation

A study proposed by Sen et al. (2018) introduced two multilingual Transformer architecture-based NMT models: many-to one (7 Indic languages to English) and one-to-many (English to 7 Indic languages). The results showed that multilingual NMT performs better than separate bilingual NMT models if the target side has only one language (English). When the target has many languages, multilingual NMT performance degrades compared to bilingual models for relatively high-resource languages. Further advancements in multilingual language translation involve the inclusion of Hindi, Telugu, Kannada and English within a single system (Chimalamarri et al., 2020). This study improved transformer-based NMT models by incorporating source-side morpho-linguistic features, which are word-based, BPE-based, and morpho-lexical features with POS tags. The results showed significant enhancements in the translation process for all language pairs by incorporating source-side morpho-linguistic features, especially morpho-lexical features with POS tags. Another important translation system based on pre-trained mT5 transformer was fine-tuned to translate between Hindi, Bengali, and English (Jha et al., 2023). That system leveraged the extensive multilingual capabilities in the mT5 model, achieving high BLEU scores for Bengali-English and English-Bengali translations.

6 Current State of Machine Transliteration for Indo-Aryan Languages

The transliteration of Indo-Aryan languages has been a challenge of research for several decades. There are various models proposed to address the complexities of converting text from one script to another. Over the years, the transliteration approaches have improved from traditional rule-based methods to modern neural and hybrid models, reflecting the increasing computational capabilities. From 2018 to 2024, there were more studies on transliteration systems for Sinhala compared to other Indo-Aryan languages.

In 2018, significant contributions were made to transliteration with the development of rule-based and modern machine-learning approaches. A rule-based transliteration system for Romanized Sinhala was proposed, using phonetic and transliteration rule bases to transliterate Romanized text into native Sinhala script. While effective, the system faced limitations in handling ambiguities, particularly with proper nouns(Vidanaralage et al., 2018). Another study experimented with Seq2Seq and LSTM models to develop a scalable transliteration pipeline for Indian languages and evaluated different language transliterations. The results showed that the Seq2Seq models outperformed traditional LSTM models, although they need large datasets for effective training (Joshi et al., 2018). Additionally, a character-level transliteration tool was created to improve Tamil to Sinhala NM,T demonstrating the utility of rule-based methods in translation tasks (Tennage et al., 2018). According to their literature, that was the first Tamil to English and Sinhala to English transliteration tool that used a rule-based approach.

In 2019, Priyadarshani et al. (2019) introduced a hybrid approach using SMT and machine learning to transliterate personal names in the Sri Lankan context using Moses SMT toolkit for Sinhala, Tamil and English languages. This system showed the importance of incorporating ethnic origin classification for personal name transliteration to improve accuracy. Another significant transliteration approach was the Gurmukhi to Roman transliteration, which used character mapping and handcrafted rules for the transliteration of Punjabi to English with a good accuracy of 99.27% (Singh and Sachan, 2019).

There were further advancements in transliteration techniques during 2020 and 2021, particularly with the use of neural networks. A rule-based method which is proposed by UCSC is combined with a trigram model trained on social media text to improve the Sinhala transliteration accuracy in the study by Liwera and Ranathunga (2020). Another study in 2021 introduced a rule-based approach for Singlish to Sinhala transliteration with an error correction module to improve accuracy (Silva and Ahangama, 2021). Singh and Bansal (2021) experimented with various neural architectures for the transliteration of Hindi and Punjabi languages. Out of those, a model with a character/grapheme level bidirectional encoder and auto-regressive decoder proved to be the best-performing architecture. In the same year, a systematic approach employing phrase-based statistical machine translation (PB-SMT) to create an English-Hindi parallel database for transliteration was introduced (Mogla et al., 2021). Another work in 2021 was the development of a Python-based algorithm to transliterate between Devanagari or Roman scripts and Brahmic scripts, and vice versa (Nair and Ahammed, 2021). Additionally with the introduction of a method for normalizing and back-transliterating Hindi-English code-switched text, this field saw further innovation (Parikh and Solorio, 2021). This system first normalized Romanized Hindi with the use of the Seq2Seq model based on an LSTM encoder-decoder architecture and then syllabified the tokens to map them to the Devanagari script. This approach could handle informal typing variations and phonetic discrepancies, improving the transliteration.

Moving into 2022, Swa-Bhasha (Athukorala and Sumanathilaka, 2022) proposed a novel approach using a combination of rule-based methods and fuzzy logic to transliterate Singlish to Sinhala even when vowels are omitted. This system has introduced a new numeric coding system to use with the Romanized Sinhala letters by matching with the recognized typing patterns. Fuzzy logic-based implementation has been used for the mapping process. Another back-transliteration system for Romanized Sinhala to Sinhala was proposed by Nanayakkara et al. (2022) utilizing a Transliteration Unit (TU) based model and a BiLSTM encoder combined with an LSTM decoder. Moreover, in 2022, a bilingual RBMT system was developed for Sanskrit-English. This system allowed users to type Sanskrit using English orthography and transliterate Sanskrit text into the English script (Sethi et al., 2022).

In 2023, Sharma et al. (2023) introduced a Generative Adversarial Networks (GANs) based system using Pix2Pix GAN architecture to transliterate ancient Indian scripts (images) like Nandinagari and Sharda into modern Devanagari script (images). Yadav and Kumar (2023) proposed a hybrid approach to transliterate Hindi to English which includes image processing and a model trained with attention. The final phase of the proposed system, which is the transliteration phrase, used the Python Indicate Transliteration library to transliterate Hindi characters into the Roman script. In the same year, Swa-Bhasha hybrid approach combining statistical methods with a Trigram and rule-based model was proposed for Singlish back transliteration (Sumanathilaka et al., 2023). Additionally, it incorporated a Trie data structure to generate word suggestions. The work by Athukorala and Sumanathilaka (2022) has achieved 0.64-word level accuracy while Liwera and Ranathunga (2020) achieved 0.52-word level accuracy. This Swa-Bhasha system has performed much more accurately with 0.84-word level accuracy compared to the existing transliteration works for Sinhala. By applying a similar hybrid approach, another back-transliteration system for Romanized Tamil, TAMZHI, was proposed by Mudiyanselage and Sumanathilaka (2024). This system achieved 93% accuracy at the character level and 70% at the word level, further demonstrating the effectiveness of this method.

In 2024, further advancement was made with the introduction of Swa Bhasha 2.0 (Dharmasiri and Sumanathilaka, 2024), which is developed to address the ambiguities of Romanized Sinhala back transliteration using GRU-based NMT. Also, the study of Swa-Bhasha Dataset (Sumanathilaka et al., 2024) introduced a rule-based transliteration tool which can annotate Sinhala words into Romanized Sinhala. This system can accommodate the various ad hoc typing patterns used by the community. Finally, in 2024, another model was proposed for accurate cross-script conversion, focusing on the hybrid model development for transliteration. This study compared two models: a hybrid of Seq2Seq with LSTM and a hybrid of rule-based and NMT approaches. Seq2Seq with an LSTM-based model demonstrated superior performance, especially in back-transliterating English text into different Indic languages (Shukla et al., 2024).

7 Gaps and Challenges in Machine Translation and Transliteration for Indo-Aryan Languages

Despite significant advancements in the field of machine translation (MT) and transliteration for Indo-Aryan languages, there are still several challenges and gaps that can be identified. Addressing these will be important to develop reliable systems for any language. This section describes some of the identified gaps and challenges in this field.

7.1 Data Scarcity

Data scarcity in low-resource languages presents significant challenges to machine translation and transliteration, especially when using neural machine translation and corpus-based translation approaches like statistical machine translation (SMT). This problem gets worse in NMT approaches because these models are even more data-hungry than SMT. Some studies have shown that when corpus size is small, SMT performs better than the NMT (Tennage et al., 2017). Even though the transformer architecture, one of the latest NMT approaches, has shown outstanding results with high-resource language pair translation, recent studies have still conducted only a small number of works on Indo-Aryan languages because of data scarcity problems.

7.2 Complex Morphological and Syntactic Structures

The complex grammatical structures and rich morphology of Indo-Aryan languages, where a single word can have multiple forms depending on tense, gender, and case, pose challenges to translation systems. Syntactic differences between Indo-Aryan languages and other language families like English also complicate the translation process, especially with idiomatic expressions.

7.3 Out-of-Vocabulary (OOV) Words

The "out of vocabulary" (OOV) issue in this field refers to the problem which occurs when a source language word is not present in the vocabulary ofthe translation/transliteration system, meaning it has not been seen or learned during training. OOV words might include rare terms, names or new slang. Techniques such as Byte Pair Encoding (BPE) have been used to address this issue in recent systems, but this issue still persists in some developments.

7.4 Code-Mixing

A significant number of people use social media in various native languages other than English. However, most of these people do not use Unicode characters to represent their languages. Instead, they use phonetic typing with the English alphabet. Therefore, people express their native languages using the English alphabet, and they even insert English words mixed up with the native language words. This phenomenon is known as code-mixing (Smith and Thayasivam, 2019). Also, sometimes, people write in their native script and insert English words using the English alphabet. Some of the current MT and transliteration systems struggle to handle mixed language inputs.

7.5 Variations in Transliteration

When people use transliterated text, especially Romanized forms of Indo-Aryan languages, the writing patterns they use to express their native language vary from person to person. Also, these typing patterns change depending on the time and the mood of uthe ser (Sumanathilaka et al., 2024). Common variations in transliterated text include ambiguous consonant transliteration, vowel dropping, long vowel transliteration, double consonant transliteration, slang and abbreviations (Parikh and Solorio, 2021). These inconsistencies make it challenging to convert the transliterated text back into the native script. Few recent developments have focused on addressing these typing variations.

7.6 Word Ambiguity

Word ambiguity, where a single word can represent multiple meanings based on the context of the sentence, remains a key challenge. Addressing this problem is known as word sense disambiguation. While SMT and NMT approaches, such as LSTM and GRU models, can retain contextual information to some extent, they have not provided an optimal solution. The transformer architecture can offer a better approach. However, only a few translation/transliteration systems have been developed with this architecture, and it seems they have not given much direct attention to this problem.

8 Conclusion

The review highlights significant advancements in machine translation and transliteration for Indo-Aryan languages. Translation systems have seen notable improvements in accuracy with the advancement of natural language processing. In transliteration, there has been progress in converting text between different scripts by managing the phonetic variations. Notably, both translation and transliteration have seen significant enhancements with the advent of transformer architecture variations, which is marking a promising direction for future research in this field. These developments are important in improving effective communication and access to information across different Indo-Aryan language communities.

Limitations

This systematic review has several limitations that need to be considered. Considering only papers published between 2018 and 2024 might have left out earlier important studies which could provide more details on how machine translation and transliteration related to Indo-Aryan languages have evolved. This review only included papers which are freely available. As a result, it might have missed important studies published in less accessible journals or conference proceedings. Additionally, using specific keywords to find relevant studies might have caused important studies which do not use these exact keywords to be missed.

References

Anupama Arukgoda, A. Weerasinghe, and Randil Pushpananda. 2019. Improving Sinhala-Tamil Translation through Deep Learning Techniques.

Maneesha Athukorala and Deshan Sumanathilaka. 2022. Swa Bhasha: Message-Based Singlish to Sinhala Transliteration.

Neha Bhadwal, Prateek Agrawal, and Vishu Madaan. 2020. A Machine Translation System from Hindi to Sanskrit Language using Rule based Approach. *Scalable Computing: Practice and Experience*, 21(3):543–554.

Akhilesh Bisht, Deepa Gupta, and Shantipriya Parida. 2023. Guided Transformer for Machine Translation: English to Hindi. In *2023 IEEE 20th India Council International Conference (INDICON)*, pages 636–641, Hyderabad, India. IEEE.

Rajitha M. D. C, Piyarathna L.L. C, Nayanajith M. M.D. S, and Surangika S. 2020. Sinhala and English Document Alignment using Statistical Machine Translation. In *2020 20th International Conference on Advances in ICT for Emerging Regions (ICTer)*, pages 29–34, Colombo, Sri Lanka. IEEE.

Santwana Chimalamarri, Dinkar Sitaram, Rithik Mali, Alex Johnson, and K A Adeab. 2020. Improving Transformer based Neural Machine Translation with Source-side Morpho-linguistic Features. In *2020 IEEE International Conference on Machine Learning and Applied Network Technologies (ICMLANT)*, pages 1–5, Hyderabad, India. IEEE.

Sachithya Dharmasiri and T.G.D.K. Sumanathilaka. 2024. Swa Bhasha 2.0: Addressing Ambiguities in Romanized Sinhala to Native Sinhala Transliteration Using Neural Machine Translation. In *2024 4th International Conference on Advanced Research in Computing (ICARC)*, pages 241–246, Belihuloya, Sri Lanka. IEEE.

Thilakshi Fonseka, Rashmini Naranpanawa, Ravinga Perera, and Uthayasanker Thayasivam. 2020. English to Sinhala Neural Machine Translation. In *2020 International Conference on Asian Language Processing (IALP)*, pages 305–309, Kuala Lumpur, Malaysia. IEEE.

Kaiser J. Giri, Nawaz Ali Lone, Rumaan Bashir, and Javaid Iqbal Bhat. 2024. English Kashmiri Machine Translation System related to Tourism Domain. In *2024 11th International Conference on Computing for Sustainable Global Development (INDIACom)*, pages 1713–1717, New Delhi, India. IEEE.

Saikiran Gogineni, G. Suryanarayana, and Sravan Kumar Surendran. 2020. An Effective Neural Machine Translation for English to Hindi Language. In *2020 International Conference on Smart Electronics and Communication (ICOSEC)*, pages 209–214, Trichy, India. IEEE.

Om Gunjal, Saurav Garje, Samir Aghav, Lavesh Jaykar, Sunil Sangve, and Saurabh Gunge. 2023. An Enhanced English to Marathi Translator using sequence-to-sequence Transformer. In *2023 4th IEEE Global Conference for Advancement in Technology (GCAT)*, pages 1–5, Bangalore, India. IEEE.

M. H. M. Hisan, A. R. Weerasinghe, and B. H. R. Pushpananda. 2020. Cross Language Information Retrieval for Accessing the English Web in Sinhala. In *2020 20th International Conference on Advances in ICT for Emerging Regions (ICTer)*, pages 244–249, Colombo, Sri Lanka. IEEE.

Abhinav Jha, Hemprasad Yashwant Patil, Sumit Kumar Jindal, and Sardar M N Islam. 2023. Multilingual Indian Language Neural Machine Translation System Using mT5 Transformer. In *2023 2nd International Conference on Paradigm Shifts in Communications Embedded Systems, Machine Learning and Signal Processing (PCEMS)*, pages 1–5, Nagpur, India. IEEE.

Shishpal Jindal, Vishal Goyal, and Jaskarn Singh Bhullar. 2018. English to Punjabi statistical machine translation using moses (Corpus Based). *Journal of Statistics and Management Systems*, 21(4):553–560.

Akshat Joshi, Kinal Mehta, Neha Gupta, and Varun Kannadi Valloli. 2018. Indian Language Transliteration Using Deep Learning. In *2018 IEEE Recent Advances in Intelligent Computational Systems (RAICS)*, pages 103–107, Thiruvananthapuram, India. IEEE.

Palakpreet Kaur and Kamal Deep Garg. 2022. Machine Transliteration for Indian languages: Survey. In *2022 Seventh International Conference on Parallel, Distributed and Grid Computing (PDGC)*, pages 462–467, Solan, Himachal Pradesh, India. IEEE.

Shaveta Khepra, Priya Kumari, Raj Gupta, Abhishek, and Vijendra Singh Bramhe. 2023. A Survey of Punjabi Language Translation using OCR and ML. In *2023 10th International Conference on Computing for Sustainable Global Development (INDIACom)*, pages 136–144.

Sahinur Rahman Laskar, Abinash Dutta, Partha Pakray, and Sivaji Bandyopadhyay. 2019. Neural Machine Translation: English to Hindi. In *2019 IEEE Conference on Information and Communication Technology*, pages 1–6, Allahabad, India. IEEE.

W.M.P. Liwera and L. Ranathunga. 2020. Combination of Trigram and Rule-based Model for Singlish to Sinhala Transliteration by Focusing Social Media Text. In *2020 From Innovation to Impact (FITI)*, pages 1–5, Colombo, Sri Lanka. IEEE.

Radha Mogla, C. Vasantha Lakshmi, and Niladri Chatterjee. 2021. A Systematic Approach for English-Hindi Parallel Database Creation for Transliteration of General Domain English Words. In *2021 IEEE 4th International Conference on Computing, Power and Communication Technologies (GUCON)*, pages 1–5, Kuala Lumpur, Malaysia. IEEE.

Anuja Dilrukshi Herath Herath Mudiyanselage and T. G. Deshan K. Sumanathilaka. 2024. TAM: Shorthand Romanized Tamil to Tamil Reverse Transliteration Using Novel Hybrid Approach. *The International Journal on Advances in ICT for Emerging Regions*, 17(1).

Muhammad Naeem, Abu Bakar Siddique, Raja Hashim Ali, Usama Arshad, Zain ul Abideen, Talha Ali Khan, Muhammad Huzaifa Shah, Ali Zeeshan Ijaz, and Nisar Ali. 2023. Performance Evaluation of Popular Deep Neural Networks for Neural Machine Translation. In *2023 International Conference on Frontiers of Information Technology (FIT)*, pages 220–225, Islamabad, Pakistan. IEEE.

Jayashree Nair and Riyaz Ahammed. 2021. English to Indian Language and Back Transliteration with Phonetic Transcription for Computational Linguistics Tools based on Conventional Transliteration Schemes. In *2021 Fourth International Conference on Electrical, Computer and Communication Technologies (ICECCT)*, pages 1–6, Erode, India. IEEE.

Rushan Nanayakkara, Thilini Nadungodage, and Randil Pushpananda. 2022. Context Aware Back-Transliteration from English to Sinhala. In *2022 22nd International Conference on Advances in ICT for Emerging Regions (ICTer)*, pages 051–056, Colombo, Sri Lanka. IEEE.

L. N. A. S. H. Nissanka, B. H. R. Pushpananda, and A. R. Weerasinghe. 2020. Exploring Neural Machine Translation for Sinhala-Tamil Languages Pair. In *2020 20th International Conference on Advances in ICT for Emerging Regions (ICTer)*, pages 202–207, Colombo, Sri Lanka. IEEE.

A. Nugaliyadde, J.K. Joseph, W.M.T. Chathurika, and Y. Mallawarachchi. 2019. Evolutionary Algorithm for Sinhala to English Translation. In *2019 National Information Technology Conference (NITC)*, pages 26–30, Colombo, Sri Lanka. IEEE.

Santanu Pal and Marcos Zampieri. 2020. Neural Machine Translation for Similar Languages: The Case of Indo-Aryan Languages. In *Proceedings of the Fifth Conference on Machine Translation*, pages 424–429, Online. Association for Computational Linguistics.

Dwija Parikh and Thamar Solorio. 2021. Normalization and Back-Transliteration for Code-Switched Data. In *Proceedings of the Fifth Workshop on Computational Approaches to Linguistic Code-Switching*, pages 119–124, Online. Association for Computational Linguistics.

Nipun Paul, Ishmam Faruki, Mutakabbirul Islam Pranto, Md. Tanvir Rouf Shawon, and Nibir Chandra Mandal. 2023. Bengali-English Neural Machine Translation Using Deep Learning Techniques. In *2023 International Conference on Electrical, Computer and Communication Engineering (ECCE)*, pages 1–6, Chittagong, Bangladesh. IEEE.

Ashmari Pramodya, Randil Pushpananda, and Ruvan Weerasinghe. 2020. A Comparison of Transformer, Recurrent Neural Networks and SMT in Tamil to Sinhala MT. In *2020 20th International Conference on Advances in ICT for Emerging Regions (ICTer)*, pages 155–160, Colombo, Sri Lanka. IEEE.

H.S. Priyadarshani, M.D.W. Rajapaksha, M.M.S.P. Ranasinghe, K. Sarveswaran, and G.V. Dias. 2019. Statistical Machine Learning for Transliteration: Transliterating names between Sinhala, Tamil and English. In *2019 International Conference on Asian Language Processing (IALP)*, pages 244–249.

Mohammad Masudur Rahman, Md. Faisal Kabir, and Mohammad Nurul Huda. 2018. A Corpus Based N-gram Hybrid Approach of Bengali to English Machine Translation. In *2018 21st International Conference of Computer and Information Technology (ICCIT)*, pages 1–6, Dhaka, Bangladesh. IEEE.

Surangika Ranathunga, Fathima Farhath, Uthayasanker Thayasivam, Sanath Jayasena, and Gihan Dias. 2018. Si-Ta: Machine Translation of Sinhala and Tamil Official Documents. In *2018 National Information Technology Conference (NITC)*, pages 1–6, Colombo. IEEE.

Jaideepsinh K. Raulji, Jatinderkumar R. Saini, Kaushika Pal, and Ketan Kotecha. 2022. A Novel Framework for Sanskrit-Gujarati Symbolic Machine Translation System. *International Journal of Advanced Computer Science and Applications*, 13(4).

Dafni Rose, K. Vijayakumar, D. Kirubakaran, R. Pugalenthi, and Gotti Balayaswantasaichowdary. 2023. Neural Machine Translation Using Attention. In *2023 International Conference on Artificial Intelligence and Knowledge Discovery in Concurrent Engineering (ICECONF)*, pages 1–7, Chennai, India. IEEE.

Dinidu Sandaruwan, Sagara Sumathipala, and Subha Fernando. 2021. Neural Machine Translation Approach for Singlish to English Translation. *International Journal on Advances in ICT for Emerging Regions (ICTer)*, 14(3):36–42.

Sonia Sarode, Raghav Thatte, Kajal Toshniwal, Jatin Warade, Ranjeet Vasant Bidwe, and Bhushan Zope. 2023. A System for Language Translation using Sequence-to-sequence Learning based Encoder. In *2023 International Conference on Emerging Smart Computing and Informatics (ESCI)*, pages 1–5, Pune, India. IEEE.

Sukanta Sen, Kamal Kumar Gupta, Asif Ekbal, and Pushpak Bhattacharyya. 2018. IITP-MT at WAT2018: Transformer-based Multilingual Indic-English Neural Machine Translation System. In *Proceedings of the 32nd Pacific Asia Conference on Language, Information and Computation: 5th Workshop on Asian Translation*, pages 1003–1007. Association for Computational Linguistics.

Nandini Sethi, Amita Dev, and Poonam Bansal. 2022. A Bilingual Machine Transliteration System for Sanskrit-English Using Rule-Based Approach. In *2022 4th International Conference on Artificial Intelligence and Speech Technology (AIST)*, pages 1–5, Delhi, India. IEEE.

Anshumani Sharma, Ayushi Verma, Chetan Shahra, and S. Indu. 2023. Ancient Indian Script Transliteration Using GANs. In *2023 10th International Conference on Signal Processing and Integrated Networks (SPIN)*, pages 621–626, Noida, India. IEEE.

Aditya Shukla, Pragati Agrawal, and Sweta Jain. 2024. Delineating Indic Transliteration: Developing A Robust Model for Accurate Cross-Script Conversion. In *2024 IEEE International Students' Conference on Electrical, Electronics and Computer Science (SCEECS)*, pages 1–6, Bhopal, India. IEEE.

Lahiru de Silva and Supunmali Ahangama. 2021. Singlish to Sinhala Transliteration using Rule-based Approach. In *2021 IEEE 16th International Conference on Industrial and Information Systems (ICIIS)*, pages 162–167, Kandy, Sri Lanka. IEEE.

Aryan Singh and Jhalak Bansal. 2021. Neural Machine Transliteration Of Indian Languages. In *2021 4th International Conference on Computing and Communications Technologies (ICCCT)*, pages 91–96, Chennai, India. IEEE.

Muskaan Singh, Ravinder Kumar, and Inderveer Chana. 2020. Corpus based Machine Translation System with Deep Neural Network for Sanskrit to Hindi Translation. *Procedia Computer Science*, 167:2534–2544.

Shailendra Kumar Singh and Manoj Kumar Sachan. 2019. GRT: Gurmukhi to Roman Transliteration System using Character Mapping and Handcrafted Rules. *International Journal of Innovative Technology and Exploring Engineering*, 8(9):2758–2763.

Shashi Pal Singh, Hemant Darbari, Ajai Kumar, Shikha Jain, and Anu Lohan. 2019. Overview of Neural

Machine Translation for English-Hindi. In *2019 International Conference on Issues and Challenges in Intelligent Computing Techniques (ICICT)*, pages 1–4, GHAZIABAD, India. IEEE.

Ian Smith and Uthayasanker Thayasivam. 2019. Language Detection in Sinhala-English Code-mixed Data. In *2019 International Conference on Asian Language Processing (IALP)*, pages 228–233, Shanghai, Singapore. IEEE.

Deshan Sumanathilaka, Nicholas Micallef, and Ruvan Weerasinghe. 2024. Swa-Bhasha Dataset: Romanized Sinhala to Sinhala Adhoc Transliteration Corpus. In *2024 4th International Conference on Advanced Research in Computing (ICARC)*, pages 189–194, Belihuloya, Sri Lanka. IEEE.

T.G.D.K. Sumanathilaka, Ruvan Weerasinghe, and Y.H.P.P. Priyadarshana. 2023. Swa-Bhasha: Romanized Sinhala to Sinhala Reverse Transliteration using a Hybrid Approach. In *2023 3rd International Conference on Advanced Research in Computing (ICARC)*, pages 136–141, Belihuloya, Sri Lanka. IEEE.

Pasindu Tennage, Achini Herath, Malith Thilakarathne, Prabath Sandaruwan, and Surangika Ranathunga. 2018. Transliteration and Byte Pair Encoding to Improve Tamil to Sinhala Neural Machine Translation. In *2018 Moratuwa Engineering Research Conference (MERCon)*, pages 390–395, Moratuwa. IEEE.

Pasindu Tennage, Prabath Sandaruwan, Malith Thilakarathne, Achini Herath, Surangika Ranathunga, Sanath Jayasena, and Gihan Dias. 2017. Neural machine translation for sinhala and tamil languages. In *2017 International Conference on Asian Language Processing (IALP)*, pages 189–192, Singapore. IEEE.

Sarubi Thillainathan, Surangika Ranathunga, and Sanath Jayasena. 2021. Fine-Tuning Self-Supervised Multilingual Sequence-To-Sequence Models for Extremely Low-Resource NMT. In *2021 Moratuwa Engineering Research Conference (MERCon)*, pages 432–437, Moratuwa, Sri Lanka. IEEE.

Gaurav Tiwari, Arushi Sharma, Aman Sahotra, and Rajiv Kapoor. 2020. English-Hindi Neural Machine Translation-LSTM Seq2Seq and ConvS2S. In *2020 International Conference on Communication and Signal Processing (ICCSP)*, pages 871–875, Chennai, India. IEEE.

Ashish Vaswani, Noam Shazeer, Niki Parmar, Jakob Uszkoreit, Llion Jones, Aidan N. Gomez, Lukasz Kaiser, and Illia Polosukhin. 2017. Attention Is All You Need. *arXiv preprint*. ArXiv:1706.03762 [cs].

A.J. Vidanaralage, A.U. Illangakoon, S.Y. Sumanaweera, C. Pavithra, and S. Thelijjagoda. 2018. Sinhala Language Decoder. In *2018 National Information Technology Conference (NITC)*, pages 1–5, Colombo. IEEE.

Haifeng Wang, Hua Wu, Zhongjun He, Liang Huang, and Kenneth Ward Church. 2022. Progress in Machine Translation. *Engineering*, 18:143–153.

Abhinav Y. Watve and Madhuri A. Bhalekar. 2023. English to Hindi Translation using Transformer. In *2023 International Conference on Innovative Data Communication Technologies and Application (ICIDCA)*, pages 993–1000, Uttarakhand, India. IEEE.

Mahima Yadav and Ishan Kumar. 2023. Transliteration from Hindi to English Using Image Processing. In *2023 3rd International Conference on Intelligent Technologies (CONIT)*, pages 1–6, Hubli, India. IEEE.

BERTopic for Topic Modeling of Hindi Short Texts: A Comparative Study

Atharva Mutsaddi, Anvi Jamkhande, Aryan Thakre, Yashodhara Haribhakta
Department of Computer Science and Engineering, COEP Technological University
{atharvaam21, jamkhandeaa21, aryanst21, ybl}.comp@coeptech.ac.in

Abstract

As short text data in native languages like Hindi increasingly appear in modern media, robust methods for topic modeling on such data have gained importance. This study investigates the performance of BERTopic in modeling Hindi short texts, an area that has been under-explored in existing research. Using contextual embeddings, BERTopic can capture semantic relationships in data, making it potentially more effective than traditional models, especially for short and diverse texts. We evaluate BERTopic using 6 different document embedding models and compare its performance against 8 established topic modeling techniques, such as Latent Dirichlet Allocation (LDA), Non-negative Matrix Factorization (NMF), Latent Semantic Indexing (LSI), Additive Regularization of Topic Models (ARTM), Probabilistic Latent Semantic Analysis (PLSA), Embedded Topic Model (ETM), Combined Topic Model (CTM), and Top2Vec. The models are assessed using coherence scores across a range of topic counts. Our results reveal that BERTopic consistently outperforms other models in capturing coherent topics from short Hindi texts.

1 Introduction

Topic modeling is a widely-used technique in text mining that identifies underlying themes within textual data. BERTopic, a newer model in this field, has demonstrated its effectiveness by using pre-trained document embedding models and unsupervised clustering algorithms to form topic groups with high semantic coherence (Grootendorst, 2022). Unlike traditional models, BERTopic's use of embeddings allows it to capture contextual information, such as identifying named entities and associating them with relevant topic clusters that older approaches struggle with (Peters et al., 2018; Liu et al., 2019). Existing research on topic modeling for Hindi texts has largely focused on traditional methods that rely on probabilistic frameworks and matrix factorisation, which often overlook natural language semantics (Ray et al., 2019). Also, these studies primarily focus on long text documents, leaving a gap in the exploration of short Hindi texts, which are increasingly common in todays digital landscape.

Topic modeling in Hindi faces several unique challenges. Hindi does not use capitalisation to differentiate proper nouns from other word forms, complicating named entity recognition. Additionally, the lack of standardised spelling leads to multiple variations of the same word (Figure 1), creating ambiguity. Hindi also often employs repetitive expressions for emphasis, which can affect tokenization and cross-language natural language processing tasks (Ray et al., 2019).

This study aims to demonstrate that traditional topic models often fall short in capturing the semantic meaning of Hindi text due to these inherent challenges and struggle with the nuances of short texts where semantic meaning is more compressed and context-dependent. The contributions of this paper are as follows:

- Conducting a comprehensive comparison of BERTopic's performance across several aspects:
  - Evaluating BERTopic using different sentence transformer models such as `HindSBERT-STS` (Joshi et al., 2022), `XLM-R` (XLM-RoBERTa) (Conneau et al., 2020), `IndicBERT` (Kakwani et al., 2020), and `mBERT` (Multilingual BERT) (Devlin et al., 2018), and analysing results using coherence metrics c_v (coherence value) (Röder et al., 2015) and c_{NPMI} (Normalised Pointwise Mutual Information) (Bouma, 2009) to identify the optimal transformer model.
  - Comparing BERTopic with traditional

Proceedings of the First Workshop on Natural Language Processing for Indo-Aryan and Dravidian Languages (IndoNLP2025), pages 22–32
January 20, 2025. ©2025 Association for Computational Linguistics

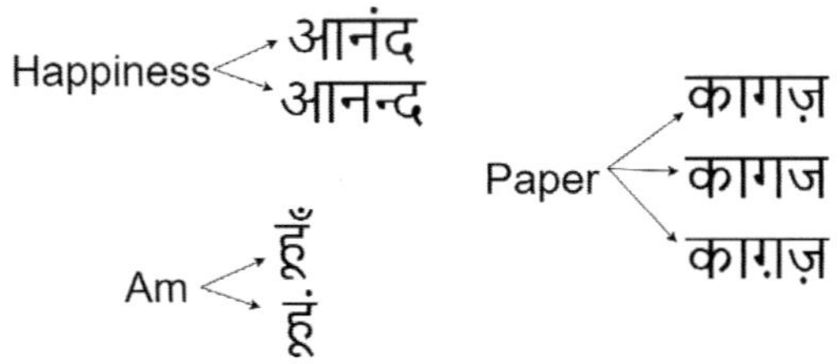

Figure 1: Multiple ways of spelling "Happiness","Paper" and "Am" in Hindi

  topic modeling methods like LDA, NMF, LSI, ARTM, and PLSA, to show that BERTopic consistently outperforms these models.
  - Exploring additional transformer-based models such as Top2vec (Angelov, 2020), Embedded Topic Model (ETM) (Dieng et al., 2020) and Combined Topic Model (CTM) (Terragni et al., 2021) to evaluate their relative performance.

- Demonstrating BERTopics effectiveness in addressing the challenges of modeling short Hindi texts by handling compressed and context-dependent semantics, as evidenced by the comparative analysis.
- Contributing to the study of under-explored languages such as Hindi, by highlighting the benefits of advanced topic models for enhancing semantic coherence and topic extraction in non-English languages.

2 Previous Work

Topic modeling studies on Hindi text have predominantly relied on traditional frameworks, such as probabilistic models and matrix factorisation techniques, while newer approaches remain largely under-explored. Furthermore, most of these studies have focused on long text documents, leaving the effectiveness of topic modeling techniques on short texts inadequately examined.

Ray et al. (2019) provided an overview of various topic modeling approaches for Hindi text, including methods like NMF (Lee and Seung, 1999), LSI (Deerwester et al., 1990), and LDA (Jelodar et al., 2019), as well as tools and Java packages used in these models. However, their work predates the development of BERTopic and does not address its application. Similarly, Srivastav and Singh (2022) investigated the use of models such as LDA, Doc2Vec, and Hierarchical Dirichlet Process (HDP) (Teh et al., 2006) for identifying the main topics in news articles in both Hindi and English. Their study, however, also did not consider newer topic modeling techniques like BERTopic. Panigrahi et al. (2018) explored an embedding-based clustering approach, using Word2Vec (Mikolov, 2013) to generate word embeddings from a corpus of Hindi Wikipedia articles, which were subsequently clustered into topic groups. While this study adopted an approach similar to BERTopic, it did not specifically focus on short texts or use more advanced document embedding models.

While BERTopic's effectiveness on Hindi texts remains unexplored, some studies have evaluated its performance in other non-English languages. Abuzayed and Al-Khalifa (2021) compared BERTopic using different sentence transformers against LDA and NMF on Arabic news articles, and found that BERTopic formed more coherent topic clusters by evaluating them using Normalised Pointwise Mutual Information (Bouma, 2009). Another study (Abdelrazek et al., 2022) compared the computational cost and topic quality of LDA, ETM, CTM, NMF, and two BERTopic variants on Arabic data, concluding that BERTopic outperformed other models in coherence scores. Although these studies focused on longer texts, Medvecki et al. (2024) demonstrated that BERTopic produced more informative clusters than LDA and NMF when applied to Serbian tweets, showing its efficiency in modeling short text data in other languages.

Although BERTopic's superior performance has been proven for some other non-English languages, its effectiveness for Hindi, especially on short texts, remains un-examined. Given Hindi's unique linguistic challenges (Ray et al., 2019) and its status as the third most spoken language globally, it is important to evaluate BERTopic's performance, particularly for Hindi short texts, which are increasingly common in modern media.

3 Methodology

This section gives an overview about the dataset we used, the topic models we evaluated and the method of evaluation used for this comparison.

3.1 Dataset

We used the IIT Patna Reviews dataset, a well-regarded dataset used for evaluating and training Hindi natural language processing models for the task of sentiment analysis. This dataset contains short text product reviews written in the Devanagari script, each mapped to its corresponding sentiment. For this study, we focused on modeling the reviews and did not use the sentiment mappings.

For pre-processing, we used the Hindi language stop words list compiled by Jha et al. (2018), to identify and remove stop words. We also removed punctuation marks, URLs, username references, extra spaces, hashtags, and leading and trailing quotations to reduce noise in the data.

3.2 Evaluation

For the performance evaluation of these topic models, we used coherence value (c_v) and Normalised Pointwise Mutual Information (c_{NPMI}) to assess the quality of topics formed (Röder et al., 2015; Bouma, 2009). The c_v metric evaluates the semantic coherence of a set of words which represent a topic using word co-occurrence graphs. The c_{NPMI} metric evaluates the word associations within a topic cluster, assessing how strongly the words are related.

For each model, the average c_v and c_{NPMI} scores were calculated across the topic clusters, and these scores were used for comparison. We perform these calculations for topic counts ranging from 5 to 210. This range was chosen because BERTopic scores generally stabilise beyond 210 topics, indicating that adding more topics does not significantly alter topic coherence. Also, considering the overall size of our dataset, 210 topic clusters were deemed sufficient for meaningful topic labeling. While BERTopic can automatically determine the optimal number of topic clusters to form, we specified the number of clusters in this comparison to ensure a consistent basis for evaluating its performance against other models, which require a predefined number of clusters.

The interpretation of coherence scores in topic modeling is subject to debate. Previous studies (He et al., 2009, 2008; Newman et al., 2011; Das Dawn et al., 2024) suggest that a lower c_v score, typically below 0.4, indicates overly generalised topic clusters, while scores above 0.7 might suggest more specialised ones. Despite this debate, there is consensus that higher c_{NPMI} scores reflect stronger word relations within the topic clusters (Abuzayed and Al-Khalifa, 2021; Medvecki et al., 2024).

3.3 BERTopic

BERTopic uses embedding models to understand the semantic meaning and context in which words are used (Grootendorst, 2022), making it well-suited for modeling Hindi short texts. It employs a dimensionality reduction algorithm like UMAP (Uniform Manifold Approximation and Projection) (McInnes et al., 2018), followed by an unsupervised clustering algorithm like HDBSCAN (Hierarchical Density-Based Spatial Clustering of Applications with Noise) (McInnes et al., 2017) or KMeans (MacQueen et al., 1967) to create coherent topic clusters. Our experiment involved using various sentence transformers with BERTopic and comparing their relative performance to choose the most optimal one for further comparisons.

The transformers we compared were:

- `XLM-R` (xlm-roberta-base) (Conneau et al., 2020)
- `IndicBERT`, which is a transformer fine-tuned for Indic languages (Kakwani et al., 2020).
- `HindSBERT-STS`, a transformer designed for semantic textual similarity tasks in Hindi (Joshi et al., 2022), using `SBERT` (Sentence-BERT) (Reimers and Gurevych, 2019).
- `mBERT` (bert-base-multilingual-cased for `mBERT-Cased` and bert-base-multilingual-uncased for `mBERT-Uncased`) (Devlin et al., 2018)

These embedding models were selected based on their ability to capture the semantic and contextual meaning of Hindi, which is essential for modeling short text reviews. Comparing language-specific and multilingual embedding models is vital for this analysis. Language-specific models, such as `HindSBERT-STS` and `IndicBERT`, are trained predominantly on Hindi corpora and are well-suited to handle features unique to Hindi, including compound verbs, spelling variations, and idiomatic expressions. On the other hand, multilingual embeddings are trained on a broader and more diverse set of languages, enabling them to leverage cross-lingual transfer for improved performance on low-resource languages by identifying shared linguistic patterns. Additionally, multilingual embeddings often exhibit greater robustness in tasks like named entity recognition and cross-lingual reference handling, making them particularly advantageous for processing multilingual or code-mixed content. This comparison highlights the distinct strengths of each approach, providing valuable insights for selecting embeddings based on specific use cases.

3.4 Comparative Models

We compared BERTopic with the following models:

- **LDA-Based Models**: These models utilise the LDA framework to identify topic distributions within the text. We compared the following variants:
  - LDA (Latent Dirichlet Allocation) (Blei et al., 2003).
  - ARTM (Additive Regularisation of Topic Models) (Vorontsov and Potapenko, 2015).
  - ETM (Embedded Topic Model) (Dieng et al., 2020) with the same sentence transformers as discussed in subsection 3.3. We consider the best transformer for further comparison with the other LDA based approaches.

  We consider the best variant of LDA for further comparison with other models.

- **Other Topic Modeling Approaches**:
  - NMF (Non-negative Matrix Factorisation) (Lee and Seung, 1999).
  - PLSA (Probabilistic Latent Semantic Analysis) (Hofmann, 1999).
  - LSI (Latent Semantic Indexing) (Deerwester et al., 1990).
  - CTM (Combined Topic Model). Specifically the `Octis` implementation of it (Terragni et al., 2021).
  - Top2Vec (Angelov, 2020). Since we cannot specify the number of topic clusters in Top2Vec, we compared the best scores it achieved with four different embedding models, namely-distiluse-base-multilingual-cased, universal-sentence-encoder, universal-sentence-encoder-multilingual and doc2vec. We later considered the best embedding model with Top2Vec for further comparison.

3.5 Implementation Details

All experiments were conducted using Google Colaboratory with the following Python tools:

- `Sklearn` for implementing ETM and NMF.
- `Gensim` for LSI and LDA Multicore.
- `Bigartm` for PLSA and ARTM.
- `Octis` library for CTM.
- `sentence-transformers` for Hugging Face models: `xlm-roberta-base`, `indic-bert`, `HindSBERT-STS`, `bert-base-multilingual-cased`, and `bert-base-multilingual-uncased`.

4 Results and Analysis

We compared 20 models, each utilising different approaches, including embedding-based models like BERTopic and ETM with the 5 embedding models mentioned in subsection 3.3, hybrid models like CTM and Top2Vec using 4 pre-trained embedding models (subsection 3.4), probabilistic models like LDA, ARTM, and PLSA, and matrix factorisation models such as NMF and LSI. Following are our findings:

4.1 Comparison of LDA-Based Models

After evaluating multiple LDA variants, we found that ETM with `HindSBERT-STS` yielded the most coherent topics, outperforming the other embedding models for majority of topic counts (Figures 2 , 3). Specifically, ETM achieved a c_v and c_{NPMI} score of 0.71 and 0.089 respectively for 205 topics.

The c_v scores for ETM model using `HindSBERT-STS` suggest a balance in topic specificity, avoiding both highly specific and overly generalised clusters (He et al., 2009, 2008; Newman et al., 2011; Das Dawn et al., 2024).

ARTM performed better than all LDA variants in terms of c_v scores, particularly in the 5 to 20 topic range, but it failed to maintain this trend for higher topic counts (Figures 4 , 5).

The performance of the traditional LDA model declined as the number of topics increased, showing its limitations in handling short text data with fewer words available for topic extraction (Qiang et al., 2022; Aggarwal and Zhai, 2012).

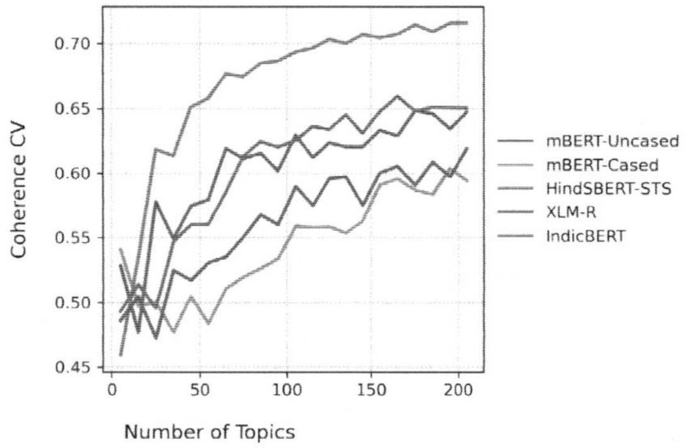

Figure 2: c_v scores of ETM with different sentence transformers

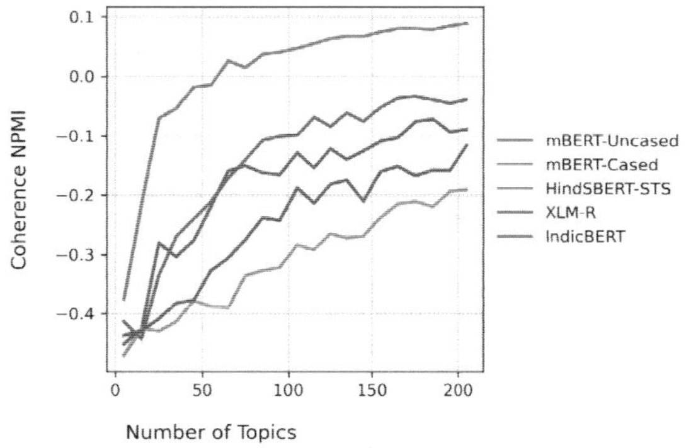

Figure 3: c_{NPMI} scores of ETM with different sentence transformers

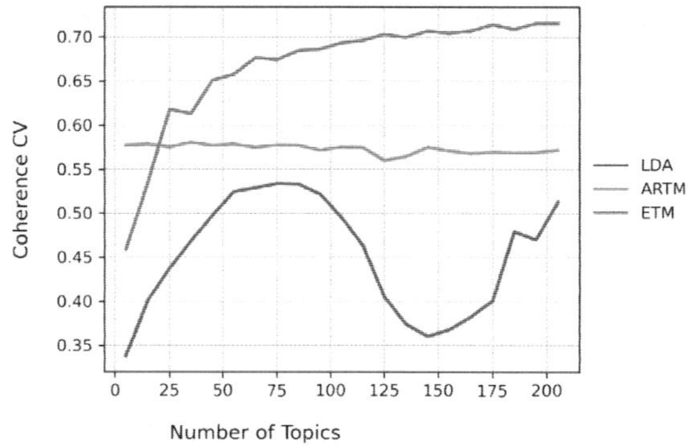

Figure 4: Comparison of c_v Scores for LDA-Based Models

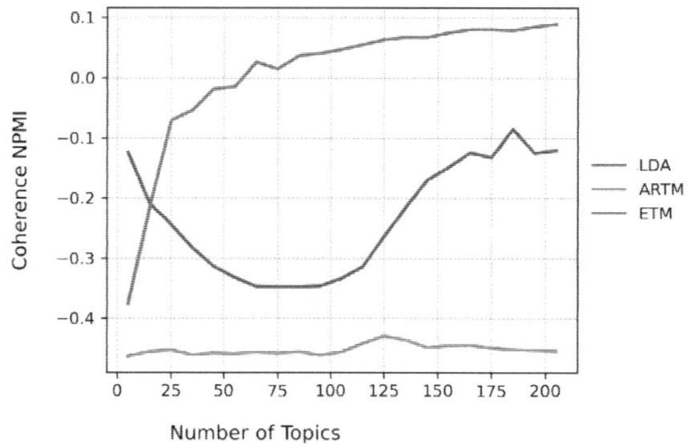

Figure 5: Comparison of NPMI Scores for LDA-Based Models

Hence we can see that ETM is the best LDA variant amongst the ones we have evaluated.

4.2 Evaluation of Embedding Models with BERTopic

Figures 6 and 7 show that `mBERT-Uncased` consistently provides better results than the other sentence transformers when used with BERTopic. The high c_v scores achieved by `mBERT-Uncased` and `XLM-R` at larger topic counts suggest the formation of dense, specialised clusters (He et al., 2009, 2008; Newman et al., 2011) with strong semantic relationships among the words within these topics (Hadiat, 2022). Although `XLM-R` barely outperforms `mBERT-Uncased` in c_v scores from 170 topics onward, its c_{NPMI} scores are significantly worse across the entire topic count range (Figure 7).

While `mBERT-Cased` performs better than the other models at lower topic counts, its scores decreased significantly as the number of topics increased, leading to its exclusion from further evaluation.

Additionally, due to poor performance, `HindSBERT-STS` and `IndicBERT` were not considered for further analysis.

4.3 Performance Analysis: Best BERTopic vs. Best LDA vs. Other Models

We found that BERTopic with the `mBERT-Uncased` embedding model outperformed other topic models for the majority of topic counts (Figures 8, 9). Table 1 presents the best coherence scores obtained by each model, along with the corresponding number of topics at which these scores were achieved.

BERTopic produced significantly higher coherence scores than all other models, with its c_v scores being, on average, 19.8% higher than those of ETM with `HindSBERT-STS`, which ranked second (Figure 8). While ETM formed topic clusters with slightly higher c_{NPMI} scores than BERTopic for 125 topics onwards, BERTopic showed better scores across most topic ranges, indicating more consistent performance.

NMF and PLSA demonstrated nearly identi-

Model	c_{NPMI}	c_v	Topic Count
BERTopic [mBERT-Uncased]	**0.07**	**0.76**	**95**
ETM [HindSBERT-STS]	0.089	0.71	205
Top2Vec [DBMC]	−0.48	0.54	45
PLSA	−0.46	0.57	45
ARTM	−0.42	0.56	125
NMF	−0.44	0.56	35
CTM	−0.38	0.48	135
LDA	−0.12	0.38	165
LSI	−0.08	0.30	15

Table 1: Best scores achieved by topic models on Hindi short text dataset

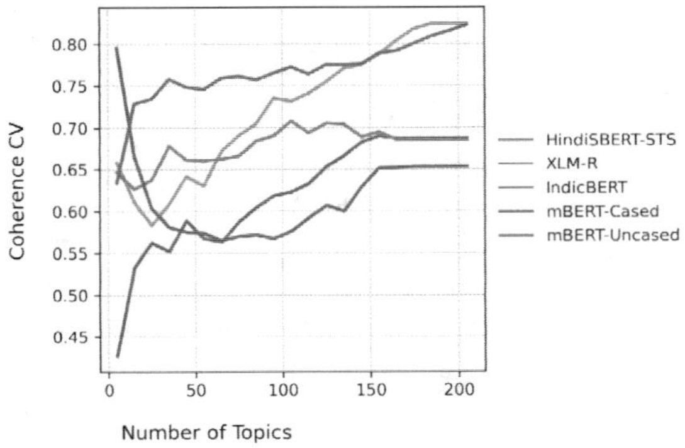

Figure 6: c_v scores for BERTopic with Different Embedding Models

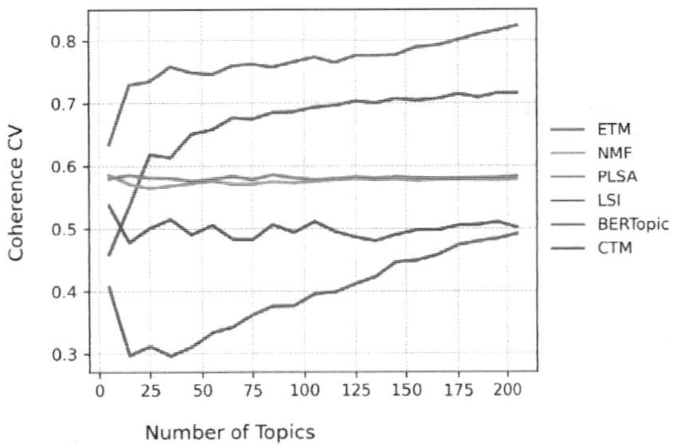

Figure 8: c_v scores of BERTopic, ETM, NMF, PLSA, LSI and CTM

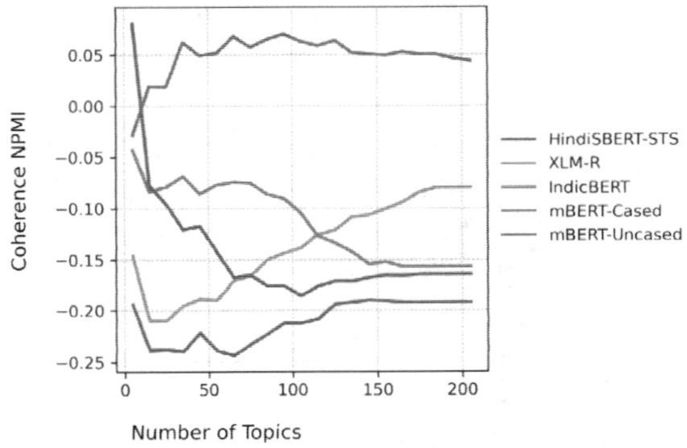

Figure 7: c_{NPMI} scores of BERTopic with Different Embedding Models

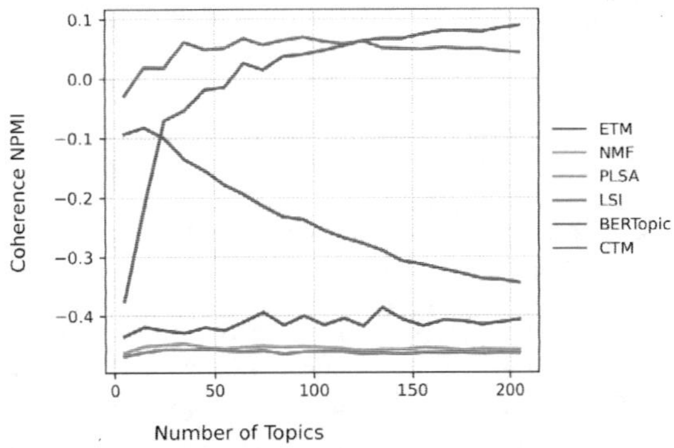

Figure 9: c_{NPMI} scores of BERTopic, ETM, NMF, PLSA, LSI and CTM

cal coherence scores, both ranking approximately third in c_v scores and last in c_{NPMI}.

For LSI, while the c_v scores of its topic clusters increased for larger topic counts, the c_{NPMI} scores declined over the same range. This suggests that as the topic count increased, LSI formed more specialised clusters with high word co-occurrence coherence. However, these clusters did not reflect strong word relations, as indicated by the decreasing c_{NPMI} scores (Bouma, 2009; Röder et al., 2015).

As mentioned previously (subsection 3.4), we

cannot specify the number of output clusters for Top2Vec, as it determines the optimal number of clusters autonomously (Angelov, 2020). Table 2 presents the best scores achieved by Top2Vec across various embedding models. We found that the distiluse-base-multilingual-cased model had the best relative performance, with a c_{NPMI} score of -0.48 and a c_v score of 0.54, for 45 topics. The universal-sentence-encoder-multilingual and universal-sentence-encoder models achieved their peak scores at 2 and 7 topics, respectively, suggesting that these models produced overly generalised topic clusters. This indicates that these embedding models were not robust enough to capture the diversity of topics present in Hindi short texts. Additionally, the low c_v score for the topic clusters generated by doc2vec highlights a general lack of semantic coherence in the clusters formed.

Embedding Model	c_{NPMI}	c_v	Topics
distiluse-base-multilingual-cased	**-0.48**	**0.54**	**45**
universal-sentence-encoder-multilingual	-0.45	0.53	2
universal-sentence-encoder	-0.44	0.51	7
doc2vec	-0.33	0.26	24

Table 2: Best scores achieved by Top2Vec using different embedding models

Overall, NMF, PLSA, LSI, CTM and Top2Vec, all had negative c_{NPMI} scores, demonstrating poor performance in modeling Hindi short texts.

4.4 Qualitative Analysis of BERTopic Clusters

Apart from using c_v and c_{NPMI}, we also qualitatively analysed the topic clusters formed by BERTopic through human evaluation, and verified the semantic coherence and relevance of the groupings. The dataset used for topic modeling encompassed a diverse range of topics, including film, tourism, and technology. For example, Figure 10 displays a word cloud for a topic cluster generated using `mBERT-Uncased` embeddings. As we can see, BERTopic successfully grouped reviews related to film and entertainment, capturing key terms such as फ़लि्म ("film") and करिदार ("character") in Hindi, reflecting its ability to form semantically coherent topic groups.

Figure 10: Word Cloud of a topic cluster formed by BERTopic

बात करें तो **एवेंजर्स: एज ऑफ अल्ट्रॉन** देखने को मिलती है।
हैदर में खोज करते हुए **नरेंद्र झा** की भूमिका है।
जेम्स वान सॉ के डायरेक्टर हैं।
हालिया रिलीज फिल्म **सैन एंड्रियास** एक ऐसी फिल्म है।
वेलकम 2 कराची एक नमूना है।

Figure 11: Some reviews belonging to the same cluster

If we examine a few reviews from this cluster (Figure 11), we see that BERTopic recognised the names of famous movies, such as एवेंजर्स: एज ऑफ अल्ट्रॉन (Avengers: Age of Ultron), हैदर (Haider), वेलकम 2 कराची (Welcome 2 Karachi), सॉ (Saw) and सैन एंड्रियास (San Andreas). It also identified the names of actors and directors, like नरेंद्र झा (Narendra Jha) and जेम्स वान (James Wan). BERTopic grouped these reviews into the same cluster, even though some had different word compositions. This indicates that the model effectively captured the contextual use of words, including named entities, with the help of advanced sentence transformers to form meaningful clusters. In contrast, traditional topic models which rely primarily on word frequency and co-occurrence, often fail to capture such semantic relationships, particularly in short texts.

5 Discussion

This study demonstrates that topic models utilising advanced sentence transformers, such as BERTopic and ETM, significantly outperform traditional models when modeling short texts. The success of these models can be attributed to their ability to capture semantic meaning beyond simple word co-occurrence patterns.

Traditional topic modeling algorithms like PLSA and LDA are widely used to uncover latent semantic structures in text corpora by relying on word co-occurrence patterns at the document level. However, these methods require a high frequency of word co-occurrences to generate meaningful topics, leading to significant performance degradation when applied to short texts where such information is sparse (Yin and Wang, 2014; Yan et al., 2013). Similarly, the performance of LSI declines over short texts as the detected topics become ambiguous, resulting in negative values in its decomposed matrices that are difficult to interpret (Murshed et al., 2023; Alghamdi and Alfalqi, 2015). Since many of these traditional models depend heavily on word frequency and co-occurrence, they are more sensitive to variations in spelling, a common issue in Hindi due to the lack of standardised spelling conventions (Ray et al., 2019). These limitations collectively undermine the reliability of traditional models in generating coherent topics from short text corpora.

6 Conclusion

We evaluated the performance of BERTopic relative to other topic models using coherence values (c_v) and normalised pointwise mutual information (c_{NPMI}) across a range of 5 to 210 topics. The results showed that BERTopic, particularly when used with `mBERT-uncased`, outperformed other models for the majority of topic counts. The ETM model, using `HindSBERT-STS`, ranked second, with better c_{NPMI} scores than BERTopic beyond 125 topics, but consistently lower c_v scores. Traditional topic models demonstrated poor performance, having negative c_{NPMI} scores for the entire topic count range.

Qualitative analysis of BERTopic clusters revealed that it effectively grouped semantically similar reviews and accurately recognised named entities, a task at which traditional models struggle. The strong performance of both ETM and BERTopic suggests that leveraging advanced sentence transformers enhances the formation of coherent topic clusters.

We conclude that BERTopic is a promising approach for topic modeling on Hindi short text corpora, particularly when using multilingual transformers fine-tuned on Hindi. Its use can produce semantically coherent topic groups and better handle the unique linguistic complexities of the language. Potential applications include trend analysis, extracting business insights, analysing customer reviews and social media comments.

7 Future Work

Future work can explore the extent to which BERTopic results can be generalised to other Indo-Aryan languages, such as Sanskrit, Prakrit, Marathi, Konkani, and Nepali. These languages share linguistic similarities, including grammatical structure, Subject-Object-Verb (SOV) sentence ordering, and their use of the Devanagari script. This exploration would depend on the availability of sentence transformer models trained specifically for these languages.

Additionally, investigating the adaptability of BERTopic to other morphologically rich and low-resource languages, such as Tamil or Punjabi, could provide valuable insights into its broader applicability. Another promising direction is applying this approach to multilingual datasets or those containing code-mixed content, which reflects the increasing prevalence of mixed-language communication in digital spaces.

It would also be interesting to study how well BERTopic performs on longer texts compared to shorter ones for Indo-Aryan languages like Hindi, as evaluating BERTopic's ability to handle such texts could provide deeper insights into its capacity to model topics in languages with complex linguistic structures and ensure its effectiveness for use cases such as document-level topic extraction.

Limitations

While this comparative study demonstrates the efficiency of BERTopic for topic modeling of Hindi short text reviews, there are some limitations to consider.

First, the IIT Patna Reviews Dataset, although a reputable and commonly used Hindi short text dataset for NLP research in Indian languages, is limited in size, containing only 5,225 reviews. Larger and domain-specific datasets could provide further insights into model performance and robustness. Due to the current lack of available benchmark datasets for Hindi short texts, we relied on this dataset for our study.

The dataset may also exhibit biases that influence the results. For instance, a representation bias exists, with a higher concentration of reviews on popular topics like movies and technology, while niche cultural or regional subjects are underrepresented. Additionally, the dataset may suffer from temporal bias, lacking significant representation of recent language trends, such as modern internet slang or code-mixed communication styles. These biases could lead the models to prioritize dominant themes, although their overall impact on topic formation appears modest.

Furthermore, the dataset spans a broad range of topics, including movies, technology, and tourism. While this diversity mirrors datasets used in prior studies, model performance may differ on more specialized datasets focused on specific types of short texts, such as reviews for a single product category.

Finally, this study primarily aimed to assess the effectiveness of BERTopic for general Hindi short texts, without targeting specific short text types such as informal conversations or mixed-language content. Future research utilizing datasets with narrowly defined topics or specialized short text variants is recommended to evaluate these models in more targeted contexts.

Acknowledgments

We sincerely thank the team at College of Engineering Pune Technological University for verifying and endorsing the quality of the results from our topic modeling pipeline. We also extend our heartfelt gratitude to the anonymous reviewers for their insightful feedback and constructive suggestions.

References

Aly Abdelrazek, Walaa Medhat, Eman Gawish, and Ahmed Hassan. 2022. Topic modeling onăarabic language dataset: Comparative study. In *Advances in Model and Data Engineering in the Digitalization Era*, pages 61–71, Cham. Springer Nature Switzerland.

Abeer Abuzayed and Hend Al-Khalifa. 2021. Bert for arabic topic modeling: An experimental study on bertopic technique. *Procedia Computer Science*, 189:191–194. AI in Computational Linguistics.

Charu C. Aggarwal and ChengXiang Zhai. 2012. *A Survey of Text Clustering Algorithms*, pages 77–128. Springer US, Boston, MA.

Rubayyi Alghamdi and Khalid Alfalqi. 2015. A survey of topic modeling in text mining. *Int. J. Adv. Comput. Sci. Appl.(IJACSA)*, 6(1).

Dimo Angelov. 2020. Top2vec: Distributed representations of topics. *arXiv preprint arXiv:2008.09470*.

David M. Blei, Andrew Y. Ng, and Michael I. Jordan. 2003. Latent dirichlet allocation. *Journal of Machine Learning Research*, 3:993–1022.

Gerlof Bouma. 2009. Normalized (pointwise) mutual information in collocation extraction. *Proceedings of GSCL*, 30:31–40.

Alexis Conneau, Kartikay Khandelwal, Naman Goyal, Vishrav Chaudhary, Guillaume Wenzek, Francisco Guzmán, Edouard Grave, Myle Ott, Luke Zettlemoyer, and Veselin Stoyanov. 2020. Unsupervised cross-lingual representation learning at scale. In *Proceedings of the 58th Annual Meeting of the Association for Computational Linguistics*.

Debapratim Das Dawn, Abhinandan Khan, Soharab Hossain Shaikh, and Rajat Kumar Pal. 2024. Likelihood corpus distribution: an efficient topic modelling scheme for bengali document class identification. *Sādhanā*, 49(3):198.

Scott Deerwester, Susan T. Dumais, George W. Furnas, Thomas K. Landauer, and Richard Harshman. 1990. Indexing by latent semantic analysis. *Journal of the American Society for Information Science*, 41(6):391–407.

Jacob Devlin, Ming-Wei Chang, Kenton Lee, and Kristina Toutanova. 2018. Bert: Pre-training of deep bidirectional transformers for language understanding. *arXiv preprint arXiv:1810.04805*.

Adji B Dieng, Francisco JR Ruiz, and David M Blei. 2020. Topic modeling in embedding spaces. *Transactions of the Association for Computational Linguistics*, 8:439–453.

Maarten Grootendorst. 2022. Bertopic: Neural topic modeling with a class-based tf-idf procedure. *arXiv preprint arXiv:2203.05794*.

Alfiuddin R Hadiat. 2022. *Topic Modeling Evaluations: The Relationship Between Coherency and Accuracy*. Ph.D. thesis.

Jiyin He, Martha Larson, and Maarten de Rijke. 2008. Using coherence-based measures to predict query difficulty. In *Advances in Information Retrieval*, pages 689–694, Berlin, Heidelberg. Springer Berlin Heidelberg.

Jiyin He, Wouter Weerkamp, Martha Larson, and Maarten de Rijke. 2009. An effective coherence measure to determine topical consistency in user-generated content. *International Journal on Document Analysis and Recognition (IJDAR)*, 12(3):185–203.

Thomas Hofmann. 1999. Probabilistic latent semantic analysis. In *Proceedings of the Fifteenth Conference on Uncertainty in Artificial Intelligence (UAI'99)*, pages 289–296.

Hamed Jelodar, Yongli Wang, Chi Yuan, Xia Feng, Xiahui Jiang, Yanchao Li, and Liang Zhao. 2019. Latent dirichlet allocation (lda) and topic modeling: Models, applications, a survey. *Multimedia Tools and Applications*, 78(11):15169–15211.

Vandana Jha, N Manjunath, P Deepa Shenoy, and K R Venugopal. 2018. Hindi language stop words list. https://doi.org/10.17632/bsr3frvvjc.1. Mendeley Data, V1.

Ananya Joshi, Aditi Kajale, Janhavi Gadre, Samruddhi Deode, and Raviraj Joshi. 2022. L3cube-mahasbert and hindsbert: Sentence bert models and benchmarking bert sentence representations for hindi and marathi. *arXiv preprint arXiv:2211.11187*.

Darshan Kakwani, Aman Arora, Simran Khanuja, Gokul Punjabi, Kushal Lakhotia, Anoop Kunchukuttan, and Pushpak Bhattacharyya. 2020. Indicnlpsuite: Monolingual corpora, evaluation benchmarks and pre-trained multilingual language models for indian languages. In *Proceedings of the 2020 Conference on Empirical Methods in Natural Language Processing*.

Daniel D. Lee and H. Sebastian Seung. 1999. Learning the parts of objects by non-negative matrix factorization. *Nature*, 401(6755):788–791.

Yinhan Liu, Pengcheng He, Weizhu Chen, and Jianfeng Gao. 2019. Linguistic knowledge and transferability of contextual representations. In *Proceedings of the 2019 Conference of the North American Chapter of the Association for Computational Linguistics: Human Language Technologies*, pages 1073–1092.

James MacQueen et al. 1967. Some methods for classification and analysis of multivariate observations. In *Proceedings of the fifth Berkeley symposium on mathematical statistics and probability*, volume 1, pages 281–297. Oakland, CA, USA.

Leland McInnes, John Healy, and Steve Astels. 2017. Hdbscan: Hierarchical density based clustering. *Journal of Open Source Software*, 2(11):205.

Leland McInnes, John Healy, and James Melville. 2018. Umap: Uniform manifold approximation and projection for dimension reduction. *arXiv preprint arXiv:1802.03426*.

Darija Medvecki, Bojana Bašaragin, Adela Ljajić, and Nikola Milošević. 2024. Multilingual transformer and bertopic for short text topic modeling: The case of serbian. In *Disruptive Information Technologies for a Smart Society*, pages 161–173, Cham. Springer Nature Switzerland.

Tomas Mikolov. 2013. Efficient estimation of word representations in vector space. *arXiv preprint arXiv:1301.3781*.

Belal Abdullah Hezam Murshed, Suresha Mallappa, Jemal Abawajy, Mufeed Ahmed Naji Saif, Hasib Daowd Esmail Al-Ariki, and Hudhaifa Mohammed Abdulwahab. 2023. Short text topic modelling approaches in the context of big data: taxonomy, survey, and analysis. *Artificial Intelligence Review*, 56(6):5133–5260.

David Newman, Edwin V Bonilla, and Wray Buntine. 2011. Improving topic coherence with regularized topic models. In *Advances in Neural Information Processing Systems*, volume 24. Curran Associates, Inc.

Sabitra Sankalp Panigrahi, Narayan Panigrahi, and Biswajit Paul. 2018. Modelling of topic from hindi corpus using word2vec. In *2018 Second International Conference on Advances in Computing, Control and Communication Technology (IAC3T)*, pages 97–100.

Matthew E Peters, Mark Neumann, Mohit Iyyer, Matt Gardner, Christopher Clark, Kenton Lee, and Luke Zettlemoyer. 2018. Deep contextualized word representations. *arXiv preprint arXiv:1802.05365*.

Jipeng Qiang, Zhenyu Qian, Yun Li, Yunhao Yuan, and Xindong Wu. 2022. Short text topic modeling techniques, applications, and performance: A survey. *IEEE Transactions on Knowledge and Data Engineering*, 34(3):1427–1445.

Santosh Kumar Ray, Amir Ahmad, and Ch Aswani Kumar. 2019. Review and implementation of topic modeling in hindi. *Applied Artificial Intelligence*, 33(11):979–1007.

Nils Reimers and Iryna Gurevych. 2019. Sentence-bert: Sentence embeddings using siamese bert-networks. In *Proceedings of the 2019 Conference on Empirical Methods in Natural Language Processing*, pages 3982–3992.

Michael Röder, Andreas Both, and Alexander Hinneburg. 2015. Exploring the space of topic coherence measures. In *Proceedings of the Eighth ACM International Conference on Web Search and Data Mining*, WSDM '15, page 399408, New York, NY, USA. Association for Computing Machinery.

Anukriti Srivastav and Satwinder Singh. 2022. Proposed model for context topic identification of english and hindi news article through lda approach with nlp technique. *Journal of The Institution of Engineers (India): Series B*, 103(2):591–597.

Yee Whye Teh, Michael I. Jordan, Matthew J. Beal, and David M. Blei. 2006. Hierarchical dirichlet processes. *Journal of the American Statistical Association*, 101(476):1566–1581.

Silvia Terragni, Elisabetta Fersini, Bruno Giovanni Galuzzi, Pietro Tropeano, and Antonio Candelieri. 2021. OCTIS: Comparing and optimizing topic models is simple! In *Proceedings of the 16th Conference of the European Chapter of the Association for Computational Linguistics: System Demonstrations*, pages 263–270. Association for Computational Linguistics.

Konstantin Vorontsov and Anna Potapenko. 2015. Additive regularization of topic models. In *Journal of Machine Learning Research: Workshop and Conference Proceedings*, volume 39, pages 1349–1357.

Xiaohui Yan, Jiafeng Guo, Yanyan Lan, and Xueqi Cheng. 2013. A biterm topic model for short texts. In *Proceedings of the 22nd International Conference on World Wide Web*, WWW '13, page 14451456, New York, NY, USA. Association for Computing Machinery.

Jianhua Yin and Jianyong Wang. 2014. A dirichlet multinomial mixture model-based approach for short text clustering. In *Proceedings of the 20th ACM SIGKDD International Conference on Knowledge Discovery and Data Mining*, KDD '14, page 233242, New York, NY, USA. Association for Computing Machinery.

Evaluating Structural and Linguistic Quality in Urdu DRS Parsing and Generation through Bidirectional Evaluation

Muhammad Saad Amin, Luca Anselma and Alessandro Mazzei
Department of Computer Science, University of Turin, Italy
{muhammadsaad.amin, luca.anselma, alessandro.mazzei}@unito.it

Abstract

Evaluating Discourse Representation Structure (DRS)-based systems for semantic parsing (Text-to-DRS) and generation (DRS-to-Text) poses unique challenges, particularly in low-resource languages like Urdu. Traditional metrics often fall short, focusing either on structural accuracy or linguistic quality, but rarely capturing both. To address this limitation, we introduce two complementary evaluation methodologies—Parse-Generate (PARS-GEN) and Generate-Parse (GEN-PARS)—designed for a more comprehensive assessment of DRS-based systems. PARS-GEN evaluates the parsing process by converting DRS outputs back to the text, revealing linguistic nuances often missed by structure-focused metrics like SMATCH. In contrast, GEN-PARS assesses text generation by converting generated text into DRS, providing a semantic perspective that complements surface-level metrics such as BLEU, METEOR, and BERTScore. Using the Parallel Meaning Bank (PMB) dataset, we demonstrate our methodology in Urdu, uncovering unique insights into the structural and linguistic interplay of Urdu. The findings show that traditional metrics frequently overlook the complexity of linguistic and semantic fidelity, especially in low-resource languages. Our dual approach offers a robust framework for evaluating DRS-based systems, improving semantic parsing and text generation quality[1].

1 Introduction

DRS is central to advanced semantic processing, providing a flexible and language-neutral framework for capturing complex semantic nuances beyond basic text interpretation (Kamp and Reyle, 1993), including phenomena such as negation and quantification (Kamp and Reyle, 2013; Jaszczolt and Jaszczolt, 2023). Its adaptability makes DRS ideal for multilingual natural language processing (NLP) systems, offering a unified way of representing meaning across languages with diverse structural and syntactic properties (Bos, 2023).

DRS parsing (van Noord et al., 2018; Noord, 2019; van Noord et al., 2019) and generation (Wang et al., 2021; Amin et al., 2022; Liu et al., 2021; Amin et al., 2024) are reversible processes which pose unique challenges, especially when working with Urdu—a morphologically rich language. Urdu exhibits different syntactic structures and semantic expressions, making accurate evaluation difficult due to the limitations of traditional structural and surface-level metrics (Butt and King, 2002; Bögel et al., 2009). Existing evaluations often fail to fully account for linguistic and structural accuracy across languages, which is essential for ensuring meaningful cross-linguistic semantic representation. This gap has motivated our development of innovative evaluation methods to bridge structural precision with linguistic adequacy in DRS-based systems.

Our research primarily aims to create evaluation frameworks that integrate both *structural* and *linguistic* (in the sense of *surface-level*) assessments. To accomplish this, we introduce two bidirectional evaluation paradigms—PARS/PARS-GEN and GEN/GEN-PARS. The former assesses parsing quality by examining the linguistic coherence of the text generated from DRS structures, moving beyond traditional metrics to provide insights into how well structural accuracy supports meaningful language representation. Conversely, the latter evaluates generation quality by analyzing the semantic consistency of parsed structures derived from generated text, offering a deeper perspective than surface-level comparisons alone.

Semantic parsing evaluation typically relies on structural metrics like SMATCH (Cai and Knight, 2013), which assesses roles or concepts-based overlaps between predicted and reference DRS

[1] https://github.com/saadamin2k13/counter-evaluations-for-urdu.

Proceedings of the First Workshop on Natural Language Processing for Indo-Aryan and Dravidian Languages (IndoNLP2025), pages 33–43
January 20, 2025. ©2025 Association for Computational Linguistics

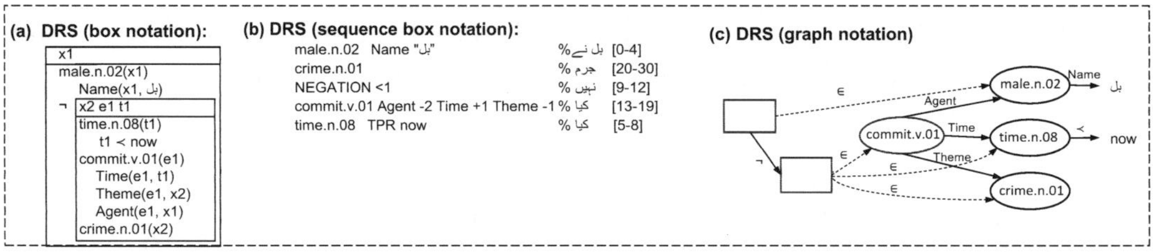

Figure 1: Different graphical representations of DRS for the text "Bill didn't commit the crime."

graphs (Kamp et al., 2010). While valuable for evaluating structural accuracy, this metric often misses essential linguistic subtleties and penalizes the overall evaluation. For instance, two DRS representations with minor structural divergences, such as `Quantity` and `Index`, obtained a significantly low SMATCH score despite near-identical semantics (Ex. 4, Table 1). Such distinctions illustrate how structural metrics alone may fall short in capturing the semantic nuances, coherence, and pragmatic meaning crucial to linguistic representation. This limitation inspired the development of the PARS/PARS-GEN approach, which leverages text generation to assess parsing quality, highlighting linguistic phenomena that structural metrics might otherwise overlook.

Text generation from DRS also poses a unique evaluation challenge. Traditional metrics like BLEU (Papineni et al., 2002), METEOR (Banerjee and Lavie, 2005), and even recent metrics like BERTScore (Hanna and Bojar, 2021) prioritize surface-level similarities between generated and reference texts. However, given the diversity of natural language, there can be multiple valid expressions for the same meaning. For example, the sentences ("*John gave Mary some money*") and ("*John gave the money to Mary*") convey similar meanings, but their syntactic variations lead to low scores under traditional evaluations, despite perfect semantic equivalence in DRS representation (Ex. 4, Table 2). To address this, we propose the GEN/GEN-PARS paradigm, which evaluates generated text by parsing it back into DRS, offering a structural evaluation perspective that complements surface-level metrics.

In this context, our research investigates several critical questions: (i) How can the evaluation of semantic parsing and text generation be improved beyond existing structural and surface-level metrics? (ii) How does structural accuracy in semantic parsing influence linguistic quality in text generation? (iii) How can surface-level evaluations be enhanced by assessing individual lexical entities? (iv) Can the reversible nature of semantic parsing and text generation be exploited for improved evaluations? and (v) Do these alternate evaluations correlate with each other and are they statistically significant?

To address these questions, this paper makes the following key contributions: (i) it introduces novel evaluation paradigms, PARS/PARS-GEN and GEN/GEN-PARS, which reveal unique insights into the language's syntactic variability and complex semantic structures that traditional metrics often overlook; (ii) the PARS/PARS-GEN paradigm uses linearized text to mitigate non-optimal outcomes in SMATCH's greedy search algorithm, enabling a more intuitive and human-centered approach to parsing evaluation; (iii) through the GEN/GEN-PARS evaluation, it identifies semantic and syntactic issues at a node level, examining lexical DRS concepts like nouns, verbs, adjectives, and adverbs within the generated DRS to provide a granular view of the generation quality, ultimately facilitating a balanced metric that captures both structural and linguistic fidelity; and (iv) it proposes a detailed Pearson correlation analysis between PARS/PARS-GEN, GEN/GEN-PARS. The observed statistically significant correlations underscore the robustness of our approach and demonstrate the effectiveness of combining structural and linguistic assessments in DRS-based semantic processing. Figure 1 contains different graphical representations of the DRS containing: (a) box format; (b) variable-free format; and (c) graph notation of the DRS. For our experimentation, we used the variable-free representation of the DRS (Figure. 1(b)) in its linearized format, as it is compatible with the sequence-to-sequence models. Additionally, we utilized its graph notation (Figure. 1(c)) to evaluate semantic parsing using SMATCH.

Ex. No	Gold Text	Gold (DRS)	PARS (DRS)	PARS (SMATCH)
1	ٹام نے ایک نیا پک اپ خریدا۔ ("Tom bought a new pickup.")	male.n.02 Name "ٹام" new.a.05 AttributeOf +1 pickup.n.01 buy.v.01 Agent -3 Theme -1 Time +1 time.n.08 TPR now	male.n.02 Name "ٹام" new.a.01 AttributeOf +1 pick_up.n.01 buy.v.01 Agent -4 Beneficiary -3 Theme -1 Time +1 time.n.08 TPR now	00.00
2	ٹام مریم کو اپنے کتے کی تصویر دکھاتا ہے۔ ("Tom shows Mary a picture of his dog.")	male.n.02 Name "ٹام" female.n.02 Name "مریم" male.n.02 ANA -2 dog.n.01 Owner -1 picture.n.01 Topic -1 show.v.04 Agent -5 Recipient -4 Theme -1 Time +1 time.n.08 TPR now	male.n.02 Name "ٹام" female.n.02 Name "مریم" female.n.02 ANA -1 dog.n.01 Owner -1 photo.n.01 Creator -1 show.v.01 Agent -4 Recipient -3 Recipient -1 Time +1 time.n.08 TPR now	69.23
3	آج میری گردن میں درد ہے۔ ("Today I have a pain in my neck.")	day.n.03 TCT now time.n.08 TIN -1 person.n.01 EQU speaker neck.n.01 pain.n.01 Location -1 have.v.16 Time -4 Experiencer -3 Stimulus -1 Time +1 time.n.08 EQU now	person.n.01 EQU speaker neck.n.01 hurt.v.01 Patient -2 Patient -1 Time +1 time.n.08 EQU now	60.00
4	تیرہ افراد کو گرفتار کر لیا گیا۔ ("Thirteen people were arrested.")	quantity.n.01 EQU 13 person.n.01 Quantity -1 arrest.v.01 Patient -1 Time +1 time.n.08 TPR now	quantity.n.01 EQU 30 person.n.01 Quantity -1 arrest.v.01 Patient -3 Time +1 time.n.08 TPR now	00.00
5	میرے پاس بہت پیسہ ہے۔ ("I have a lot of money.")	person.n.01 EQU speaker money.n.01 Quantity + get.v.01 Pivot -2 Theme -1 Time +1 time.n.08 TPR now	person.n.01 EQU speaker have.v.01 Pivot -1 Theme +2 Time +3 quantity.n.01 EQU +1 quantity.n.01 EQU +1 money.n.01 Quantity + time.n.08 EQU now	57.89

Table 1: Structural overlap-based evaluation measures: highlighting limitations of SMATCH. English translations are mentioned in brackets. PARS scores are in %.

The remaining sections are organized as follows: Section 2 discusses the limitations of current evaluation approaches in detail. Section 3 presents our novel evaluation methodologies and describes the experimental setup and implementation details. Section 4 presents reversible evaluation measures and correlation analysis. Finally, Section 5 concludes with limitations.

2 Limitations in Current Evaluations

The evaluation of semantic parsing and text generation system presents unique challenges that conventional metrics often struggle to address comprehensively. This section examines these limitations in detail and establishes the motivation for our proposed evaluation approaches.

Parsing Limitations: Traditional evaluation metrics, such as SMATCH (Cai and Knight, 2013), SMATCH++ (Opitz, 2023), and SemBLEU (Song and Gildea, 2019), focus on assessing structural similarities between predicted and reference DRS. SMATCH, for instance, employs a greedy hill-climbing algorithm that matches nodes across logical structures. This approach, however, often results in suboptimal evaluations, especially in cases where structural differences do not reflect actual semantic deviations. For example, SMATCH assigns a zero score to the DRS representation for ("*Tom bought a new pickup*"), despite the semantic content being essentially equivalent in both gold and predicted DRS. The low-score is due to minor structural differences, underscoring a limitation of SMATCH's focus on structural alignment rather than semantic equivalence (Ex. 1, Table 1).

Additionally, SMATCH's handling of semantic relationships is limited, as it treats DRS nodes as isolated entities. This limitation is evident in Ex. 2 ("*Tom shows Mary a picture of his dog*"), where differences in role modifiers like ("`Topic`" and "`Creator`") for "picture" results in a SMATCH score of 69.23. The metric's penalty for these isolated structural variations, without accounting for the underlying semantic alignment, highlights its tendency to overlook contextually equivalent expressions when modifiers are altered or substituted. This penalization is further illustrated in Ex. 3 ("*Today I have a pain in my neck*"), where SMATCH deducts points based on minor discrepancies in the verb sense, yielding a score of 60.00 despite the overall message being well-preserved across both DRS.

In Ex. 4 ("*Thirteen people were arrested*"), SMATCH once again assigns a score of zero, this time due to an inconsistency in the numerical value between gold (13) and predicted (30) DRS. This significant deduction overlooks that the core event—people being arrested—is accurately conveyed. Ex. 5 ("*I have a lot of money*") further emphasizes SMATCH's limitations, where minor numerical and role-discrepancies lead to a score of 57.89, despite the intended meaning being largely retained. These examples collectively underscore that SMATCH's sensitivity to structural changes can cause unfairly low scores even when semantic content is mostly preserved.

Ex. No.	Gold DRS	Gold Text	GEN Text	GEN Scores				
				BLEU	METEOR	ROUGE	chrF	B_Scr.
1	person.n.01 EQU speaker ashamed.a.01 Experiencer -1 Time +1 NEGATION <1 time.n.08 EQU now	میں شرمندہ نہیں ہوں. ("I am not ashamed.")	میں ابھی تک شرمندہ نہیں ہوں. ("I'm not shy yet.")	16.67	11.90	19.99	21.95	78.96
2	person.n.01 EQU speaker quantity.n.01 EQU 24 pencil.n.01 Quantity -1 buy.v.01 Agent -3 Theme -1 Time +1 time.n.08 TPR now	میں نے دو درجن پنسلیں خریدیں۔ ("I bought two dozen pencils.")	میں نے 24 پنسلیں خریدیں۔ ("I bought 24 pencils.")	49.12	43.31	54.54	39.79	92.09
3	NEGATION <1 person.n.01 NEGATION <1 leave.v.01 Theme -1 Time +1 time.n.08 TPR now	سب چلے گئے۔ ("Everyone left.")	اب سب چلے گئے ہیں۔ ("All have now left.")	50.00	32.25	57.14	29.38	88.74
4	male.n.02 Name "جان" female.n.02 Name "مریم" money.n.01 give.v.03 Agent -3 Recipient -2 Theme -1 Time +1 time.n.08 TPR now	جان نے مریم کو کچھ پیسے دیے۔ ("John gave Mary some money.")	جان نے رقم مریم کو دی۔ ("John gave the money to Mary.")	56.43	57.52	61.54	48.84	89.99
5	male.n.02 time.n.08 YearOfCentury '198X' bear.v.02 Patient -2 Time -1 Time +1 time.n.08 TPR now	وہ اسی کی دہائی میں پیدا ہوئے۔ ("He was born in the eighties.")	وہ استی میں پیدا ہوئے۔ ("He was born in 198X.")	42.32	37.04	44.15	34.12	79.26

Table 2: Semantic overlap-based evaluation measures: highlighting limitations of automatic evaluation metrics for text generation. Note: B_Scr. = BERTScore.

To address these limitations, our PARS-GEN approach rephrases DRS outputs as natural language text, enabling the use of complementary evaluation metrics like chrF, METEOR, and BERTScore, which emphasizes semantic accuracy. By generating interpretable text from DRS, PARS-GEN provides a holistic evaluation of parsing quality and captures linguistic nuances that structural metrics like SMATCH often miss. Through this approach, we enhance the accessibility and interpretability of semantic fidelity assessment, ensuring a more accurate and inclusive evaluation across diverse language structures and semantics.

Generation Limitations: Traditional evaluation metrics for Urdu text generation, like BLEU, METEOR, and ROUGE, primarily rely on n-gram overlaps, limiting their ability to capture semantic alignment beyond lexical matches. This is particularly evident in our DRS-to-text generation examples in Table 2. For instance, BLEU assigns a score of 16.67 to the generated translation ("*I am not ashamed yet*") compared to the gold reference ("*I'm not shy yet*") (Ex. 1, Table 2). While the generated text conveys the same core meaning, the BLEU score is low due to slight lexical variations in the choice of words like "ashamed" vs. "shy." This highlights BLEU's emphasis on lexical overlap over capturing the overall meaning of the sentence.

Similarly, for the translation ("*I bought two dozen pencils*") compared to ("*I bought 24 pencils*"), both sentences convey the same meaning but are penalized due to different representations i.e., "two dozen" vs. "24." This exemplifies the metric's failure to acknowledge acceptable paraphrases or equivalent expressions in the target language, further underscoring its limitations in multilingual contexts. In both cases, SMATCH indicates complete semantic alignment with a score of 1.0, highlighting the gap in traditional metrics' sensitivity to semantic fidelity. METEOR, which improves on BLEU by considering synonym matching and stemming, does provide higher scores for the same example (43.31 vs. BLEU's 49.12), but it is not immune to limitations. METEOR still struggles with capturing fine-grained semantic differences, as seen in Ex. 5 in Table 2, where the score of 37.04 fails to distinguish between "*He was born in 198X*" and "*He was born in the eighties*". Despite both sentences being semantically similar, METEOR's score is lower because it does not consider the subtleties of temporal expressions in Urdu and fails to fully match the corresponding time entities. The chrF score (which focuses on character-level n-gram overlap) in this context, with scores ranging from 21.95 (Ex. 1) to 39.79 (Ex. 2), similarly fails to capture the underlying semantic similarity. While chrF is more effective for languages with complex morphology, such as Urdu, it still penalizes minor differences in word structure and morphology, even when the generated text accurately conveys the intended meaning. In Ex. 1, "ashamed" vs. "shy" shows small morphological differences that affect chrF's performance, despite the generated text being semantically correct.

BERTScore, which attempts to measure semantic similarity using pre-trained language models, is better suited for capturing the deeper semantic relationships between words. However, even this metric struggles when dealing with syntactic and morphological variations in Urdu. For instance, in Ex. 3, "*Everyone left*" and "*All have now left*" exhibit a difference in tense and aspect, yet the meaning remains intact. BERTScore performs better here with scores of 88.74, but still faces challenges when evaluating minor syntactic differences that do not affect the overall meaning.

These examples underscore the need for an evaluation approach that emphasizes semantic quality. Our GEN-PARS approach addresses this by focusing on whether generated texts preserve the semantic content of the original DRS. Across all examples analyzed, where traditional metrics like BLEU fluctuate significantly (ranging from 16.67 to 56.43), GEN-PARS achieves perfect SMATCH scores of 1.0 by parsing generated texts back to DRS. This validates semantic equivalence despite surface differences as evident in Table 6.

3 Methods and Results

This study presents two novel evaluation methodologies for assessing the quality of DRS parsing and generation in Urdu: (1) evaluating parsing through generation capabilities (PARS-GEN) and (2) assessing generation through semantic parsing (GEN-PARS). Unlike conventional metrics that often focus on surface-level text similarity or structural alignment, these methodologies offer a deeper, cross-task approach that assesses both structural and linguistic fidelity in Urdu semantic processing. To complement our cross-task evaluations, we also computed the Pearson correlation between metrics across the PARS/PARS-GEN and GEN/GEN-PARS evaluations. This correlation analysis helps us understand the relationship between structural accuracy (e.g., SMATCH F1 scores) and linguistic quality metrics (e.g., BLEU, METEOR, BERTScore).

PMB[2] is a multilingual dataset comprising semantic representations in English, Italian, German, Dutch, and Chinese. Leveraging the language-neutral nature of DRS, we transformed English DRS-Text pairs into Urdu through a systematic approach involving syntactic structure, concept and word alignment, grammatical genders, and cross-lingual adaptation through named entities. This methodology resulted in the first comprehensive semantic resource for Urdu, comprising 3,000 gold-standard (fully manually annotated) data instances. The dataset transformation employed a hybrid methodology: DRS transformations utilized rule-based techniques and human annotation, while text translations were generated using Google Translate API. The dataset was partitioned into 1,200 training, 900 development, and 900 test examples. To enhance dataset diversity and complexity, we applied multi-dimensional augmentation strategies, including named entities, lexical (encompassing common nouns, adjectives, adverbs, and verbs), and grammatical augmentations. This approach expanded the dataset to 10,800 training examples, supplemented by 6,857 silver (partially manually annotated) instances.

For bidirectional evaluation—converting PARS to PARS-GEN and vice versa—we employed byT5-based parsing and generation models, fine-tuned using our comprehensive augmented dataset[3]. We implemented a two-stage fine-tuning strategy consistent with (van Noord et al., 2020). The first stage involved fine-tuning the model on silver data for 3 epochs to establish foundational DRS knowledge. The second stage focused on gold data fine-tuning for 10 epochs. Experimental parameters included AdamW optimizer, polynomial learning rate decay (1e−4), batch size of 32, maximum sequence length of 512, and GeGLU activation function. These models achieved state-of-the-art performance in Urdu DRS processing, facilitating reversible data generation.

For the PARS/PARS-GEN evaluations in Urdu (see Table 3), we achieved a SMATCH F1 score of 79.77, indicating a moderate level of structural accuracy in parsing Urdu texts into DRS. When this parsed DRS output was subsequently evaluated through generation (PARS-GEN), performance varied across different metrics, highlighting the challenges posed by Urdu's morphological complexity. Notably, the PARS-GEN evaluation returned a BLEU score of 45.48, a METEOR score of 41.39, chrF of 40.57, BERTScore of 85.36, and ROUGE of 49.55. Among these metrics, BERTScore showed the highest correlation

[2]The PMB is developed at the University of Groningen as part of the NWO-VICI project "Lost in Translation—Found in Meaning" (Project number 277-89-003), led by Johan Bos. Urdu PMB is not part of the official website yet, but can be provided freely for scientific purposes.

[3]Our Urdu semantic parsing and text generation models are publically available for research purposes.

with the PARS structural evaluation (SMATCH), suggesting that it better captures semantic consistency across the tasks. However, lower scores in BLEU, METEOR, and chrF reflect the challenge of generating text that matches reference structures while accounting for Urdu's flexible syntax and morphology.

PARS	PARS-GEN				
S-F1	BLU	MET	chrF	B_Scr	RUG
79.77	45.48	41.39	40.57	85.36	49.55

Table 3: Experimental results of PARS and PARS-GEN on standard test sets for Urdu. Underlined are the results with hightest correlation. Note: S-F1 = SMATCH F1-Score; BLU = BLEU; MET = METEOR; B_Scr = BERTScore; RUG = ROUGE.

In the GEN/GEN-PARS evaluations (see Table 4), we assessed how well the generated Urdu text preserved the intended DRS semantics by parsing it back into a DRS representation. Here, the GEN approach achieved moderate scores, with BLEU at 53.31, METEOR at 53.07, chrF at 51.49, BERTScore at 88.33, and ROUGE at 59.40. The GEN-PARS evaluation returned a SMATCH score of 74.83, emphasizing that maintaining full semantic accuracy is challenging in text-to-DRS parsing for Urdu, possibly due to its unique syntactic structures. BERTScore again showed the strongest correlation with GEN-PARS results, indicating it is more aligned with the structural preservation needed in semantic evaluations.

GEN					GPAR
BLU	MET	chrF	B_Scr	RUG	S-F1
53.31	53.07	51.49	88.33	59.40	74.83

Table 4: Experimental results of GEN and GEN-PARS approaches on standard test sets for Urdu. Underlined are the results with hightest correlation. Note: GPAR = GEN-PARS; S-F1 = SMATCH F1-Score.

These results underscore that traditional metrics alone may not fully capture the linguistic intricacies in Urdu DRS parsing and generation. The relatively lower scores in some linguistic metrics, such as BLEU and METEOR, indicate that while structural preservation (PARS) aligns moderately well with these scores, morphological and syntactic differences specific to Urdu lead to lower alignment in n-gram-based and surface-level metrics. This suggests the potential benefit of incorporating additional language-specific evaluation strategies when working with morphologically complex languages like Urdu.

4 Analysis and Discussion

To further emphasize the usefulness of the reversible evaluation approaches, we have analyzed examples present in Table 1 and Table 2 by performing the reverse evaluations, i.e., PARS through PARS-GEN and GEN through GEN-PARS. Furthermore, we have performed Pearson correlation analysis on the reversible evaluation measures.

Reversible Evaluation Measures: While Sections 2 highlighted the limitations of traditional parsing and generation metrics individually, in this section we present the cases where our proposed evaluation approaches (PARS-GEN and GEN-PARS) provide complementary evidence of semantic and structural preservation. Through detailed analysis, we demonstrate how low scores in one type of evaluation (PARS or GEN) can be counter-verified by evaluating it in the reverse direction, revealing semantic equivalences that would have been missed.

Evaluating PARS through PARS-GEN: In analyzing DRS with structural overlap metrics like SMATCH, certain limitations in capturing the full semantic equivalence between the gold standard and generated DRS is evident. Table 1 highlights this issue through examples where PARS (DRS) scores do not adequately reflect semantic alignment despite the intended meaning being correctly represented. These examples underscore a critical drawback of relying solely on structural metrics, as they may fail to capture essential meaning alignment between generated and gold structures.

To address these limitations, PARS-GEN (text generation from DRS) evaluations in Table 5 supplement structural assessments with semantic overlap metrics, including BLEU, METEOR, ROUGE, chrF, and BERTScore, which provide a finer-grained view of how well the generated text aligns with the gold text. In Ex. 1, PARS-GEN achieves a BERTScore of 97.30 and METEOR of 69.14, capturing the semantic fidelity of the phrase "*Tom bought a new pickup*". Although SMATCH did not register structural similarity, the text-based evaluations in PARS-GEN reveal a strong overlap in meaning. Similarly, Ex. 2 achieves perfect PARS-GEN score across all metrics (BLEU:

Ex. No.	PARS DRS	PARS (SMATCH)	PARS GEN Text	Gold Text	GEN Scores				
					BLEU	METEOR	ROUGE	chrF	B_Scr.
1	male.n.02 Name "ٹام" new.a.01 AttributeOf +1 pick_up.n.01 buy.v.01 Agent -4 Beneficiary -3 Theme -1 Time +1 time.n.08 TPR now	00.00	ٹام نے ایک نیا پک اپ خریدا۔ ("Tom bought a new pickup.")	ٹام نے ایک نیا پک اپ خریدا۔ ("Tom bought a new pickup.")	71.43	69.14	71.43	64.14	97.30
2	male.n.02 Name "ٹام" female.n.02 Name "مریم" female.n.02 ANA -1 dog.n.01 Owner -1 photo.n.01 Creator -1 show.v.01 Agent -4 Recipient -3 Recipient -1 Time +1 time.n.08 TPR now	69.23	ٹام مریم کو اپنے کتے کی تصویر دکھاتا ہے۔ ("Tom shows Mary a picture of his dog")	ٹام مریم کو اپنے کتے کی تصویر دکھاتا ہے۔ ("Tom shows Mary a picture of his dog.")	100	99.93	99.99	100	100
3	person.n.01 EQU speaker neck.n.01 hurt.v.01 Patient -2 Patient -1 Time +1 time.n.08 EQU now	60.00	میری گردن میں اب بھی درد ہے۔ ("My neck still hurts.")	آج میری گردن میں درد ہے۔ ("Today I have a pain in my neck.")	57.14	61.47	61.54	48.07	87.11
4	quantity.n.01 EQU 30 person.n.01 Quantity -1 arrest.v.01 Patient -3 Time +1 time.n.08 TPR now	00.00	تیس افراد کو گرفتار کر لیا گیا۔ ("Thirty people were arrested.")	تیرہ افراد کو گرفتار کر لیا گیا۔ ("Thirteen people were arrested.")	56.43	54.35	61.54	61.72	94.55
5	person.n.01 EQU speaker have.v.01 Pivot -1 Theme +2 Time +3 quantity.n.01 EQU +1 quantity.n.01 EQU +1 money.n.01 Quantity + time.n.08 EQU now	57.89	میرے پاس بہت پیسہ ہے۔ ("I have a lot of money.")	میرے پاس بہت پیسہ ہے۔ ("I have a lot of money.")	83.33	80.66	83.33	76.08	97.63

Table 5: Evaluating PARS through PARS-GEN by taking examples from Table 1. Note: B_Scr. = BERTScore.

100, METEOR: 99.93, ROUGE: 99.99, chrF: 100, BERTScore: 100), demonstrating that, despite SMATCH's inability to capture semantic alignment, PARS-GEN accurately reflects the intended message that the `Owner` showed the `Recipient` a picture of dog.

Furthermore, Ex. 3 in Table 1 highlights a nuanced challenge where SMATCH (60.00) underestimates the semantic alignment due to complex relational and sentiment-bearing expressions. Here, the DRS encodes the phrase "*My neck still hurts*" yet this overlap is inadequately represented by the structural metric. In contrast, PARS-GEN scores in Table 5, with a BERTScore of 87.11, provides a closer approximation of the intended meaning, thereby validating the DRS from a semantic standpoint. Similarly, Ex. 5 also demonstrates this phenomenon, where a SMATCH score of 57.89 misses subtle lexical differences in phrases like ("*I have a lot of money*"), PARS-GEN BLEU (83.33) and BERTScore (97.63) confirm semantic equivalence, which structural evaluation alone failed to capture.

This analysis reveals that PARS-GEN complements structural metrics by providing a more robust measure of semantic fidelity in text generation tasks. By using both PARS and PARS-GEN, we gain a comprehensive understanding of meaning overlap, particularly in cases where linguistic nuances or variations may obscure the structural alignment but are nonetheless captured through text-based evaluations. Together, PARS and PARS-GEN offer a dual approach that effectively bridges the gap between structural and semantic overlap, enhancing the accuracy and reliability of DRS evaluation.

Evaluating GEN through GEN-PARS: The evaluation of generated text against gold DRS (after performing GEN-PARS) using semantic overlap metrics reveal critical insights into the limitations of traditional automatic metrics for text generation. Table 2 outlines these issues, showcasing several examples where semantic alignment is assessed through automatic word-overlap-based measures, e.g., BLEU, METEOR, ROUGE, chrF, and BERTScore. This discrepancy suggests that, traditional evaluation metrics for Urdu text focus on n-gram matching, they may not adequately capture the semantic richness and structural sequences represented in the DRS.

Transitioning to Table 6, which focuses on structural overlap metrics, we observe the implementation of GEN-PARS, which assesses the generated text against the original DRS. Notably, all examples (1-5) yield a perfect SMATCH score of 100, signifying that the generated structures align perfectly with the gold DRS. For instance, in Ex. 1, the transition from "*I'm not shy yet*" in GEN to the corresponding GEN-PARS representation maintains the event structure intact, reinforcing the idea that the generated text retains all necessary elements for a correct DRS encoding.

Furthermore, Ex. 3 and Ex. 4 reveal similar patterns. Both examples demonstrate that the generated text aligns seamlessly with the DRS structure, as evidenced by the SMATCH scores of 100. The transformation from "*All have now left*" and "*John gave the money to Mary*" to their DRS representations encapsulate the essential semantic components, reinforcing the effectiveness of GEN-PARS

Ex. No.	GEN Text	GEN-PARS (DRS)	Gold DRS	GPARS (SMATCH)
1	میں ابھی تک شرمندہ نہیں ہوں. ("I'm not shy yet.")	person.n.01 EQU speaker ashamed.a.01 Experiencer -1 Time +1 NEGATION <1 time.n.08 EQU now	person.n.01 EQU speaker ashamed.a.01 Experiencer -1 Time +1 NEGATION <1 time.n.08 EQU now	100
2	میں نے 24 پنسلیں خریدیں۔ ("I bought 24 pencils.")	person.n.01 EQU speaker quantity.n.01 EQU 24 pencil.n.01 Quantity -1 buy.v.01 Agent -3 Theme -1 Time +1 time.n.08 TPR now	person.n.01 EQU speaker quantity.n.01 EQU 24 pencil.n.01 Quantity -1 buy.v.01 Agent -3 Theme -1 Time +1 time.n.08 TPR now	100
3	اب سب چلے گئے ہیں۔ ("All have now left.")	NEGATION <1 person.n.01 NEGATION <1 leave.v.01 Theme -1 Time +1 time.n.08 TPR now	NEGATION <1 person.n.01 NEGATION <1 leave.v.01 Theme -1 Time +1 time.n.08 TPR now	100
4	جان نے رقم مریم کو دی۔ ("John gave the money to Mary.")	male.n.02 Name "جان" female.n.02 Name "مریم" money.n.01 give.v.03 Agent -3 Recipient -2 Theme -1 Time +1 time.n.08 TPR now	male.n.02 Name "جان" female.n.02 Name "مریم" money.n.01 give.v.03 Agent -3 Recipient -2 Theme -1 Time +1 time.n.08 TPR now	100
5	وہ اسّی میں پیدا ہوئے۔ ("He was born in 198X.")	male.n.02 time.n.08 YearOfCentury 198X bear.v.02 Patient -2 Time -1 Time +1 time.n.08 TPR now	male.n.02 time.n.08 YearOfCentury '198X' bear.v.02 Patient -2 Time -1 Time +1 time.n.08 TPR now	100

Table 6: Evaluating GEN through GEN-PARS by taking examples from Table 2. Note: GPARS = GEN-PARS

in maintaining structural integrity while providing a high-quality semantic output.

The role of word order and the presence of synonyms in model-generated outputs (either DRS or text) significantly influence the model performance and should be carefully considered. In the SMATCH evaluation, the impact of word order is generally minimal because SMATCH emphasizes structural overlap rather than the precise sequence of words. However, in cases where the meaning of a sentence is heavily based on its syntactic arrangement, SMATCH may not adequately capture the nuances, making it less effective for parsing evaluation. Similarly, SMATCH evaluates exact lexical entities, leading to penalties for synonymous expressions that maintain semantic equivalence but differ in lexical choice. To address these limitations, our cross-task evaluation approach (PARS/PARS-GEN) generates textual representations of DRSs and evaluates these using n-gram overlaps to assess word order and metrics like METEOR and BERTScore, which account for synonyms and contextual embeddings, respectively.

On the other hand, metrics such as BLEU, commonly used for evaluating text generation, impose strict penalties for variations in word order and the use of synonyms due to their reliance on n-gram-based overlap. To mitigate these issues, our counter-evaluation method for generation through parsing (GEN/GEN-PARS) transforms textual outputs into DRS representations, allowing evaluation through structural overlaps that are less sensitive to word order, as measured by SMATCH. This analysis elucidates the necessity of integrating both semantic (GEN) and structural (GEN-PARS) evaluations in understanding the quality of generated texts. While GEN metrics highlight the challenges posed by conventional evaluations in capturing semantic nuances, GEN-PARS effectively illustrates how generated structures can align with DRS, thus ensuring that the meaning is preserved. By leveraging both sets of metrics, we obtained a more nuanced view of the strengths and limitations of text-generation processes, fostering improvements in model training and evaluation methodologies.

Correlation Analysis: In evaluating DRS-based systems for Urdu, it is essential to analyze both quantitative performance measures and how well the system preserves underlying semantic content. Traditional metrics provide an initial foundation, but correlation analysis enables deeper insights into whether automatic evaluations effectively capture semantic quality and structural coherence. By analyzing correlations across automated measures such as PARS/PARS-GEN and GEN/GEN-PARS, we assess how reliably these metrics reflect true semantic accuracy in generated outputs.

We used Pearson correlation to examine the relationships between PARS/PARS-GEN and GEN/GEN-PARS scores. This analysis reveals the extent to which different metrics align—such as whether improvements in parsing accuracy correspond to enhancements in generation quality. A high positive Pearson correlation would indicate that the metrics consistently capture similar aspects of semantic and structural accuracy.

PARS/PARS-GEN Correlation: Our analysis for Urdu reveals statistically significant correlations across all metrics, despite the language's morphological complexity. BERTScore exhibited the highest correlation ($r = 0.2832$, $p < 4.55e\text{-}18$), suggesting that neural-based metrics, like contextual embeddings, may more effectively capture semantic relationships in morphologically rich languages (see Table 7). This strong correlation with BERTScore implies that it could be particularly effective for evaluating the semantic quality of generated Urdu text, as it appears more sensitive to the subtle linguistic variations present in Urdu.

PARS vs. PARS-GEN	Corr-val	P-val
Pars vs BLEU	0.2318†	1.87e-12
Pars vs METEOR	0.1949†	3.69e-9
Pars vs ROUGE	0.2023†	9.12e-10
Pars vs chrF	0.2042†	6.25e-10
Pars vs BERTScore	0.2832†	4.55e-18

Table 7: Correlation results for PARS and PARS-GEN. Underlined values represent the strongest correlation. † indicates that the values are highly significant.

The remaining metrics also demonstrated significant, albeit weaker, correlations: BLEU (r = 0.2318), ROUGE (r = 0.2023), chrF (r = 0.2042), and METEOR (r = 0.1949). While these correlations are weaker, they remain highly significant, indicating that even traditional generation metrics can offer valuable insights into parsing performance. However, BERTScore's stronger correlation emphasizes the advantages of using contextual embeddings for capturing semantic fidelity in Urdu. The consistently positive and significant correlations across metrics affirm the reliability of our PARS-GEN approach for Urdu, demonstrating that parsing accuracy align well with generation quality metrics, with BERTScore emerging as particularly effective for assessing complex semantic content.

GEN/GEN-PARS Correlation: We extended the correlation analysis to GEN/GEN-PARS, examining how well generation metrics predict parsing performance, adding a complementary perspective on the relationship between these processes. BERTScore demonstrated the highest correlation in the GEN/GEN-PARS evaluation (r = 0.4073, p < 2.75e-37), indicating a moderate and highly significant relationship between generation quality and parsing accuracy (see Table 8). This high correlation suggests that neural-based embeddings are particularly effective at preserving semantic content that can be recognized by parsing models, even when dealing with morphologically rich languages. BLEU followed with a notable correlation (r = 0.3414, p < 5.36e-26), further highlighting its utility as a predictor of parsing performance.

GEN vs. GEN-PARS	Corr-val	P-val
BLEU vs Gen-Pars	0.3414‡	5.36e-26
METEOR vs Gen-Pars	0.2936‡	2.30e-19
ROUGE vs Gen-Pars	0.3043‡	9.82e-21
chrF vs Gen-Pars	0.2987‡	5.25e-20
BERTScore vs Gen-Pars	0.4073‡	2.75e-37

Table 8: Correlation results for GEN and GEN-PARS. Underlined values represent the strongest correlation. ‡ shows that the values are highly significant.

Other metrics also demonstrated significant correlations, albeit to a lesser extent. ROUGE (r = 0.3043), chrF (r = 0.2987), and METEOR (r = 0.2936) maintained positive and statistically significant correlations. These findings suggest that even traditional generation metrics capture some degree of semantic alignment in Urdu, but neural metrics like BERTScore remain more robust.

5 Conclusion

DRS parsing and generation are reversible processes that can be exploited in cross-task evaluations. Traditional metrics often fall short in capturing the true structural and linguistic quality required for accurate assessment. To address the limitations, we introduced two complementary methodologies, PARS-GEN and GEN-PARS, which offer a bidirectional framework to evaluate Urdu DRS processing more holistically. The PARS-GEN approach assesses parsing quality by generating text from parsed DRS, revealing linguistic nuances that purely structural metrics may miss. In parallel, GEN-PARS transforms generated text back into DRS, providing a structural and semantic evaluation of generation quality that goes beyond surface evaluations. Applying these methods to Urdu has yielded significant insights: (i) Urdu exhibits stronger correlations between generation quality and parsing accuracy than the reverse, indicating that high-quality generation is a reliable predictor of parsing performance; (ii) BERTScore shows the highest correlations, demonstrating their effectiveness in capturing Urdu's complex linguistic features; and (iii) The positive, statistically significant correlations across both evaluation directions validate the bidirectional parsing-generation relationship for Urdu.

Limitations The cross-task evaluations conducted for DRS parsing and generation offer a foundational approach to assessing the structural and linguistic quality of Urdu semantic processing comprehensively. However, the transformation process from DRS to text and text to DRS relies heavily on the capabilities of the underlying pre-trained language models. These models must demonstrate sufficient generalizability and robustness to achieve accurate and high-quality data transformations between DRS and text formats. Model biases or limitations in the pre-trained architecture may adversely impact performance, potentially resulting in evaluations that deviate from gold-standard outputs. This reliance on model quality underscores the need for continued refinement and bias mitigation in pre-trained models to ensure reliable and unbiased semantic transformation and evaluation.

Acknowledgments

The research is conducted at the Department of Computer Science, University of Turin, Italy, and is partially funded by the "HARMONIA" project (M4-C2, I1.3 Partenariati Estesi - Cascade Call - FAIR). The project is supported under the NextGenerationEU program, with the funding identification details CUP C63C22000770006 - PE PE0000013. We extend our gratitude to prof. Viviana Patti, the principal investigator of the HARMONIA research initiative, for facilitating the funding of this work.

References

Muhammad Saad Amin, Luca Anselma, and Alessandro Mazzei. 2024. Exploring data augmentation in neural DRS-to-text generation. In *Proceedings of the 18th Conference of the European Chapter of the Association for Computational Linguistics (Volume 1: Long Papers)*, pages 2164–2178, St. Julian's, Malta. Association for Computational Linguistics.

Muhammad Saad Amin, Alessandro Mazzei, and Luca Anselma. 2022. Towards data augmentation for DRS-to-text generation. In *Proceedings of the Sixth Workshop on Natural Language for Artificial Intelligence (NL4AI 2022) co-located with 21th International Conference of the Italian Association for Artificial Intelligence (AI*IA 2022), Udine, November 30th, 2022*, volume 3287 of *CEUR Workshop Proceedings*, pages 141–152. CEUR-WS.org.

Satanjeev Banerjee and Alon Lavie. 2005. METEOR: An automatic metric for MT evaluation with improved correlation with human judgments. In *Proceedings of the ACL workshop on intrinsic and extrinsic evaluation measures for machine translation and/or summarization*, pages 65–72.

Tina Bögel, Miriam Butt, Annette Hautli, and Sebastian Sulger. 2009. Urdu and the modular architecture of pargram. In *Proceedings of the Conference on Language and Technology*, volume 70.

Johan Bos. 2023. The sequence notation: Catching complex meanings in simple graphs. In *15th International Conference on Computational Semantics*, pages 195–208. Association for Computational Linguistics (ACL).

Miriam Butt and Tracy Holloway King. 2002. Urdu and the parallel grammar project. In *COLING-02: The 3rd Workshop on Asian Language Resources and International Standardization*.

Shu Cai and Kevin Knight. 2013. Smatch: an evaluation metric for semantic feature structures. In *Proceedings of the 51st Annual Meeting of the Association for Computational Linguistics (Volume 2: Short Papers)*, pages 748–752.

Michael Hanna and Ondřej Bojar. 2021. A fine-grained analysis of BERTScore. In *Proceedings of the Sixth Conference on Machine Translation*, pages 507–517, Online. Association for Computational Linguistics.

Kasia M Jaszczolt and Katarzyna Jaszczolt. 2023. *Semantics, pragmatics, philosophy: a journey through meaning*. Cambridge University Press.

Hans Kamp and Uwe Reyle. 1993. *From Discourse to Logic: Introduction to Modeltheoretic Semantics of Natural Language, Formal Logic and Discourse Representation Theory*. Kluwer Academic Publishers, Dordrecht.

Hans Kamp and Uwe Reyle. 2013. *From discourse to logic: Introduction to modeltheoretic semantics of natural language, formal logic and discourse representation theory*, volume 42. Springer Science & Business Media.

Hans Kamp, Josef Van Genabith, and Uwe Reyle. 2010. Discourse representation theory. In *Handbook of Philosophical Logic: Volume 15*, pages 125–394. Springer.

Jiangming Liu, Shay B. Cohen, and Mirella Lapata. 2021. Text generation from discourse representation structures. In *Proceedings of the 2021 Conference of the North American Chapter of the Association for Computational Linguistics: Human Language Technologies*, pages 397–415, Online. Association for Computational Linguistics.

Rik van Noord. 2019. *Neural boxer at the IWCS shared task on DRS parsing*. in Proc. IWCS Shared Task on Semantic Parsing, Gothenburg, Sweden. Association for Computational Linguistics.

Juri Opitz. 2023. SMATCH++: Standardized and extended evaluation of semantic graphs. In *Findings of the Association for Computational Linguistics: EACL 2023*, pages 1595–1607, Dubrovnik, Croatia. Association for Computational Linguistics.

Kishore Papineni, Salim Roukos, Todd Ward, and Wei-Jing Zhu. 2002. BLEU: a method for automatic evaluation of machine translation. In *Proceedings of the 40th annual meeting of the Association for Computational Linguistics*, pages 311–318.

Linfeng Song and Daniel Gildea. 2019. SemBleu: A robust metric for AMR parsing evaluation. In *Proceedings of the 57th Annual Meeting of the Association for Computational Linguistics*, pages 4547–4552, Florence, Italy. Association for Computational Linguistics.

Rik van Noord, Lasha Abzianidze, Hessel Haagsma, and Johan Bos. 2018. Evaluating scoped meaning representations. In *Proceedings of the Eleventh International Conference on Language Resources and Evaluation (LREC 2018)*, Miyazaki, Japan. European Language Resources Association (ELRA).

Rik van Noord, Antonio Toral, and Johan Bos. 2019. Linguistic information in neural semantic parsing with multiple encoders. In *Proc. 13th International Conference on Computational Semantics-Short Papers*, pages 24–31. Association for Computational Linguistics (ACL).

Rik van Noord, Antonio Toral, and Johan Bos. 2020. Character-level representations improve DRS-based semantic parsing even in the age of BERT. In *Proceedings of the 2020 Conference on Empirical Methods in Natural Language Processing (EMNLP)*, pages 4587–4603, Online. Association for Computational Linguistics.

Chunliu Wang, Rik van Noord, Arianna Bisazza, and Johan Bos. 2021. Evaluating text generation from discourse representation structures. In *Proceedings of the 1st Workshop on Natural Language Generation, Evaluation, and Metrics (GEM 2021)*, pages 73–83, Online. Association for Computational Linguistics.

Studying the Effect of Hindi Tokenizer Performance on Downstream Tasks

Rashi Goel
Manipal Institute of Technology
Manipal Academy of Higher Education, India
rashigoel2017@gmail.com

Fatiha Sadat
Université du Québec à Montréal
Montréal, Québec, Canada
sadat.fatiha@uqam.ca

Abstract

This paper deals with a study on the effect of training data size and tokenizer performance for Hindi language on the eventual downstream model performance and comprehension. Multiple monolingual Hindi tokenizers are trained for large language models such as BERT and intrinsic and extrinsic evaluations are performed on multiple Hindi datasets. The objective of this study is to understand the precise effects of tokenizer performance on downstream task performance to gain insight on how to develop better models for low-resource languages.

1 Introduction

Large Language Models (LLMs) have shown extraordinary performance in a range of Natural Language Processing (NLP) tasks, including both text classification and text generation. They are made use of across the world. After the success of many monolingual LLMs such as BERT (Devlin, 2018) and GPT, multilingual LLMs were built over these foundational models, increasing the number of languages they were pre-trained on, using different architectures and expanding the number of parameters. Some multilingual language models such as mBERT, mBART (Liu, 2020), Llama (Touvron et al., 2023), the more recent GPT versions, BLOOM (Workshop et al., 2022) have been trained on more than hundred languages. However, there is a skewed distribution in the quantity of the different languages they have been trained, causing bias in their predictions, in terms of languages as well as cultures. For Indic languages in specific, many LLMs have been built by using the aforementioned models trained on large corpora of multiple Indian languages. These include IndicBERT (Doddapaneni et al., 2022), IndicBART (Dabre et al., 2021), MuRIL (Khanuja et al., 2021), OpenHathi (sar). While India has hundreds of languages, most of them are however very low-resource, making training on them very hard.

The process of pre-training these LLMs involve processing large amounts of text data and make them perform tasks like Masked Language Modeling (MLM) and Next Sentence Prediction (NSP) to learn semantic embeddings of the sentences that are input. While a lot of work has been done for the mechanisms and architecture of the models, a relatively under-investigated aspect of tokenizers is the impact of the tokenizer performance on the performance of the model.

Tokenizer performance plays a crucial role in the performance of LLMs. The quality of tokenization can have a huge effect on the contextual understanding and linguistic ability of the model. This project aims to investigate the effect of tokenizer performance on LLMs for Indian Languages. Since there are hundreds of Indian Languages, for this project, only Hindi was chosen as a representative language to conduct experimentation and evaluate results. Initial rudimentary investigations showed that there exist issues even with existing Indian LLMs. Hindi represents its vowel sounds within a word using 'matras' for the vowel letters, as do many other Indian Languages. However, these are encoded as accent marks in digital representations. It was seen that when IndicBERT (Doddapaneni et al., 2022) was used to tokenize Hindi text, it removed these accents as part of its pre-tokenization. The removal of these 'matras' would remove a lot of the semantic sense behind the words, equivalent to removing all the vowel characters from English words. Furthermore, it can also be seen in Figure 1 that the model splits the words very frequently into small-length tokens, to an average of around 2-4 characters, essentially removing the meaning behind the words, to simply represent repeating character groups. Such tokenization would deprive the model of any semantic understanding of the words, and would not allow it to gain meaningful context of the given text in order to perform its

Proceedings of the First Workshop on Natural Language Processing for Indo-Aryan and Dravidian Languages (IndoNLP2025), pages 44–49
January 20, 2025. ©2025 Association for Computational Linguistics

desired task.

This project thus extensively investigates the effect of the training data and tokenizer performance on subsequent downstream task performance by developing several monolingual tokenizers and models in Hindi, making use of different training data sizes as well as tokenization algorithms.
The remainder of the paper is structured as follows. Section 2 discusses related studies of tokenizer parameters and their effect on low-resource languages, section 3 outlines the methodology of the research in terms of tokenizers used, models trained and intrinsic and extrinsic evaluations performed along with the data used. Finally, section 4 presents the results of the experiments. Section 5 highlights the final findings and inferences and section 6 discusses limitations of the current research with future scope.

2 Related Work

Tokenizers are a relatively unexplored aspect in the training of LLMs. Ali et al. (2023) investigated the intrinsic and extrinsic performance of tokenizers in monolingual and multilingual settings for 5 European languages. 24 tokenizers were trained with corresponding transformer-based decoder models making use of them, which were fine-tuned on a range of downstream tasks. There experiments showed that there was some correlation between certain metrics and downstream task performance, however, a more fine-grained analysis was required.
Kaya and Tantuğ (2024) also investigate tokenizers for Turkish, a morphologically rich and relatively less-studied language. They studied the fine-grained effect of tokenization granularity based on the training data, vocabulary size and algorithm. They displayed that these factors play a role in tokenization quality as well as downstream task performance, especially for morphologically complex words so the model can attain contextually meaningful tokens.
Rajab (2022) investigated the effect of the tokenization algorithm on low-resource African languages for Neural Machine Translation. Being agglutinative languages, they showed the improvement in performance when SentencePiece BPE was used instead of BPE tokenization, since it encodes the whitespace character and does not require words to be space separated.

3 Methodology

3.1 Tokenizers

To carry out the experimentation, several monolingual tokenizers were trained from a Hindi corpus. Four tokenization algorithms were used:

- Wordpiece (Schuster and Nakajima, 2012)
- Unigram (Kudo, 2018b)
- Byte-pair encoding (BPE) (Sennrich, 2015)
- Sentencepiece BPE (Kudo, 2018a)

These are all subword-based tokenizers, which deal with the challenges faced by word based tokenization and character based tokenization. Word-based tokenizers usually require large vocabularies and are unable to handle out-of-vocabulary words. Character-based tokenizers output long tokenized sequences with less meaningful individual tokens. Subword tokenizers use the training corpus to learn split or merge rules, based on their algorithm, to effectively separate given words, more often than not, into their stem and suffixes, so more meaningful tokens are created and it can deal with variations of the same word.
For each algorithm, a tokenizer was developed with a subset of 2M sentences from the raw corpus. The same dataset and vocabulary size was used for each of the algorithms.

3.2 Models

For each tokenizer, a subsequent BERT (Bidirectional Encoder Representation from Transformers) model was pre-trained for a Masked Language Modeling task. To save on computation, smaller BERT models were developed. These consisted of only 6 attention heads instead of 12, with a total of 82M parameters. The same architecture was used for all tokenizers with the intent of simply performing ablations of data and tokenizer performance on downstream tasks. The models were fine-tuned on multiple tasks, such as Sentiment Analysis and Named-Entity Recognition. Sentiment analysis involves classifying a text as having either positive, negative or neutral sentiment, by making use of the words, semantics as well as tone of the text. Named-Entity Recognition locates and classifies the individual words of a text as Named Entities such as person (PER), location (LOC), etc. To fine-tune for these tasks, a classification head was also

	Text	Tokenization
1	तब वह मोटी थी और जेरी ने उस पर ध्यान नहीं दिया था।	_तब, _वह, _मट, _थ, _और, _जर, _न, _उस, _पर, _ध, यन, _न, ह, _द, य, _थ, ।,
2	अक्षरा हासन इस फिल्म से अपना डेब्यू कर रही हैं।	_अक, ष, र, _हसन, _इस, _फल, म, _स, _अपन, _डब, य, _कर, _रह, _ह, ।,
3	साजन और इला हिंदी फिल्मों के नियमित किरदार नहीं हैं।	_स, जन, _और, _इल, _हद, _फल, म, _क, _न, यम, त, _कर, दर, _न, ह, _ह, ।,

Figure 1: Tokenization of sample texts by IndicBERT

added to the model, consisting of linear layers followed by the final softmax layer. Fine-tuning was performed for 15 epochs.

3.3 Evaluations

Once developed, several intrinsic and extrinsic evaluations were carried out on the tokenizers and models respectively. The tokenizer performance was evaluated using 3 primary metrics:

- Number of unique tokens : This is number of unique tokens the model splits the text in the dataset into. A higher number of unique tokens indicates that the model captures the different words more effectively. A large number of repeated tokens (fewer unique tokens), conversely, indicates that the model splits the words into a large number of smaller repeating units, which would take away some of the semantic sense of the different words.

- Subword fertility ratio: It measures the average number of subwords per word in the text, as a ratio of the total number of tokens produced and the number of words in the text. A higher value means the model is producing a larger number of subwords per word, leading to over-segmentation and lesser contextual value due to the lower sequence length.

- Proportion of continued words: This is the ratio of words the tokenizer splits into two or more subwords, that is, the ratio of continued words in the tokenizer output and the total number of words in the text. While the fertility ratio gives a measure of the extent to which each word is split, this metric indicates how often words in the text are split. A higher value means the tokenizer is segmenting a large proportion of words and has not captured many words in the language.

These metrics provide a broad view of the effectiveness of the tokenizers in terms of how well they can segment meaningful subwords from texts to garner generalizability to unseen data while still retaining semantic sense. They are calculated on a held-out test set. The finetuned models are then evaluated on their performance in their respective tasks, using the accuracy of predictions as the metric, since these tasks are both multi-class classification tasks. Further, for Sentiment Analysis, the quality of the sentence embeddings were also examined. Sentence embeddings are usually extracted as the embedding of the [CLS] token from the pooler layer of the model. This embedding passes to the classification head to be segregated into its corresponding sentiment label. These sentence embeddings were examined to see how well they represented the positive, negative or neutral sentiment of the text by checking how well they cluster into their ground truth labels. The silhouette score for each model was calculated to evaluate how well sentences sharing similar sentiments were clustering. The silhouette score provides a metric over the inter-class and within-class distance. A high score indicates low intra-class distance and high inter-class distance. Ideally, sentences sharing similar sentences in the fine-tuned models should align closely with each other, and be far apart from the clusters of other sentiments.

3.4 Data

Several sources of digital Hindi text data were used to carry out the experiments in the project. The raw text corpus for training the tokenizers and pre-training the BERT models was obtained from the IndicNLP corpus (Git). This is a corpus developed by AI4Bharat, a research lab in IIT Madras which develops tools, models and datasets for NLP in Indian Languages. The corpus consists of crawled data from numerous web sources, including news-

papers, books and magazines in several Indian languages. The Hindi subset of this corpus was used, which in total consisted of 62.9M sentences.
For sentiment analysis, AI4Bharat's Hindi movie reviews dataset was used. This is part of the Indic_GLUE (Kakwani et al., 2020) dataset which consists of datasets for several Natural Language Understanding tasks to evaluate model performance. The sentiment analysis dataset consists of movie reviews, collected by IIT Patna, with each review annotated with its corresponding sentiment (positive, neutral or negative).
For Named-Entity Recognition, AI4Bharat's Naamapadam dataset (Mhaske et al., 2023) was used. This consists of annotated data for 11 Indian Languages. The data is produced by using the English-Indian Language parallel corpus and transferring the labels from the English side to the correct corresponding word on the Indian Language side.

4 Results

To carry out evaluations, intrinsic tokenizer metrics were first calculated for a held-out test corpus of text, which consisted of 54961 words. Table 1 shows the intrinsic metrics of the 4 tokenizers created using the corresponding algorithms.

Tokenizer	Unique Tokens	Fertility	Continued Words
Unigram	6990	1.2768	0.1307
Wordpiece	6961	1.1599	0.0219
BPE	1938	3.3367	0.8735
SentencePiece	7724	1.2082	0.0787

Table 1: Intrinsic metrics

It can be seen that Wordpiece shows the best performance in both subword fertility and proportion of continued words. The results of SentencePiece and Unigram are also comparable. BPE shows the worst performance, with the lowest number of unique tokens and the highest subword fertility and proportion of continued words. This suggests that it splits each word in the text into a large number of small, repeating units which would likely fail to capture the semantics or nuances of the words.
It can be seen from Table 2 that the monolingual Hindi Unigram, Wordpiece and SentencePiece tokenizers perform better than tokenizers of benchmark LLMs, IndicBERT and mBERT, despite being trained on a significantly lower amount of data.

Tokenizer	Unique Tokens	Fertility	Continued Words
IndicBERT	1327	1.6643	0.4589
mBERT	1280	2.0424	0.4284

Table 2: Intrinsic metrics of benchmark LLMs

Table 3 shows the performance of the BERT models, pretrained from the corresponding tokenizer, fine-tuned for the Sentiment Analysis task. While the models trained on the Unigram, Wordpiece and Sentencepiece algorithm show comparable performance, there is a large drop in the performance of the BPE tokenizer based BERT model. This follows the hypothesis that the poor tokenizer performance caused worse downstream task performance, as all other factors in the models were kept constant.

Tokenizer	Accuracy	Silhouette score
Unigram	0.6355	0.1160
Wordpiece	0.6483	0.1263
BPE	0.5774	0.0706
SentencePiece	0.6581	0.1141

Table 3: Results of Sentiment Analysis

The silhouette scores of the sentence embeddings (before being processed through the classification head) also show similar trends, being the lowest for BPE, and comparable for the other 3 algorithms. This indicates the model's inherent understanding of the language based on how well it can represent the sentences. Table 4 shows the performance of the models fine-tuned for the Named Entity Recognition task. Once again, the Unigram, Wordpiece and SentencePiece based models show comparable performance, whereas there is a drop in the performance of the BPE based model. This shows a significant correlation between the quality of the tokenizer and the downstream performance of the model.

Tokenizer	Accuracy
Unigram	0.9384
Wordpiece	0.9381
BPE	0.8878
SentencePiece	0.9400

Table 4: Results of Named Entity Recognition

5 Conclusion

In this paper, fine grained analysis of the impact of tokenizer performance on downstream performance of BERT models in Hindi was conducted. The results showed that there is a significant correlation between intrinsic tokenizer performance and extrinsic downstream task performance. The Unigram, Wordpiece and SentencePiece models that showed the best tokenizer performance also showed the best results in Sentiment Analysis as well as in Named-Entity Recognition tasks. This suggests that the quality of words in the models' vocabulary allows it to segment words in the input text more meaningfully, thereby allowing it to learn better semantics during the pre-training phase and subsequently when being fine-tuned for the downstream tasks.

6 Limitations

This research investigates the effect of several tokenizer algorithms on downstream task performance of the model, specifically for the Hindi language. While the results strongly back the hypothesis, the research is limited in its scope. Due to computation requirements, the tokenizers and models were trained on only a limited subset of the raw corpus, for only a single language. Further, only two downstream tasks were evaluated. Investigation can still be done into the effect of tokenizer vocabulary size as well as the amount training data to form a learning a learning curve. The research can also be extended to more Indian languages, which are morphologically rich and more low-resourced. Further manual evaluations could help to better understand the nuanced analysis as well as the strengths and shortcomings of the tokenizers by observing the types of subwords and splits generated for the input text, especially for morphologically complex languages.

References

Github - ai4bharat/indicnlp_corpus: Description describes the indicnlp corpus and associated datasets. `https://github.com/AI4Bharat/indicnlp_corpus`. (Accessed on 09/17/2024).

sarvamai/openhathi-7b-hi-v0.1-base · hugging face. `https://huggingface.co/sarvamai/OpenHathi-7B-Hi-v0.1-Base`. (Accessed on 09/17/2024).

Mehdi Ali, Michael Fromm, Klaudia Thellmann, Richard Rutmann, Max Lübbering, Johannes Leveling, Katrin Klug, Jan Ebert, Niclas Doll, Jasper Schulze Buschhoff, et al. 2023. Tokenizer choice for llm training: Negligible or crucial? *arXiv preprint arXiv:2310.08754*.

Raj Dabre, Himani Shrotriya, Anoop Kunchukuttan, Ratish Puduppully, Mitesh M Khapra, and Pratyush Kumar. 2021. Indicbart: A pre-trained model for indic natural language generation. *arXiv preprint arXiv:2109.02903*.

Jacob Devlin. 2018. Bert: Pre-training of deep bidirectional transformers for language understanding. *arXiv preprint arXiv:1810.04805*.

Sumanth Doddapaneni, Rahul Aralikatte, Gowtham Ramesh, Shreya Goyal, Mitesh M Khapra, Anoop Kunchukuttan, and Pratyush Kumar. 2022. Towards leaving no indic language behind: Building monolingual corpora, benchmark and models for indic languages. *arXiv preprint arXiv:2212.05409*.

Divyanshu Kakwani, Anoop Kunchukuttan, Satish Golla, NC Gokul, Avik Bhattacharyya, Mitesh M Khapra, and Pratyush Kumar. 2020. Indicnlpsuite: Monolingual corpora, evaluation benchmarks and pre-trained multilingual language models for indian languages. In *Findings of the Association for Computational Linguistics: EMNLP 2020*, pages 4948–4961.

Yiğit Bekir Kaya and A Cüneyd Tantuğ. 2024. Effect of tokenization granularity for turkish large language models. *Intelligent Systems with Applications*, 21:200335.

Simran Khanuja, Diksha Bansal, Sarvesh Mehtani, Savya Khosla, Atreyee Dey, Balaji Gopalan, Dilip Kumar Margam, Pooja Aggarwal, Rajiv Teja Nagipogu, Shachi Dave, et al. 2021. Muril: Multilingual representations for indian languages. *arXiv preprint arXiv:2103.10730*.

T Kudo. 2018a. Sentencepiece: A simple and language independent subword tokenizer and detokenizer for neural text processing. *arXiv preprint arXiv:1808.06226*.

Taku Kudo. 2018b. Subword regularization: Improving neural network translation models with multiple subword candidates. *arXiv preprint arXiv:1804.10959*.

Y Liu. 2020. Multilingual denoising pre-training for neural machine translation. *arXiv preprint arXiv:2001.08210*.

Arnav Mhaske, Harshit Kedia, Sumanth Doddapaneni, Mitesh M. Khapra, Pratyush Kumar, Rudra Murthy, and Anoop Kunchukuttan. 2023. Naamapadam: A large-scale named entity annotated data for Indic languages. In *Proceedings of the 61st Annual Meeting of the Association for Computational Linguistics (Volume 1: Long Papers)*, pages 10441–10456, Toronto, Canada. Association for Computational Linguistics.

Jenalea Rajab. 2022. Effect of tokenisation strategies for low-resourced southern african languages. In *3rd Workshop on African Natural Language Processing*.

Mike Schuster and Kaisuke Nakajima. 2012. Japanese and korean voice search. In *2012 IEEE international conference on acoustics, speech and signal processing (ICASSP)*, pages 5149–5152. IEEE.

Rico Sennrich. 2015. Neural machine translation of rare words with subword units. *arXiv preprint arXiv:1508.07909*.

Hugo Touvron, Thibaut Lavril, Gautier Izacard, Xavier Martinet, Marie-Anne Lachaux, Timothée Lacroix, Baptiste Rozière, Naman Goyal, Eric Hambro, Faisal Azhar, et al. 2023. Llama: Open and efficient foundation language models. *arXiv preprint arXiv:2302.13971*.

BigScience Workshop, Teven Le Scao, Angela Fan, Christopher Akiki, Ellie Pavlick, Suzana Ilić, Daniel Hesslow, Roman Castagné, Alexandra Sasha Luccioni, François Yvon, et al. 2022. Bloom: A 176b-parameter open-access multilingual language model. *arXiv preprint arXiv:2211.05100*.

Adapting Multilingual LLMs to Low-Resource Languages using Continued Pre-training and Synthetic Corpus: A Case Study for Hindi LLMs

Raviraj Joshi, Kanishk Singla, Anusha Kamath, Raunak Kalani, Rakesh Paul, Utkarsh Vaidya, Sanjay Singh Chauhan, Niranjan Wartikar, Eileen Long
NVIDIA
{ravirajj, kanishks, anushak, rkalani, rapaul, uvaidya schauhan, nwartikar, elong}@nvidia.com

Abstract

Multilingual LLMs support a variety of languages; however, their performance is suboptimal for low-resource languages. In this work, we emphasize the importance of continued pre-training of multilingual LLMs and the use of translation-based synthetic pre-training corpora for improving LLMs in low-resource languages. We conduct our study in the context of the low-resource Indic language Hindi. We introduce Nemotron-Mini-Hindi 4B, a bilingual SLM supporting both Hindi and English, based on Nemotron-Mini 4B. The model is trained using a mix of real and synthetic Hindi + English tokens, with continuous pre-training performed on 400B tokens. We demonstrate that both the base and instruct models achieve state-of-the-art results on Hindi benchmarks while remaining competitive on English tasks. Additionally, we observe that the continued pre-training approach enhances the model's overall factual accuracy.

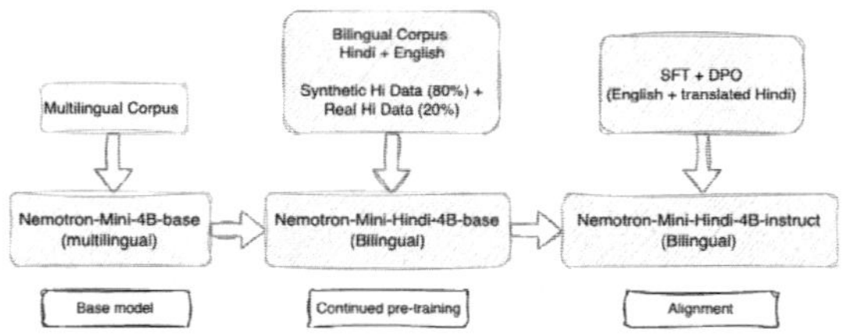

Figure 1: Adaptation of multilingual Nemotron-Mini-4B model (also known as Minitron-4B).

1 Introduction

The accuracy and utility of large language models (LLMs) have continuously improved over time. Both closed and open-source LLMs have demonstrated strong performance in English and several other languages. Open models such as Nemotron (Adler et al., 2024), Gemma (Team et al., 2024), and Llama (Dubey et al., 2024) are inherently multilingual. For instance, the Nemotron-4 15B model was pre-trained on 8 trillion tokens, of which 15% were multilingual (Parmar et al., 2024). However, the proportion of multilingual data is limited, which in turn affects the accuracy of these models on non-English languages.

The model's performance further diminishes as we move from high-resource to low-resource languages. In this work, we specifically focus on the Indic language Hindi as our target low-resource language. Out of the 8 trillion tokens used to train the Nemotron-4 models, only 20 billion tokens are in Hindi. As a result, while the model can understand and generate Hindi content to a reasonable extent, the usability of such a multilingual LLM for specific low-resource languages remains questionable. Frequent hallucinations, meaningless sentences, and mixing of English content often occur when responding to purely Hindi queries in the Devanagari script. There is a strong need to adapt multilingual LLMs to target languages to enhance their usability.

Recently, in the context of Indic languages, target language Supervised Fine-Tuning (SFT) has become a common practice to adapt LLMs to specific languages (Gala et al., 2024). However, it remains to be studied whether language-specific SFT tuning improves LLMs' understanding in regional contexts. Some studies suggest that SFT can introduce LLMs to new domain knowledge, though it is typically used to enhance the model's instruction-following capability (Mecklenburg et al., 2024). SFT on translated English instruction tuning data is widely used to develop regional LLMs for Indic languages. While this may improve instruction-following in the target language, it may not enhance LLMs' understanding of regional contexts (Balachandran, 2023). Another approach to updating LLM knowledge is continued pre-training, but the limited availability of tokens for low-resource languages makes this both infeasible and prone to

Proceedings of the First Workshop on Natural Language Processing for Indo-Aryan and Dravidian Languages (IndoNLP2025), pages 50–57
January 20, 2025. ©2025 Association for Computational Linguistics

Model	Layers	Hidden Size	Att. Heads	Query Groups	MLP Hidden	Parameters
Nemotron 4B	32	3072	24	8	9216	4.19B

Table 1: Architecture details of Nemotron-Mini-4B model.

overfitting.

In this work, we focus on a continued pre-training approach using a mix of real and synthetic corpora. We demonstrate that a robust base model can be adapted to the target language with a small continued pre-training corpus. This approach is particularly relevant for low-resource languages, where the amount of training data is limited. The synthetic pre-training dataset is curated by translating high-quality generic English corpora into the target language. To further expand the corpus and support Roman script queries in the target language, the text is transliterated into Roman script and used for pre-training. The base model is then aligned using supervised fine-tuning (SFT), followed by preference tuning with Direct Preference Optimization (DPO). We observe that the continued pre-training approach is particularly useful for reducing hallucinations, improving regional knowledge of LLMs, and enhancing response capabilities in the target language. The high-level process is outlined in Figure 1,

Based on this approach, we present Nemotron-Mini-Hindi-4B-Base[1] and Nemotron-Mini-Hindi-4B-Instruct[2][3], state-of-the-art Small Language Models (SLMs) for the Hindi language. These SLMs support Hindi, English, and Hinglish. The Hindi models are based on the multilingual Nemotron-Mini-4B (also known as Minitron-4B), adapted with continued pre-training on 400 billion Hindi and English tokens. The data blend used equal proportions of both languages. The instruct version of the model was developed using SFT and DPO techniques. The model outperforms all similarly sized models on various IndicXTREME, IndicNLG benchmark tasks and popular translated English benchmarks such as MMLU, Hellaswag, ARC-C, and ARC-E (Gala et al., 2024). We also perform LLM-based evaluations using the benchmark datasets IndicQuest (Rohera et al., 2024) and in-house SubjectiveEval, with GPT-4 serving as the judge LLM. This is the first study to present and evaluate bilingual language models of this nature. We provide a thorough study of the models in both languages.

2 Related Work

In this section, we review various approaches for adapting LLMs to different languages. Several efforts have focused on adapting LLaMA models to Indic languages. A common method involves extending the vocabulary, followed by SFT or PEFT (LoRA) using translated and available SFT corpora in Indic languages. Examples of such work include OpenHathi, Airavata (Gala et al., 2024), Tamil-LLaMA (Balachandran, 2023), Navarasa[4], Ambari, MalayaLLM, and Marathi-Gemma (Joshi, 2022). Notably, some of these efforts employ bilingual next-word prediction, alternating between English and the target language in the pre-training corpus. Airavata also introduced an evaluation framework[5] for Indic LLMs, which we leverage to evaluate Nemotron-Mini-Hindi 4B and other multilingual models.

Apart from Indic languages, similar efforts have been made for other languages, including Chinese LLaMA (Cui et al., 2023), LLaMATurk (Toraman, 2024), FinGPT (Luukkonen et al., 2023), and RedWhale (Vo et al., 2024) for Chinese, Turkish, Finnish, and Korean, respectively. These LLMs use one or more techniques such as tokenizer extension, secondary pretraining, and supervised fine-tuning. The key distinction of our work lies in its emphasis on developing bilingual LLMs, whereas the aforementioned efforts concentrate on creating monolingual LLMs.

Cahyawijaya et al. (2024) show that large language models can learn low-resource languages effectively using in-context learning and few-shot examples, improving performance through cross-lingual contexts without extensive tuning. Gurgurov et al. (2024) enhance multilingual LLMs for low-resource languages by using adapters with data from ConceptNet, boosting performance in sentiment analysis and named entity recognition.

[1] https://huggingface.co/nvidia/Nemotron-4-Mini-Hindi-4B-Base

[2] https://huggingface.co/nvidia/Nemotron-4-Mini-Hindi-4B-Instruct

[3] https://build.nvidia.com/nvidia/nemotron-4-mini-hindi-4b-instruct

[4] https://huggingface.co/Telugu-LLM-Labs/Indic-gemma-7b-finetuned-sft-Navarasa-2.0

[5] https://github.com/AI4Bharat/IndicInstruct

3 Methodology

In this section, we describe our methodology for adapting multilingual LLMs to target languages to improve performance in those languages. Specifically, we build a bilingual SLM that supports both Hindi and English. We conduct our adaptation experiments using the multilingual Nemotron-Mini-4B model (also known as Minitron-4B). The model undergoes continuous pre-training with an equal mixture of Hindi and English data, consisting of 200B tokens per language. The original Nemotron-4B model was primarily trained on English tokens and had seen only 20B Hindi tokens. Given the limited amount of Hindi data, adapting an existing multilingual model rather than training from scratch is an effective strategy, allowing us to leverage the knowledge learned from the pre-trained model. Additionally, as Nemotron-4B employs a large 256k tokenizer, we did not need to extend the tokenizer. The fertility ratio for Hindi text is 1.7, which is better than that of its Llama (2.64) and Gemma (1.98) counterparts.

3.1 Synthetic Data Curation

One of the key aspects of our work is the creation of a synthetic Hindi pre-training dataset. This synthetic data is generated using machine translation and transliteration. We first select high-quality English data sources and translate them into Hindi using a custom document translation pipeline. This pipeline preserves the document structure, including elements like bullet points and tables, and employs the IndicTrans2 model (Gala et al.) for sentence translation. However, since the translated data may contain noise, we use an n-gram language model to filter out low-quality samples. This model, trained on MuRIL-tokenized (Khanuja et al., 2021) real Hindi data, applies perplexity scores to identify and exclude noisy translations. Around 2% of the documents were discarded post-filtering.

The translated Hindi data comprises approximately 60 billion tokens. We then combine this synthetic data with around 40 billion real tokens (web-scraped data) to create a dataset totaling 100 billion Hindi tokens. Additionally, this entire Hindi text is transliterated into Roman script, expanding the total dataset to 220 billion tokens. The transliterated tokens are included to enable the model to support Hinglish queries. This Hindi data is further combined with 200 billion English tokens for continued pre-training. Including the English dataset helps prevent catastrophic forgetting of English capabilities and contributes to training stability. Fuzzy deduplication is performed on the entire text using NeMo-Curator[6] to eliminate similar documents. The real Hindi data sources include internal web-based datasets and Sangraha Corpus (Khan et al., 2024). The English dataset is a subset of the pre-training corpus used for the Nemotron-15B model. All the datasets used in this work are commercially friendly.

3.2 Continued Pre-training

The Nemotron-Mini-4B base model is used for continuous pre-training, and its architecture details are presented in Table 1. The Nemotron-Mini-4B model is derived from the Nemotron-15B model using compression techniques such as pruning and distillation, consisting of 2.6B trainable parameters (Muralidharan et al., 2024). Re-training is performed using a standard causal modeling objective. The dataset consists of 400B tokens, with an equal mix of Hindi and English. During batch sampling, greater weight is given to real data compared to synthetic data. We use the same optimizer settings and data split as (Parmar et al., 2024), with a cosine learning rate decay schedule from 2e-4 to 4.5e-7. This model is referred to as Nemotron-Mini-Hindi-4B, a base model where Hindi is the primary language. The re-training was performed using the Megatron-LM library (Shoeybi et al., 2020) and 128 Nvidia A100 GPUs.

3.3 Model Alignment

The first alignment stage is Supervised Fine-Tuning (SFT). We use a general SFT corpus with approximately 200k examples, comprising various tasks as outlined in (Adler et al., 2024). The model is trained for one epoch with a global batch size of 1024 and a learning rate in the range of [5e-6, 9e-7], using cosine annealing. Due to the lack of a high-quality Hindi SFT corpus, we leverage English-only data for SFT. We also experimented with translated English data (filtered using back-translation-based methods) for SFT, but did not observe any improvements with this addition. We found that using the English-only SFT corpus enhances instruction-following capabilities in Hindi, highlighting the cross-lingual transferability of these skills.

After SFT stage, the model undergoes a preference-tuning phase, where it learns from

[6]https://github.com/NVIDIA/NeMo-Curator

Base models	Metric	Nemotron-Mini-Hindi-4B	Nemotron-Mini-4B	Sarvam-1 2B	Gemma 2-2B	Openhathi	Llama-3.1 8B	Gemma 2-9B
IndicSentiment	F1 - NLU	84.31	72.47	96.36	91.90	72.89	92.06	94.90
IndicCopa	F1 - NLU	81.86	62.50	51.63	58.65	68.69	61.87	72.58
IndicXNLI	F1 - NLU	49.67	40.39	36.08	16.67	16.67	16.67	16.79
IndicXParaphrase	F1 - NLU	37.09	16.27	80.99	26.60	71.72	72.75	71.38
Indic QA (With Context) 1 shot	F1 - NLG	18.32	15.10	35.81	33.37	20.69	35.92	46.27
Indic Headline 1 shot	BLEURT - NLG	0.50	0.46	0.36	0.27	0.47	0.38	0.27
IndicWikiBio 1 shot	BLEURT - NLG	0.62	0.59	0.53	0.60	0.52	0.60	0.63
MMLU	Acc - NLU	49.89	38.20	45.65	35.05	32.27	44.84	55.08
BoolQ	Acc - NLU	71.71	70.79	56.08	66.00	58.56	61.00	61.00
ARC Easy	Acc - NLU	78.81	58.25	76.85	52.31	44.28	67.05	85.69
Arc Challenge	Acc - NLU	65.02	47.87	59.04	40.78	32.68	54.10	76.02
Hella Swag	Acc - NLU	31.66	25.31	37.13	27.50	25.59	33.50	42.40

Table 2: Performance metrics for various base models across different Hindi tasks. The results are zero-shot unless otherwise specified.

Instruct models	Metric	Nemotron-Mini-Hindi-4B	Nemotron-Mini-4B	Airavata	Navarasa 2B	Gemma-2 2B	Navarasa 7B	Llama-3.1 8B	Gemma-2 9B
IndicSentiment	F1 - NLU	97.62	90.01	95.81	93.62	94.32	95.99	98.59	99.09
IndicCopa	F1 - NLU	80.1	66.01	63.75	38.83	27.64	62.59	59.08	89.89
IndicXNLI	F1 - NLU	53.77	39.25	73.26	16.67	17.33	38.19	31.27	39.71
IndicXParaphrase	F1 - NLU	67.93	83.74	76.53	43.82	43.06	44.58	77.72	61.38
Indic QA (With Context) 1 shot	F1 - NLG	37.51	42.56	37.69	3.3	62.95	19.09	40.03	59.83
Indic Headline 1 shot	BLEURT - NLG	0.44	0.18	0.38	0.24	0.39	0.3	0.26	0.25
IndicWikiBio 1 shot	BLEURT - NLG	0.6	0.49	0.43	0.3	0.49	0.45	0.42	0.24
MMLU	Acc - NLU	50.5	38.66	34.96	23.1	39.39	40	45.85	57.35
BoolQ	Acc - NLU	67.86	60.00	64.5	60.31	70	78.1	80	84
ARC Easy	Acc - NLU	79.97	60.14	54	38.8	59.76	61.24	71.55	91.16
Arc Challenge	Acc - NLU	65.53	49.83	35.92	31.66	48.55	48.29	59.64	81.23
Hella Swag	Acc - NLU	39.9	39.69	25.37	25.3	34.7	30.8	35.5	54.6
IndicQuest (En)	Score (1-5)	4.01	3.94	3.75	3.78	4.1	4.07	4.2	4.4
IndicQuest (Hi)	Score (1-5)	4.15	2.72	3.1	3.18	3.58	3.6	4.02	4.23
SubjectiveEval (Hi)	Score (1-5)	4.35	1.64	2.24	1.75	3.66	2.97	3.98	4.5

Table 3: Performance metrics for various instruct models across different Hindi tasks. The results are zero-shot unless otherwise specified.

Task	Nemotron-Mini-Hindi-4B-Base	Nemotron-Mini-4B-Base	Gemma-2 2b
MMLU (5)	56.37	58.60	51.3
arc_challenge (25)	46.08	50.90	55.4
hellaswag (10)	74.64	75.00	73
truthfulqa_mc2 (0)	41.05	42.72	-
winogrande (5)	70.09	74.00	70.9
xlsum_english (3)	29.71	29.62	-

Table 4: Performance of base models on English Benchmarks

triplets consisting of a prompt, a preferred response, and a rejected response. In this stage, we apply the Direct Preference Optimization (DPO) (Rafailov et al., 2024) algorithm, which trains the policy network to maximize the reward difference between the preferred and rejected responses. We train the model for one epoch with a global batch size of 512 and a learning rate in the range of [9e-6, 9e-7], utilizing cosine annealing. For the DPO stage, we use approximately 200k English samples and 60k synthetic Hindi samples. The synthetic Hindi samples were created by translating the English samples and then filtered using back-translation methods. We observe that incorporating synthetic Hindi samples during this stage improves the overall performance of the model. The aligned model is referred to as Nemotron-Mini-Hindi-4B-Instruct. Both the SFT and DPO stages are carried out using Nemo Aligner (Shen et al., 2024) and 64 Nvidia A100 GPUs.

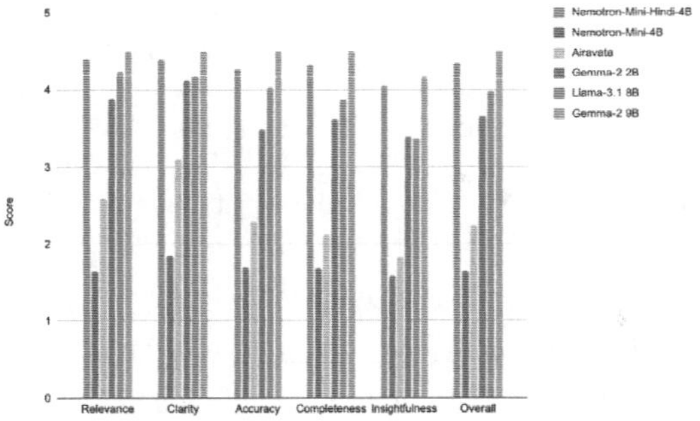

Figure 2: Comparison of different instruct models on various parameters using SubjectiveEval.

3.4 Evaluation Datasets

We evaluate Nemotron-Mini-Hindi-4B and other multilingual LLMs using both native Hindi benchmarks and translated English benchmarks. The native benchmarks include tasks from IndicXTREME, IndicNLG, and IndicQuest, while the translated English benchmarks include popular datasets like MMLU and Hellaswag. Additionally, we curate an open-ended QnA dataset termed SubjectiveEval to assess the model's generation capabilities in the Hindi language. Human evaluation is also conducted using the translated MT-Bench dataset.

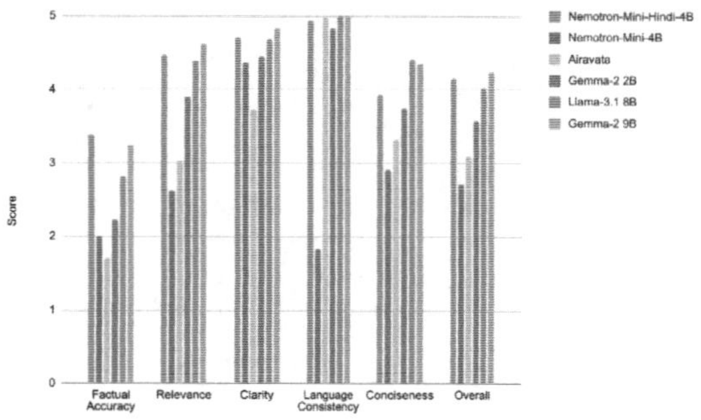

Figure 3: Comparison of different instruct models on various parameters using IndicQuest-Hi.

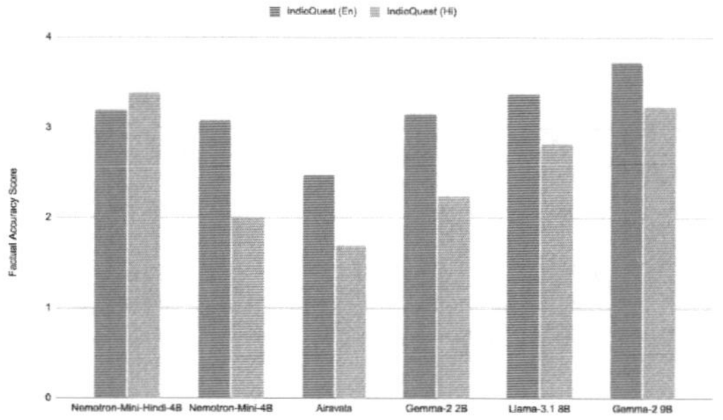

Figure 4: Comparison of different instruct models on Factuality score of IndicQuest. The ground truth answers from IndicQuest are provided as a reference to GPT4 for better scoring. The Nemotron-Mini-Hindi-4B provides comparable scores for Hindi and English whereas other models provide better factuality for English.

- **IndicXTREME**: The benchmark consists of different Natural Language Understanding (NLU) tasks in Indic languages (Doddapaneni et al., 2023). We consider different tasks like IndicSentiment, IndicCopa, IndicXNLI, and IndicXParaphrase.

- **IndicNLG**: The IndicNLG benchmark (Kumar et al., 2022) consists of various tasks for evaluating the generation capabilities of the model. We consider IndicHeadline, IndicWikiBio, and IndicQA covering text summarization and question-answering tasks.

- **IndicQuest**: IndicQuest (Rohera et al., 2024) is a gold-standard fact-based question-answering benchmark designed to evaluate multilingual language models ability to capture regional knowledge across various Indic languages. It focuses on factual questions related to India in domains such as Literature, History, Geography, Politics, and Economics. The dataset is available in English as well as several Indic languages, including Hindi, allowing for language-specific evaluations. For LLM-as-a-judge evaluation, the ground truth facts are passed to the evaluator LLM as a reference.

- **SubjectiveEval**: This in-house Hindi evaluation dataset features open-ended questions across various Indian domains, including History, Geography, Agriculture, Food, Culture, Religion, Science and Technology, Mathematics, and Thinking Ability. It offers broader coverage compared to the fact-based questions in IndicQuest. It assesses a model's understanding, generative capabilities, coherence, and insightfulness. Questions include 'what', 'how', and 'why' types, varying from brief one-word answers to detailed explanations. The dataset also tests analytical and problem-solving skills with hypothetical scenarios. Model responses are evaluated using an LLM as a judge.

- **Translated English Benchmarks**: We use translated versions of popular benchmarks for exhaustive evaluation of our models. The benchmarks include MMLU, Hella Swag, BoolQ, Arc-Easy, and Arc-Challenge.

- **Human Evaluation**: For human evaluation, we utilized a translated version of the multi-turn MT-Bench dataset (Zheng et al., 2023). The prompts were first translated into Hindi using the Google Translate API and then manually filtered to remove problematic prompts or those relying on English-specific semantics. During evaluation, human judges conducted A/B testing, where they were presented with randomized, pair-wise model responses for comparison.

4 Results and Discussion

The results for the base models are shown in Table 2 and Table 4. The Nemotron-Mini-Hindi-4B Base delivers state-of-the-art performance on nearly all benchmarks compared to similarly sized models. Additionally, it outperforms larger models like Gemma-2-9B and Llama-3.1-8B on more than half of the benchmarks. Hindi-specific continued pre-training significantly enhances the model's performance on Hindi tasks compared to the base

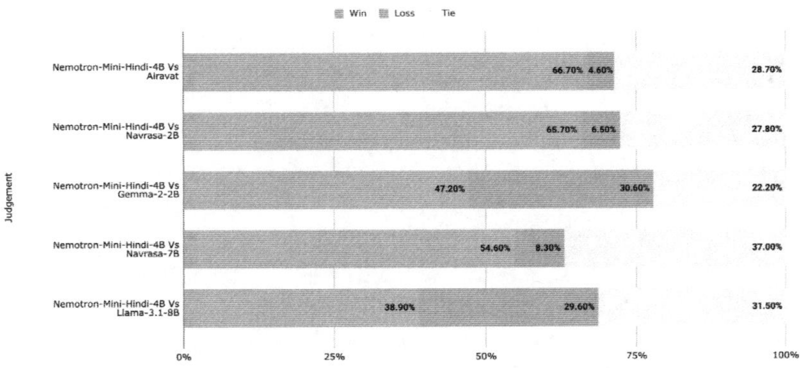

Figure 5: Results of human evaluation on translated MT-Bench. A win indicates Nemotron-Mini-Hindi-4B model is preferred.

Nemotron-Mini-4B model. There is some degradation on English benchmarks, though the results remain competitive. This underscores the importance of dual-language continued pre-training.

We observe similar results with the instruct model on IndicXTREME, IndicNLG, and translated English benchmarks. The results are presented in Table 3. The instruct model is also evaluated using LLM-as-a-judge on IndicQuest and SubjectiveEval. On these benchmarks, we see improvements in both English and Hindi compared to the Nemotron-Mini-4B-Instruct model. The model outperforms all baseline models except for Gemma-2-9B. Notably, we observe improvements in the model's factuality and language consistency. These results are shown in Figure 2, 3, and 4. Furthermore, during human evaluations, responses from Nemotron-Mini-4B-Hindi were consistently preferred over those from other models, as shown in Figure 5.

5 Conclusion

We present Nemotron-Mini-Hindi-4B-Base and Nemotron-Mini-Hindi-4B-Instruct, state-of-the-art SLMs primarily designed for the Hindi language. These models have been continuously pre-trained and aligned using a combination of Hindi and English data. The Hindi corpus includes both real and synthetic data, with the synthetic data generated through translation. The models outperform similarly sized models on various Hindi benchmarks, as assessed through reference-based and LLM-as-a-judge evaluations. They also perform competitively on English benchmarks. We emphasize the importance of pre-training to reduce hallucinations and enhance the factuality of the models.

Limitations

The model was trained on internet data that includes toxic language and biases, which means it might reproduce these biases and generate toxic responses, particularly if prompted with harmful content. It may also produce inaccurate, incomplete, or irrelevant information, potentially leading to socially undesirable outputs. The problem could be worsened if the suggested prompt template is not used.

To mitigate these issues to some extent, we have implemented safety alignment during the DPO stage to guide the model away from responding to toxic or harmful content. Additionally, we conduct safety evaluations using benchmarks such as Aegis[7] (Ghosh et al., 2024), Garak[8] (Derczynski et al., 2024), and Human Content red-teaming, and our findings indicate that the model's responses remain within permissible limits.

Acknowledgements

This work would not have been possible without contributions from many people at NVIDIA. To mention a few: Asif Ahamed, Ayush Dattagupta, Umair Ahmed, Yoshi Suhara, Ameya Mahabaleshwarkar, Zijia Chen, Varun Singh, Vibhu Jawa, Saurav Muralidharan, Sharath Turuvekere Sreenivas, Marcin Chochowski, Rohit Watve, Oluwatobi Olabiyi, Mostofa Patwary, and Oleksii Kuchaiev.

[7]https://huggingface.co/datasets/nvidia/Aegis-AI-Content-Safety-Dataset-1.0

[8]https://github.com/leondz/garak

References

Bo Adler, Niket Agarwal, Ashwath Aithal, Dong H Anh, Pallab Bhattacharya, Annika Brundyn, Jared Casper, Bryan Catanzaro, Sharon Clay, Jonathan Cohen, et al. 2024. Nemotron-4 340b technical report. *arXiv preprint arXiv:2406.11704*.

Abhinand Balachandran. 2023. Tamil-llama: A new tamil language model based on llama 2. *arXiv preprint arXiv:2311.05845*.

Samuel Cahyawijaya, Holy Lovenia, and Pascale Fung. 2024. Llms are few-shot in-context low-resource language learners. In *Proceedings of the 2024 Conference of the North American Chapter of the Association for Computational Linguistics: Human Language Technologies (Volume 1: Long Papers)*, pages 405–433.

Yiming Cui, Ziqing Yang, and Xin Yao. 2023. Efficient and effective text encoding for chinese llama and alpaca. *arXiv preprint arXiv:2304.08177*.

Leon Derczynski, Erick Galinkin, Jeffrey Martin, Subho Majumdar, and Nanna Inie. 2024. garak: A framework for security probing large language models. *arXiv preprint arXiv:2406.11036*.

Sumanth Doddapaneni, Rahul Aralikatte, Gowtham Ramesh, Shreya Goyal, Mitesh M Khapra, Anoop Kunchukuttan, and Pratyush Kumar. 2023. Towards leaving no indic language behind: Building monolingual corpora, benchmark and models for indic languages. In *Proceedings of the 61st Annual Meeting of the Association for Computational Linguistics (Volume 1: Long Papers)*, pages 12402–12426.

Abhimanyu Dubey, Abhinav Jauhri, Abhinav Pandey, Abhishek Kadian, Ahmad Al-Dahle, Aiesha Letman, Akhil Mathur, Alan Schelten, Amy Yang, Angela Fan, et al. 2024. The llama 3 herd of models. *arXiv preprint arXiv:2407.21783*.

Jay Gala, Pranjal A Chitale, AK Raghavan, Varun Gumma, Sumanth Doddapaneni, Janki Atul Nawale, Anupama Sujatha, Ratish Puduppully, Vivek Raghavan, Pratyush Kumar, et al. Indictrans2: Towards high-quality and accessible machine translation models for all 22 scheduled indian languages. *Transactions on Machine Learning Research*.

Jay Gala, Thanmay Jayakumar, Jaavid Aktar Husain, Mohammed Safi Ur Rahman Khan, Diptesh Kanojia, Ratish Puduppully, Mitesh M Khapra, Raj Dabre, Rudra Murthy, Anoop Kunchukuttan, et al. 2024. Airavata: Introducing hindi instruction-tuned llm. *arXiv preprint arXiv:2401.15006*.

Shaona Ghosh, Prasoon Varshney, Erick Galinkin, and Christopher Parisien. 2024. Aegis: Online adaptive ai content safety moderation with ensemble of llm experts. *arXiv preprint arXiv:2404.05993*.

Daniil Gurgurov, Mareike Hartmann, and Simon Ostermann. 2024. Adapting multilingual llms to low-resource languages with knowledge graphs via adapters. In *Proceedings of the 1st Workshop on Knowledge Graphs and Large Language Models (KaLLM 2024)*, pages 63–74.

Raviraj Joshi. 2022. L3cube-mahanlp: Marathi natural language processing datasets, models, and library. *arXiv preprint arXiv:2205.14728*.

Mohammed Safi Ur Rahman Khan, Priyam Mehta, Ananth Sankar, Umashankar Kumaravelan, Sumanth Doddapaneni, Sparsh Jain, Anoop Kunchukuttan, Pratyush Kumar, Raj Dabre, Mitesh M Khapra, et al. 2024. Indicllmsuite: A blueprint for creating pre-training and fine-tuning datasets for indian languages. *arXiv preprint arXiv:2403.06350*.

Simran Khanuja, Diksha Bansal, Sarvesh Mehtani, Savya Khosla, Atreyee Dey, Balaji Gopalan, Dilip Kumar Margam, Pooja Aggarwal, Rajiv Teja Nagipogu, Shachi Dave, et al. 2021. Muril: Multilingual representations for indian languages. *arXiv preprint arXiv:2103.10730*.

Aman Kumar, Himani Shrotriya, Prachi Sahu, Amogh Mishra, Raj Dabre, Ratish Puduppully, Anoop Kunchukuttan, Mitesh M Khapra, and Pratyush Kumar. 2022. Indicnlg benchmark: Multilingual datasets for diverse nlg tasks in indic languages. In *Proceedings of the 2022 Conference on Empirical Methods in Natural Language Processing*, pages 5363–5394.

Risto Luukkonen, Ville Komulainen, Jouni Luoma, Anni Eskelinen, Jenna Kanerva, Hanna-Mari Kupari, Filip Ginter, Veronika Laippala, Niklas Muennighoff, Aleksandra Piktus, et al. 2023. Fingpt: Large generative models for a small language. In *Proceedings of the 2023 Conference on Empirical Methods in Natural Language Processing*, pages 2710–2726.

Nick Mecklenburg, Yiyou Lin, Xiaoxiao Li, Daniel Holstein, Leonardo Nunes, Sara Malvar, Bruno Silva, Ranveer Chandra, Vijay Aski, Pavan Kumar Reddy Yannam, et al. 2024. Injecting new knowledge into large language models via supervised fine-tuning. *arXiv preprint arXiv:2404.00213*.

Saurav Muralidharan, Sharath Turuvekere Sreenivas, Raviraj Joshi, Marcin Chochowski, Mostofa Patwary, Mohammad Shoeybi, Bryan Catanzaro, Jan Kautz, and Pavlo Molchanov. 2024. Compact language models via pruning and knowledge distillation. *arXiv preprint arXiv:2407.14679*.

Jupinder Parmar, Shrimai Prabhumoye, Joseph Jennings, Mostofa Patwary, Sandeep Subramanian, Dan Su, Chen Zhu, Deepak Narayanan, Aastha Jhunjhunwala, Ayush Dattagupta, et al. 2024. Nemotron-4 15b technical report. *arXiv preprint arXiv:2402.16819*.

Rafael Rafailov, Archit Sharma, Eric Mitchell, Christopher D Manning, Stefano Ermon, and Chelsea Finn. 2024. Direct preference optimization: Your language model is secretly a reward model. *Advances in Neural Information Processing Systems*, 36.

Pritika Rohera, Chaitrali Ginimav, Akanksha Salunke, Gayatri Sawant, and Raviraj Joshi. 2024. L3cube-indicquest: A benchmark question answering dataset for evaluating knowledge of llms in indic context. *arXiv preprint arXiv:2409.08706*.

Gerald Shen, Zhilin Wang, Olivier Delalleau, Jiaqi Zeng, Yi Dong, Daniel Egert, Shengyang Sun, Jimmy Zhang, Sahil Jain, Ali Taghibakhshi, et al. 2024. Nemo-aligner: Scalable toolkit for efficient model alignment. *arXiv preprint arXiv:2405.01481*.

Mohammad Shoeybi, Mostofa Patwary, Raul Puri, Patrick LeGresley, Jared Casper, and Bryan Catanzaro. 2020. Megatron-lm: Training multi-billion parameter language models using model parallelism. *Preprint*, arXiv:1909.08053.

Gemma Team, Morgane Riviere, Shreya Pathak, Pier Giuseppe Sessa, Cassidy Hardin, Surya Bhupatiraju, Léonard Hussenot, Thomas Mesnard, Bobak Shahriari, Alexandre Ramé, et al. 2024. Gemma 2: Improving open language models at a practical size. *arXiv preprint arXiv:2408.00118*.

Cagri Toraman. 2024. Llamaturk: Adapting open-source generative large language models for low-resource language. *arXiv preprint arXiv:2405.07745*.

Anh-Dung Vo, Minseong Jung, Wonbeen Lee, and Daewoo Choi. 2024. Redwhale: An adapted korean llm through efficient continual pretraining. *arXiv preprint arXiv:2408.11294*.

Lianmin Zheng, Wei-Lin Chiang, Ying Sheng, Siyuan Zhuang, Zhanghao Wu, Yonghao Zhuang, Zi Lin, Zhuohan Li, Dacheng Li, Eric Xing, et al. 2023. Judging llm-as-a-judge with mt-bench and chatbot arena. *Advances in Neural Information Processing Systems*, 36:46595–46623.

OVQA: A Dataset for Visual Question Answering and Multimodal Research in Odia Language

Shantipriya Parida[1], **Shashikanta Sahoo**[2], **Sambit Sekhar**[3],**Kalyanamalini Sahoo**[4], **Ketan Kotwal**[5], **Sonal Khosla**[3], **Satya Ranjan Dash** [6], **Aneesh Bose**[7], **Guneet Singh Kohli**[8], **Smruti Smita Lenka**[3], **Ondřej Bojar**[9]

[1]Silo AI, Finland; [2]Government College of Engineering Kalahandi, India; [3]Odia Generative AI, India; [4] University of Artois, France; [5]Idiap Research Institute, Switzerland; [6]KIIT University, India; [7]Microsoft, India; [8]Thapar University, India; [9]Charles University, MFF, ÚFAL, Czech Republic;
correspondence: shantipriya.parida@silo.ai

Abstract

This paper introduces OVQA, the first multimodal dataset designed for visual question-answering (VQA), visual question elicitation (VQE), and multimodal research for the low-resource Odia language. The dataset was created by manually translating 6,149 English question-answer pairs, each associated with 6,149 unique images from the Visual Genome dataset. This effort resulted in 27,809 English-Odia parallel sentences, ensuring a semantic match with the corresponding visual information. Several baseline experiments were conducted on the dataset, including visual question answering and visual question elicitation. The dataset is the first VQA dataset for the low-resource Odia language and will be released for multimodal research purposes and also help researchers extend for other low-resource languages.

1 Introduction

Visual Question Answering (VQA) is a complex task at the intersection of computer vision and natural language processing, requiring models to understand and reason about visual content and formulate accurate responses to textual questions. Despite significant advances in this field, the majority of VQA research has been focused on a handful of widely spoken languages, primarily English. This language bias limits the accessibility and applicability of VQA technologies to non-English speaking populations.

To address this gap, we introduce OVQA, the first multimodal dataset specifically designed for VQA tasks in the Odia language. Odia, an official language of India, is currently spoken by approximately 50 million people.[1] However, it has been largely underrepresented in the realm of natural language processing and VQA research. By developing a VQA dataset in Odia, we aim to broaden the inclusivity of AI technologies and foster advancements in multilingual and multimodal AI systems.

The OVQA dataset was built by translating 6,149 English question-answer pairs from the widely used Visual Genome dataset into Odia. Each question-answer pair is associated with a unique image, resulting in a robust dataset of 27,809 English-Odia parallel sentences. This ensures a strong semantic alignment between the visual content and the textual data in both languages.

Our contributions are threefold:

- Dataset Creation: We present OVQA, a comprehensive dataset that enriches the multilingual VQA landscape and provides a valuable resource for the Odia language.
- Baseline Experiments: We establish baseline performance metrics through various experiments including visual question answering, and visual question elicitation. These baselines will serve as a reference for future research and development.
- Semantic Alignment: We ensure high-quality translation and semantic consistency between the English and Odia texts, enhancing the dataset's reliability and usability for multimodal learning tasks.

The development of OVQA is a significant step towards bridging the linguistic divide in AI research. By making this dataset publicly available, we hope to inspire further research in multilingual VQA and contribute to the creation of more inclusive AI systems.

For our work, the Visual Genome dataset introduced by Krishna et al. (2016), has been used. It is a large-scale collection of images and associated descriptive data designed to facilitate

[1]https://www.britannica.com/topic/Oriya-language

Proceedings of the First Workshop on Natural Language Processing for Indo-Aryan and Dravidian Languages (IndoNLP2025), pages 58–66
January 20, 2025. ©2025 Association for Computational Linguistics

research in computer vision and natural language processing.

We explored the *PaliGemma* (Beyer et al., 2024) model which can be used for various tasks such as VQA, detecting objects on images, or even generating segmentation masks. Here, we have explored the capability of *PaliGemma* for low-resource language on the VQA task. Although *PaliGemma* has zero-shot capabilities – meaning the model can identify objects without fine-tuning, Google strongly recommends fine-tuning the model for optimal performance in specific domains.

2 Related Work

Parida et al. (2023a) created HaVQA, a multimodal dataset for visual question answering for the low-resource Hausa language. The dataset demonstrates several use cases utilizing text and images including multimodal machine translation, visual question answering, and visual question elicitation. Romero et al. (2024) proposed a culturally diverse multilingual Visual Question Answering (CVQA) benchmark which includes culturally driven images and questions from across 28 countries on four continents, covering 26 languages with 11 scripts, providing a total of 9k questions. Gupta et al. (2020) proposed a framework for multilingual and code-mixed VQA for Hindi and English.

3 Focused Language

Odia is an Indo-Aryan language predominantly spoken in Odisha, a state located in eastern India. It is part of the Indo-Aryan language family, which evolved in the Indian subcontinent through three distinct phases: Old Indo-Aryan (1500 BC to 600 BC), Middle Indo-Aryan (600 BC to 1000 AD), and Modern Indo-Aryan (after 1000 AD). Languages that emerged during the Modern Indo-Aryan period include Odia, Bangla, Assamese, Hindi, Urdu, Punjabi, Gujarati, Sindhi, Bhojpuri, Marathi, Sinhali, and Maithili. Odia is thought to have developed around 1000 AD, and it serves as the official language of Odisha, recognized as one of the 22 languages in the Indian constitution. According to the 2011 Census, approximately 42 million people speak Odia. The language features several dialects, with Mughalbandi (Standard Odia) recognized as the standard dialect used in education. The script employed for writing Odia is called the Oriya/Odia script.

3.1 Odia Parts of Speech and Syntax

The primary parts of speech in Odia include nouns, pronouns, verbs, adjectives, and postpositions, along with minor categories such as classifiers, complementizers, and conjunctions (Sahoo, 2001). Odia follows a Subject-Object-Verb (SOV) order, where a simple sentence typically starts with a subject and concludes with a finite verb, placing objects between the subject and the verb, with the indirect object preceding the direct object. Modifiers come before the words they modify: adjectives precede nouns, and adverbs come before verbs. While word scrambling is permitted, the typical structure adheres to V-final patterns, except in poetic contexts.

Example 1:
ମିଲି ମୋତେ ଗୋଟିଏ ବହି ଦେଲା
mili mote goTie bahi delaa
Mili me a book gave
'Mili gave me a book.'

Example 2:
ମିଶିଯାଏ ଯଥା ପ୍ରଭାତୀ ତାରା ରବି କିରଣେ
misijaae jathaa prabhaati taaraa rabi kiraNe
unites as morning star sun ray-PP

ମିଶିଯାଏ ଯଥା ଜୀବାତ୍ମା ପରମାତ୍ମା ଚରଣେ
misijaae jathaa jibaatmaa paramaatmaa charaNe
unites as individual soul great soul of God feet-PP

For instance, Example (1) displays a straightforward sentence, while Example (2) demonstrates poetic inversion, where the verb appears at the beginning of the clause; this inversion is included in our corpus due to the variety of poetic forms.

3.2 Grammatical Features of Odia

Odia features three genders: masculine, feminine, and neuter; two numbers: singular and plural; and eight cases: nominative, vocative, accusative, instrumental, dative, genitive, and locative. There are also three persons: first, second, and third. The subject noun phrase agrees with the verb in terms of person, number, and honorificity. Odia employs a natural gender system, where gender does not influence other grammatical forms like pronouns or verbs. Although gender is explicitly marked in nouns and adjectives, pronouns do not show overt gender distinctions; they are generally neutral. The gender of a pronoun is determined by the noun or adjective it associates with (Parida et al., 2023b). In Odia, there is a four-fold tense distinction: past, present, future, and hypothetical, based on whether an event occurs before, during, after, or in a hypothetical context. The present tense marker is not morphologically expressed, while the other three are indicated by -il (past), -ib (future), and -ant (hypothetical) (Sahu et al., 2022; Parida et al., 2020; Nayak, 1987).

4 Odia VQA Dataset

In this section, we delve into the various stages involved in the OdiaVQA dataset creation process, including collection, annotation, validation, and data analysis.

4.1 Data Collection and Annotation

For the creation of new dataset, we utilized the Visual Genome Dataset[2] as our primary source of images, supplemented with question-answer pairs. This dataset offers a rich multimodal context comprising images and relevant captions. To gather data for the VQA task, we developed a specific web interface. With the assistance of seven native Odia speakers to manually translate the QA pairs, we annotated the dataset via this web interface.

The interface was thoughtfully designed to integrate an Odia keyboard as shown in Fig. 1, facilitating easy access to special characters in Odia. A detailed guideline was provided to the annotators to minimize errors during the annotation process. Notably, annotations were not supposed to be generated using translation tools, and annotators were required to view the images before annotating the QA pairs. These measures were implemented to reduce errors in annotations, ensuring the authenticity and overall quality of the dataset.

4.2 Data Validation

Concurrently with the annotation process, each question-answer pair underwent validation to ensure translation consistency and quality. The validation process included basic spelling and grammar checks using the interface. We engaged seven native Odia speakers to validate the entire dataset simultaneously with the annotation process. A separate interface was employed for the validation process that simultaneously displayed images and translated question-answer pairs to the validators. Validators could update question-answer pairs in case of errors, and any changes made were directly reflected in the back-end as well.

Item	Count
Number of Images	6,149
Number of Questions	27,809
Number of Answers	27,809
Number of Wh-Questions	26,939
Number of Counting Questions	70
Others	800

Table 1: Statistics of the OVQA Dataset.

4.3 Data Analysis

Within the OVQA dataset, the Odia Natural Language Processing (ONLP)[3] toolkit alongside a Basic Tokenizer has been employed for Odia text tokenization. Table 1 presents pertinent statistics, Question and answer length in OVQA dataset is shown in Figure 2.

Odia	Gloss	Percentage (%)
କଣ	What	56.67
କେଉଁଠାରେ	Where	16.30
କିପରି	How	12.83
କିଏ (କାହାର)	Who (whose)	6.04
କେବେ	When	5.24
କାହିଁକି	Why	3.15

Table 2: Statistics of the OVQA Dataset based on the Question Types.

4.4 Question

In the original English dataset, there are various question types, which can be classified into two main categories: wh-questions and counting questions. Wh-questions typically begin with words such as 'What,' 'Where,' 'When,' 'Whens,' 'Who,' 'How,' and 'Whose.' The statistics for different types of *wh*-questions are presented in Table 2. Odia questions range from as short as two words to as long as eleven words. The distribution of question lengths is illustrated in Fig. 3.

[2]https://homes.cs.washington.edu/~ranjay/visualgenome/index.html

[3]https://github.com/nlpodisha/oriya-nlp

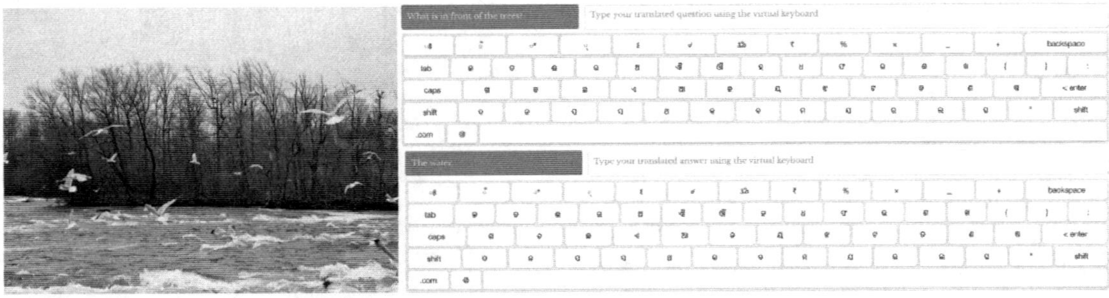

Figure 1: Odia Visual Question Answer (OVQA) Annotation Interface

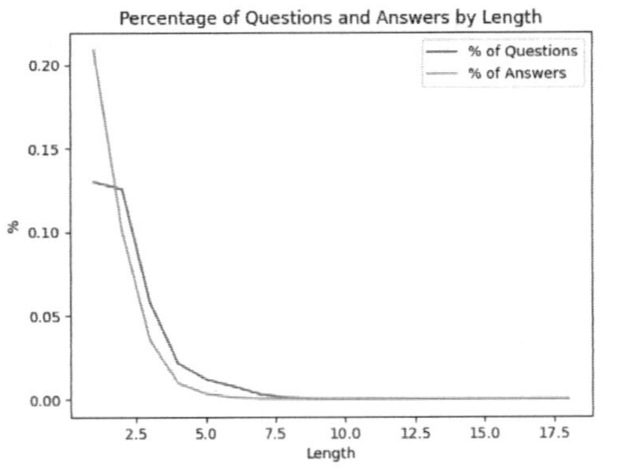

Figure 2: Percentage of Questions and Answers by length.

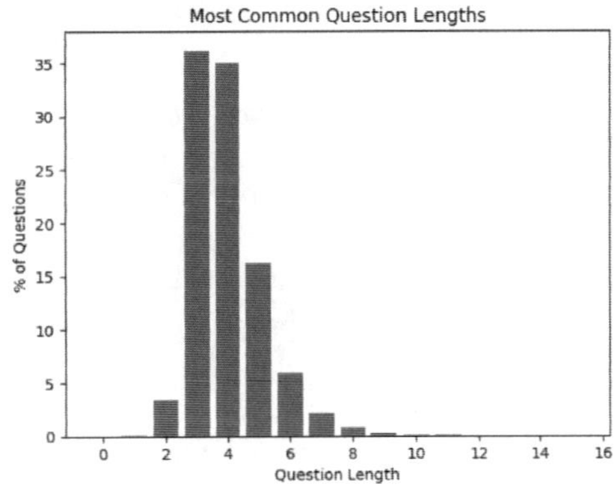

Figure 3: Distribution of Question Length.

4.5 Answers

Depending on the questions in OVQA dataset, different lengths of answers are included. In the majority of the cases (60% cases out of more than 20k QA pairs), the shortest answer is just one word or just a number; however, the longest answer is eight words. The distribution of the length of the answers is shown in Fig. 4 for different types of questions.

5 Baselines for Use Cases

5.1 Visual Question Answering

We used *PaliGemma-3b-448mix* [4] from Google for model fine-tuning on the VQA task. *PaliGemma* is a 3B vision-language model composed of a SigLIP vision encoder and a Gemma language decoder linked by a multimodal linear projection (Beyer et al., 2024; Fedorov et al., 2022).

We prepared the dataset into an instruction set format for fine-tuning.

We used Deepspeed[5] for training on GPU. For GPU, we used AMD Instinct MI250X Accelerator where each node has 60GB GPU memory and we have 1*8 nodes.

We used supervised fine-tuning (SFT) for the full fine-tuning. The hyperparameters are shown in Table 3 and learning curve in Fig. 6.

Hyper Parameter	Value
Train Batch Size (per device)	2
Gradient Accumulation Steps	4
Warm-sup step	50
Learning Rate	$3e^{-4}$
LR_Scheduler	Cosine
Epochs	10
Cutoff Length	1536
bf16	True

Table 3: Training Hyperparameters for VQA

5.2 Visual Question Elicitation

We used the images and associated questions to train an automatic VQE model (Fedorov et al., 2022). We extracted visual features using the images and fed them to an LSTM decoder.

[4] https://huggingface.co/google/paligemma-3b-mix-448

[5] https://github.com/microsoft/DeepSpeed

The decoder generates the tokens of the caption autoregressively using a greedy search approach (Soh, 2016). Trained to minimize the cross-entropy loss on the questions from the training data (Yu et al., 2019a) was minimized.

Image encoder All the images were resized to 224×224 pixels, and features from the whole image were extracted to train the model. The feature vector is the output of the final convolutional layer of ResNet-50. It is a 2048-dimensional feature representation of the image. The encoder module is a fixed feature extractor and, thus, non-trainable.

LSTM decoder A single-layer LSTM, with a hidden size of 256, was used as a decoder. The dropout is set to 0.3. During training, for the LSTM decoder, the cross-entropy loss is minimized and computed using the output logits and the tokens in the gold caption. Weights are optimized using the Adam optimizer (Kingma and Ba, 2014) with an initial learning rate of 0.001. Training is halted when the validation loss does not improve for ten epochs. We trained the model for 100 epochs.

6 Discussion and Analysis

6.1 Visual Question Elicitation

Since it is challenging to assess the quality of the generated questions using automatic evaluation metrics, we conducted a manual evaluation with the assistance of a native Odia speaker. Around 10% of the generated questions were sampled and manually reviewed. Each question was categorized as 'Exact,' 'Correct,' 'Nearly Correct,' or 'Wrong.' The distribution of these categories

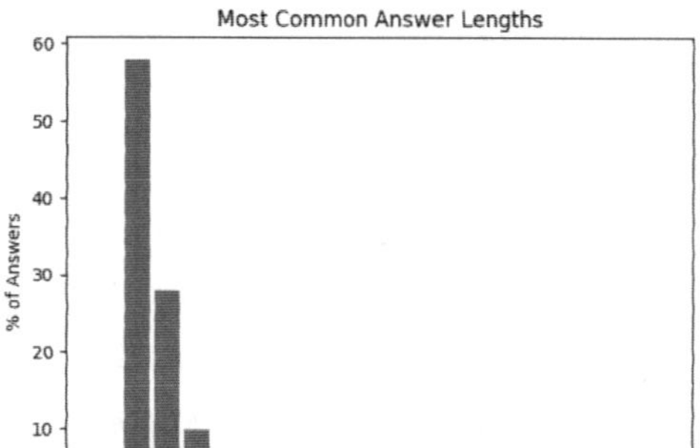

Figure 4: Distribution of Answer Length.

[{ "content": "ଫଟୋରେ କେତୋଟି ଜେବ୍ରା ଅଛି?", "role": "user" }, { "content": "୨ |", "role": "assistant" }]

Figure 5: Dataset Sample

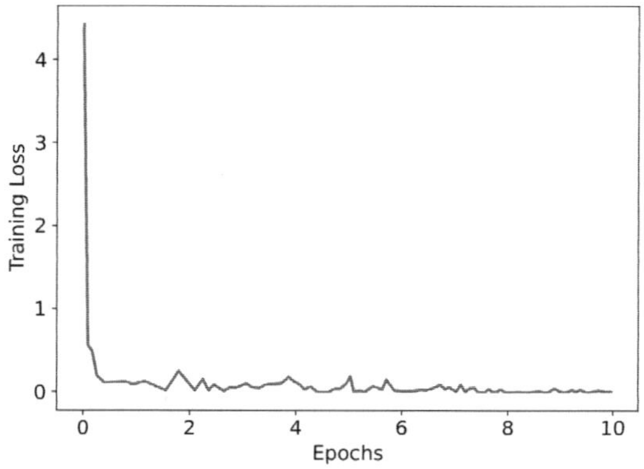

Figure 6: Learning Curve for VQA Training

is shown in Figure 8, with additional sample questions provided in Part A in the Appendix.

All the generated predictions were valid and reasonable questions, with 99.5% of them (all but 3) correctly ending with a question mark ('?'). The distribution of question types is as follows: "କଣ" (what)–60.1%, "କେଉଁଠାରେ" (where)–26.4%, "କେବେ" (when)–4.8%, "କିଏ" (who)–3.7%, "କାହିଁକି" (why)–1.5%, "କେତେ" (how much)–2.32%, and "କିପରି" (how)–1.2%.

7 Availability

The OVQA dataset can be accessed via LINDAT at: http://hdl.handle.net/11234/1-5820.

Additionally, the OVQA dataset, designed for multimodal LLM training in an instruction set format, is available on Hugging Face:

Dataset: https://huggingface.co/datasets/odiagenmllm/odia_vqa_en_odi_set

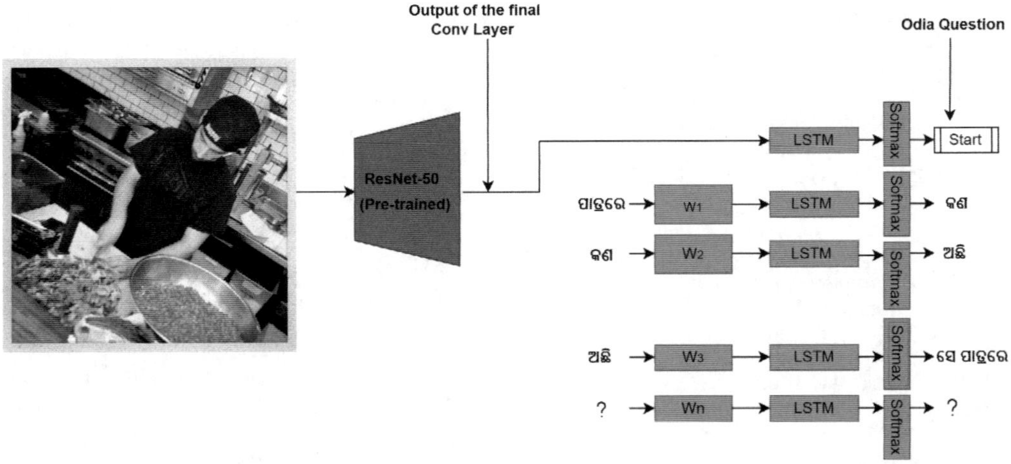

Figure 7: Architecture of Visual Question Elicitation using ResNet-50 (Koonce and Koonce, 2021) and LSTM (Yu et al., 2019b). The training question was "ପାତ୍ରରେ କଣ ଅଛି ?" (gloss: What is in the bowl?). During inference, when the image was passed through the system, the generated question was "କଣ ଅଛି ସେପାତ୍ରରେ?" (gloss: What is in the container?).

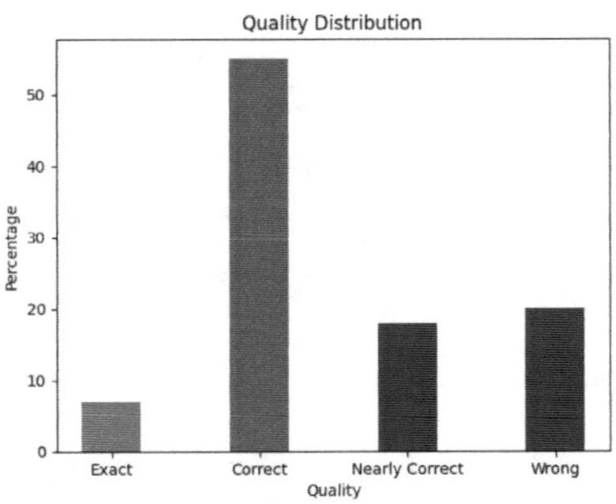

Figure 8: Quality Distribution of Automatically Generated Questions.

8 Conclusion

In this work, we presented **OVQA**: a multimodal dataset suitable for various NLP tasks for the Odia language. Some examples of these tasks include VQA, VQE, and other research tasks based on multimodal analysis.

The OVQA dataset is available for research and non-commercial use under the Creative Commons Attribution-NonCommercial-ShareAlike 4.0 License.[6]

Our planned future work includes: *i)* extending the dataset with more images depicting regional, and cultural aspects and QA pairs *ii)* providing ground truth for all images for image captioning experiments, and *iii)* organizing a shared task using the OVQA dataset.

[6] https://creativecommons.org/licenses/by-nc-sa/4.0/

Ethics Statement

We do not envisage any ethical concerns. The dataset does not contain any personal, or personally identifiable, information, the source data is already open source, and there are no risks or harm associated with its usage.

Limitations

The most important limitation of our work lies in the size of the OVQA dataset. However, substantial further funding would be needed to resolve this.

Acknowledgements

The work on this project was supported by Odia Generative AI, India, and partially supported by the grant CZ.02.01.01/00/23_020/0008518 of the Ministry of Education of the Czech Republic.

References

Lucas Beyer, Andreas Steiner, André Susano Pinto, Alexander Kolesnikov, Xiao Wang, Daniel Salz, Maxim Neumann, Ibrahim Alabdulmohsin, Michael Tschannen, Emanuele Bugliarello, et al. 2024. Paligemma: A versatile 3b vlm for transfer. *arXiv preprint arXiv:2407.07726*.

Dmitry A Fedorov, Bo Peng, Niranjan Govind, and Yuri Alexeev. 2022. Vqe method: a short survey and recent developments. *Materials Theory*, 6(1):2.

Deepak Gupta, Pabitra Lenka, Asif Ekbal, and Pushpak Bhattacharyya. 2020. A unified framework for multilingual and code-mixed visual question answering. In *Proceedings of the 1st Conference of the Asia-Pacific Chapter of the Association for Computational Linguistics and the 10th International Joint Conference on Natural Language Processing*, pages 900–913, Suzhou, China. Association for Computational Linguistics.

Diederik P. Kingma and Jimmy Ba. 2014. Adam: A method for stochastic optimization. Cite arxiv:1412.6980Comment: Published as a conference paper at the 3rd International Conference for Learning Representations, San Diego, 2015.

Brett Koonce and Brett Koonce. 2021. Resnet 50. *Convolutional neural networks with swift for tensorflow: image recognition and dataset categorization*, pages 63–72.

Ranjay Krishna, Yuke Zhu, Oliver Groth, Justin Johnson, Kenji Hata, Joshua Kravitz, Stephanie Chen, Yannis Kalantidis, Li-Jia Li, David A. Shamma, Michael S. Bernstein, and Fei-Fei Li. 2016. Visual genome: Connecting language and vision using crowdsourced dense image annotations. *Preprint*, arXiv:1602.07332.

Rath Nayak. 1987. *Non-finite clauses in Oriya*. Doctoral dissertation, Central Institute of English and Foreign Languages (CIEFL), Hyderabad, India.

Shantipriya Parida, Idris Abdulmumin, Shamsuddeen Hassan Muhammad, Aneesh Bose, Guneet Singh Kohli, Ibrahim Said Ahmad, Ketan Kotwal, Sayan Deb Sarkar, Ondřej Bojar, and Habeebah Kakudi. 2023a. HaVQA: A dataset for visual question answering and multimodal research in Hausa language. In *Findings of the Association for Computational Linguistics: ACL 2023*, pages 10162–10183, Toronto, Canada. Association for Computational Linguistics.

Shantipriya Parida, Ondřej Bojar, and Satya Ranjan Dash. 2020. Odiencorp: Odia–english and odia-only corpus for machine translation. In *Smart Intelligent Computing and Applications: Proceedings of the Third International Conference on Smart Computing and Informatics, Volume 1*, pages 495–504. Springer.

Shantipriya Parida, Alakananda Tripathy, Satya Ranjan Dash, and Shashikanta Sahoo. 2023b. Mdolc: Multi dialect odia song lyric corpus.

David Romero, Chenyang Lyu, Haryo Akbarianto Wibowo, Teresa Lynn, Injy Hamed, Aditya Nanda Kishore, Aishik Mandal, Alina Dragonetti, Artem Abzaliev, Atnafu Lambebo Tonja, et al. 2024. Cvqa: Culturally-diverse multilingual visual question answering benchmark. *arXiv preprint arXiv:2406.05967*.

Kalyanamalini Sahoo. 2001. *Oriya Verb Morphology and Complex Verb Constructions*. Ph.d dissertation, Norwegian University of Science and Technology, Trondheim, Norway.

Anupama Sahu, Sarojananda Mishra, and Kalyan Kumar Jena. 2022. Classification of odia and other text printed images usingmachine intelligence based approach. *NeuroQuantology*, 20(9):764.

Moses Soh. 2016. Learning cnn-lstm architectures for image caption generation.

Jun Yu, Jing Li, Zhou Yu, and Qingming Huang. 2019a. Multimodal transformer with multi-view visual representation for image captioning. *IEEE transactions on circuits and systems for video technology*, 30(12):4467–4480.

Yong Yu, Xiaosheng Si, Changhua Hu, and Jianxun Zhang. 2019b. A review of recurrent neural networks: Lstm cells and network architectures. *Neural computation*, 31(7):1235–1270.

A Visual Question Elicitation Sample Predictions

Example 1: Exact	Example 2: Correct

Ref Que.: ସେଠାରେ କେତେଗୁଡ଼ିଏ ଫ୍ୟାକେଟ୍ ଅଛି? **Gloss:** How many faucets are there? **Pred Que.:** ସେଠାରେ କେତେ ଫ୍ୟାକେଟ୍ ଅଛି? **Gloss:** How many faucets are there?	**Ref Que.:** ଆକାଶରେ ମେଘର କେଉଁ ରଙ୍ଗ? **Gloss:** What color are the clouds in the sky? **Pred Que.:** ମେଘର ରଙ୍ଗ କ'ଣ? **Gloss:** What is the color of the clouds?
Example 3: Nearly Correct	**Example 4: Wrong**

Ref Que.: ବିମାନରେ ଥିବା ଫିନ୍ ଉପରେ ଅକ୍ଷରଗୁଡ଼ିକ କ'ଣ? **Gloss:** What are the letters on the fin on the airplane? **Pred Que.:** ବିମାନରେ ଅକ୍ଷରଗୁଡ଼ିକ କ'ଣ? **Gloss:** What are the letters on the airplane?	**Ref Que.:** ସବୁଜ ପରିବାଟି କଣ? **Gloss:** What is the green vegetable? **Pred Que.:** ବ୍ରୋକଲି ଟିକେଉଁଠାରେ ଅଛି? **Gloss:** Where is the broccoli?

Table 4: Visual Question Elicitation Sample Predictions

B Recruitment of Annotators and Validators

We selected native Odia speakers from the Odia Generative AI (OdiaGenAI) research group, which consists of experienced translators, to serve as annotators and validators. The annotation team comprised 4 women and 3 men, while the validation team included 3 women and 4 men. Each team member holds at least an undergraduate degree and resides in various regions across Odisha state of India.

C Annotation Guidelines

The following instructions were provided to the Odia annotators and validators:

1. Review the Odia typing guidelines carefully. Before beginning the annotation, perform a quick test and report any issues encountered.
2. Ensure that the annotator is a native speaker of the Odia language.
3. View the image before proceeding with annotation.
4. Aim to understand the task fully—translate both questions and answers into Odia.
5. Refrain from using any machine translation tools for annotation.
6. Do not enter dummy entries for testing the interface.

7. Data will be saved at the backend.
8. Press the Shift Key on the virtual keyboard for complex consonants.
9. Contact the coordinator for any clarification/support.

Advancing Multilingual Speaker Identification and Verification for Indo-Aryan and Dravidian Languages

Braveenan Sritharan
Dept. of Computer Science & Engineering, University of Moratuwa
Sri Lanka
braveenans.22@cse.mrt.ac.lk

Uthayasanker Thayasivam
Dept. of Computer Science & Engineering, University of Moratuwa
Sri Lanka
rtuthaya@cse.mrt.ac.lk

Abstract

Multilingual speaker identification and verification is a challenging task, especially for languages with diverse acoustic and linguistic features such as Indo-Aryan and Dravidian languages. Previous models have struggled to generalize across multilingual environments, leading to significant performance degradation when applied to multiple languages. In this paper, we propose an advanced approach to multilingual speaker identification and verification, specifically designed for Indo-Aryan and Dravidian languages. Empirical results on the Kathbath dataset show that our approach significantly improves speaker identification accuracy, reducing the performance gap between monolingual and multilingual systems from 15% to just 1%. Additionally, our model reduces the equal error rate for speaker verification from 15% to 5% in noisy conditions. Our method demonstrates strong generalization capabilities across diverse languages, offering a scalable solution for multilingual voice-based biometric systems.

1 Introduction

In today's world, biometric recognition is revolutionizing how we identify and verify individuals. Traditional methods, such as passwords, personal identification numbers, or signatures, are often inconvenient because they can be forgotten, stolen, or forged (Jain et al., 2004). In contrast, biometric traits are unique to each individual, making them difficult to replicate or steal. These systems rely on either physiological characteristics, such as fingerprints, iris patterns, or facial features, or behavioral traits, such as handwriting, voice, or keystroke patterns, to identify a person (Tolba et al., 2006).

Among these biometric traits, voice-based recognition offers clear advantages. Two factors make it a strong choice: First, speech is a natural and easy signal for users to provide. Second, the wide availability of phones and low-cost microphones make voice capture accessible and convenient for many applications (Reynolds, 2002). In voice-based biometric recognition, there are two distinct modes of operation: speaker identification, which typically involves recognizing an individual from a larger pool, and speaker verification, which focuses on validating a specific identity claim (Togneri and Pullella, 2011).

Voice-based recognition systems can be classified by their language handling capabilities into monolingual and multilingual systems (Nagaraja and Jayanna, 2012). Monolingual systems are trained and tested within a single language, offering high accuracy but limited flexibility outside that specific linguistic context. Multilingual systems, on the other hand, are designed to recognize speakers across multiple languages within a single model, eliminating the need for separate models for each language. This versatility makes multilingual systems well-suited for environments where multiple languages are spoken.

Recent advancements in self-supervised learning (SSL) have significantly enhanced the performance and robustness of voice-based recognition systems. SSL models, particularly in the context of the upstream model, play a crucial role in feature extraction. Here, rich speech features are captured and transferred to a downstream model, which is responsible for tasks such as speaker identification and verification (wen Yang et al., 2021). By separating the feature extraction and task-specific components, SSL models offer greater flexibility, improving the performance of voice recognition systems, particularly in multilingual applications.

Despite these advances, multilingual systems still lag behind their monolingual counterparts in terms of accuracy (Javed et al., 2023). This performance gap is particularly significant in multilingual countries such as India, where linguistic diversity presents a unique challenge. India's population speaks languages from four main language fam-

Proceedings of the First Workshop on Natural Language Processing for Indo-Aryan and Dravidian Languages (IndoNLP2025), pages 67–73
January 20, 2025. ©2025 Association for Computational Linguistics

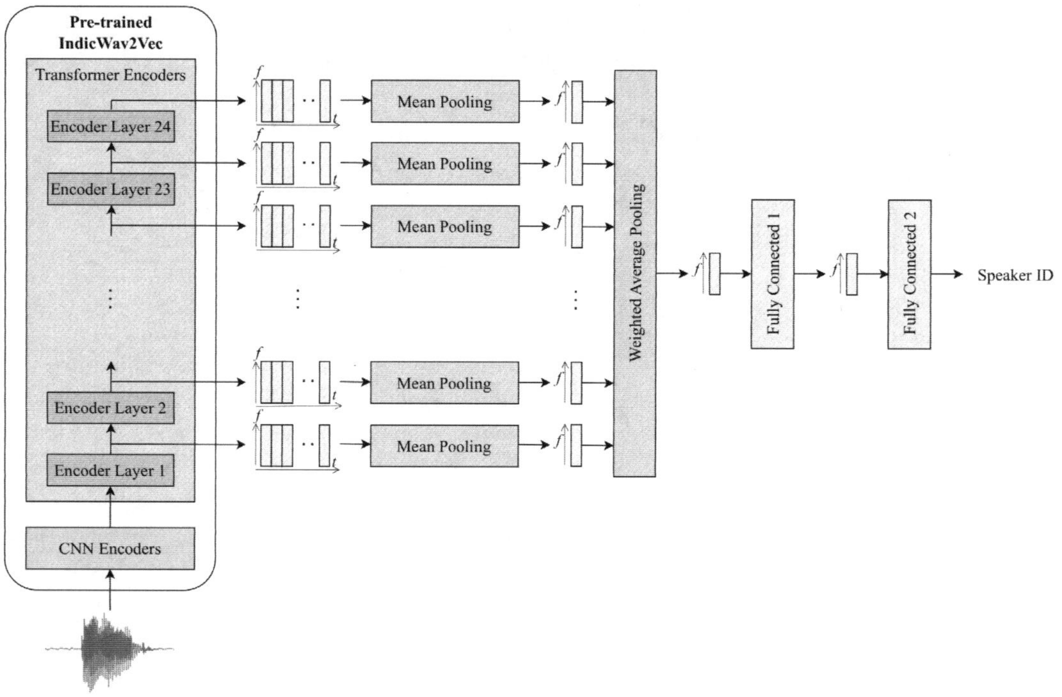

Figure 1: Architecture of our speaker identification model. The model processes an input speech signal in .m4a format (sampled at 16 kHz) using the pre-trained IndicWav2Vec model (Javed et al., 2023) to generate 24 frame-level representations. These are then mean-pooled along the time axis to create utterance-level representations. A weighted average pooling is applied across the 24 utterance-level representations to produce the final representation, which is passed through two fully connected layers to predict speaker identity. Layer dimensions and additional hyper-parameters are detailed in Section 3.

ilies, with approximately 96% of speakers using languages from the Indo-Aryan and Dravidian families, while the remaining languages have smaller speaker bases (Kakwani et al., 2020). In this context, a multilingual voice recognition system capable of handling multiple languages within a single model is crucial. It would eliminate the need for separate models for each language, streamlining speaker identification and verification processes across India's diverse linguistic landscape.

In this paper, we propose a novel architecture for voice-based biometric recognition using the pre-trained IndicWac2Vec model (Javed et al., 2023) to enhance both speaker identification and verification. Our model was tested under two conditions: clean and noisy environments. While there was a slight improvement in monolingual speaker identification accuracy, the major gain was in multilingual speaker identification accuracy, where the performance gap between monolingual and multilingual systems decreased from around 15% to 1%. Additionally, instead of creating a separate speaker verification model, we used the speaker embeddings from our speaker identification model for verification. Compared to the standard approach, our method reduced the equal error rate from 15% to 5% on unknown data in both clean and noisy conditions, demonstrating improved multilingual voice-based recognition.

2 Methodology

Our speaker identification model builds upon the architecture proposed by Javed et al.. To enhance the model's performance on speaker identification and verification tasks, we have introduced two key modifications, as illustrated in Figure 1.

2.1 Weighted Average Pooling Strategy

The original model employs mean pooling, which averages representations from all transformer encoder layers to generate a single vector. While straightforward, this approach assumes equal contribution from all layers, which may not align with the properties of speech representations. Prior stud-

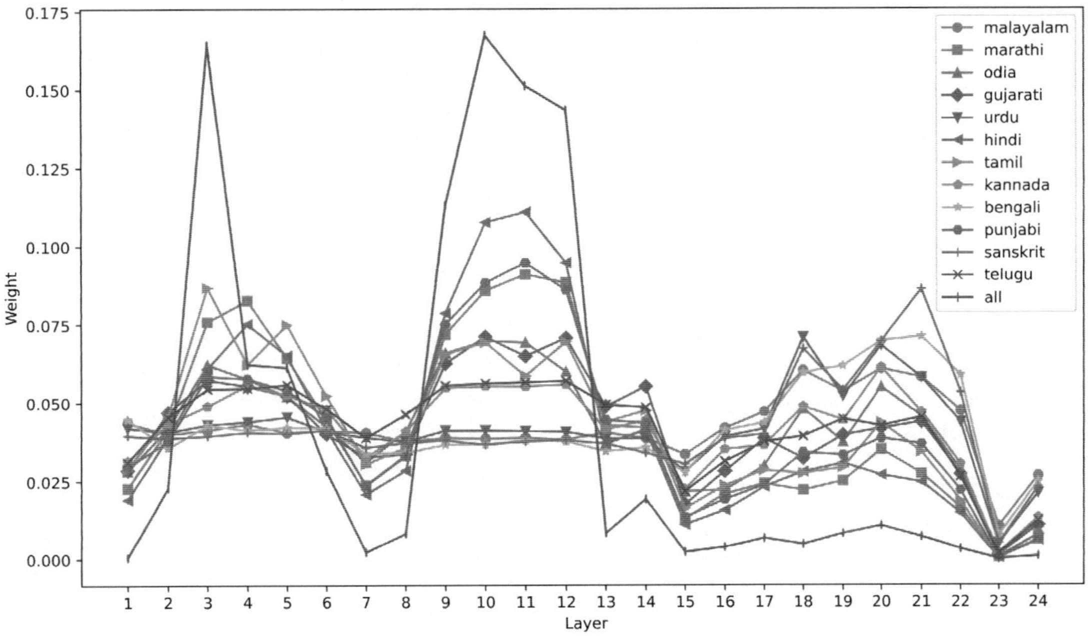

Figure 2: Encoder layer-wise representation weights for speaker identification models trained on specific languages and a multi-language dataset. The figure contains 13 subplots: each of the first 12 subplots shows a model trained exclusively on one language, labeled by the language name. The final subplot, labeled "all," displays results from a model trained on a combined dataset incorporating all 12 languages. This visualization highlights the variation in layer importance across language-specific models and the multi-language model.

ies (Chen et al., 2022) have shown that middle layers of transformer-based models often capture speaker-specific features more effectively than the initial or final layers.

To address this limitation, we employ a weighted average pooling strategy, which assigns learnable weights to each layer's representation. This approach enables the model to emphasize layers that capture speaker-specific features while reducing the contribution of less relevant layers. By prioritizing these layers, the model effectively exploits the hierarchical structure of transformer outputs, as supported by the findings in (Chen et al., 2022), which highlight the importance of middle layers for speaker-related tasks.

2.2 Additional Embedding Layer

In the baseline architecture, the aggregated representation is passed directly to the classifier. To enhance the model's ability to refine speaker-related features, we introduce an additional embedding layer, a linear transformation applied to the pooled representation before classification. This layer refines the pooled representation to better distinguish speaker-specific features, leveraging the hypothesis that increased depth improves feature separability (Shi et al., 2020). Additionally, the refined embeddings support both speaker identification and verification, providing a unified representation that enhances the model's accuracy and robustness.

The resulting model improves accuracy and robustness for speaker identification and verification. Details on layer dimensions and other hyperparameters are in Section 3.

3 Experimental Setup

Our speaker identification model consists of two main components: an upstream model and a downstream model. The upstream model, IndicWav2Vec, is a Wav2Vec-based model pretrained on half a million hours of raw speech data across 128 Indian languages (Javed et al., 2023). Following standard practice in speech processing benchmarks, such as SUPERB (wen Yang et al., 2021), we freeze the upstream model and train only the downstream model. This approach allows us to use the rich, pre-trained representations while reducing computational complexity, as only the downstream model is updated to predict speaker

Language	SID - Mono		SID - Multi					
	Clean	Noise	Dravidian		Indo-Aryan		All	
			Clean	Noise	Clean	Noise	Clean	Noise
Bengali	**99.64**	**99.63**	-	-	99.54	99.44	99.54	99.37
Gujarati	97.73	**95.97**	-	-	97.63	95.68	**97.79**	94.94
Hindi	**99.39**	**99.08**	-	-	99.23	98.68	99.17	98.62
Kannada	98.54	99.86	**99.00**	**100.00**	-	-	98.91	**100.00**
Malayalam	**99.94**	**99.93**	**99.94**	99.65	-	-	99.77	99.58
Marathi	**94.11**	97.97	-	-	**94.11**	98.39	93.82	**98.47**
Odia	98.17	**98.39**	-	-	**98.24**	97.82	98.10	97.37
Punjabi	**99.41**	99.24	-	-	99.13	99.19	98.94	**99.37**
Sanskrit	99.82	99.56	-	-	**99.94**	99.24	**99.94**	**99.62**
Tamil	96.41	96.73	**96.96**	**96.85**	-	-	96.12	96.65
Telugu	93.61	**96.48**	**94.81**	95.83	-	-	94.73	95.66
Urdu	**99.72**	**99.29**	-	-	99.62	99.20	99.27	99.23

Table 1: Performance of different languages on the Speaker Identification (SID) tasks, specifically for the Mono and Multi language settings, evaluated on both clean and noisy datasets. In the SID-Multi task, languages are grouped into three categories: Dravidian (a model trained on all Dravidian languages and tested on each language individually), Indo-Aryan (a model trained on all Indo-Aryan languages and tested on each language individually), and All (a model trained on all languages combined and tested on each language individually)

identity. [1] [2].

As the speaker identification task is framed as a classification problem, we use cross-entropy as the loss function and accuracy as the evaluation metric. In the speaker verification task, we first train the model for multilingual speaker identification, then extract speaker embeddings. These embeddings are compared using cosine similarity, and performance is evaluated using the Equal Error Rate (EER), which represents the point at which the false acceptance rate equals the false rejection rate. Hyper-parameter tuning, performed using grid search, was applied to both tasks to optimize the model's performance [3].

For evaluating our model's performance, we select the Kathbath dataset (Javed et al., 2023), which is particularly well-suited for speaker identification tasks involving Indo-Aryan and Dravidian languages. This dataset is the largest available for Indian languages, making it an ideal choice for multilingual speaker identification. It includes 8 Indo-Aryan languages—Gujarati, Marathi, Bengali, Odia, Hindi, Punjabi, Sanskrit, and Urdu—and 4 Dravidian languages—Kannada, Malayalam, Tamil, and Telugu. All 12 languages are widely spoken, ensuring the model's generalization across a diverse set of linguistic and acoustic features. The dataset is divided into four categories: Clean Known, Noise Known, Clean Unknown, and Noise Unknown, which allows for robust evaluation under varying conditions of noise and speaker familiarity. The "Clean" and "Noise" labels distinguish between clean and noisy audio, while "Known" and "Unknown" indicate whether the speaker is seen or unseen during training. We follow the recommended train-test splits for each dataset.

4 Results and Discussion

A key architectural modification in our model is the use of weighted average pooling for features extracted from the pre-trained IndicWav2Vec model, replacing traditional mean pooling. Figure 2 demonstrates that layer contributions are not uniform; notably, layers 9 through 12 consistently receive higher weights across all models. This suggests that these deeper layers play a substantial role in encoding speaker identity, as they may capture more abstract, speaker-specific features that are essential for accurate identification.

Furthermore, there is a strong correlation between the weight patterns in monolingual and multilingual models. Layers with relatively small weights in monolingual models appear even smaller in the multilingual model, while those with higher

[1]Our model was implemented using PyTorch.

[2]All experiments were conducted on an NVIDIA Quadro RTX 6000 GPU with 30GB of RAM.

[3]The fully connected layer has a dimension of 1500, with a batch size of 32 and a learning rate of 2.5×10^{-3}.

Model	Clean - Known	Clean - Unknown	Noisy - Known	Noisy - Unknown
Speaker Identification Monolingual (SID-Mono) - Accuracy				
XLS-R	94.2	-	92.4	-
IndicWav2Vec	95.6	-	95.2	-
Ours	**98.04**	-	**98.51**	-
Speaker Identification Multilingual (SID-Multi) - Accuracy				
XLS-R	70.71	-	69.22	-
IndicWav2Vec	79.26	-	78.08	-
Ours	**97.96**	-	**98.12**	-
Automatic Speaker Verification - EER				
XLS-R	2.15	12.05	2.83	11.58
IndicWav2Vec	**2.08**	15.33	**2.11**	15.39
Ours	4.61	**5.15**	5.23	**5.55**

Table 2: Performance comparison of different models on various tasks, including Speaker Identification (SID) in both monolingual (SID-Mono) and multilingual (SID-Multi) settings, and Automatic Speaker Verification (ASV). For SID-Mono and SID-Multi, the accuracy is reported for both clean and noisy conditions on known speakers. For ASV, the Equal Error Rate (EER) is reported for clean and noisy conditions on both known and unknown speakers. Ours denotes the model proposed in this work, which outperforms the other models, XLS-R and IndicWav2Vec, in most settings.

weights tend to be accentuated in the multilingual setting. This consistency suggests that the multilingual model captures a generalizable layer-wise structure across languages, reinforcing the importance of weighted pooling in effectively leveraging essential layers for robust speaker representation. These findings demonstrate that our approach preserves key features across languages, enhancing speaker identification accuracy.

Table 1 presents the performance of our model on the SID task across monolingual and multilingual settings, evaluated on both clean and noisy datasets. In the monolingual setting, the model achieves high accuracy on several languages, with Bengali, Hindi, and Malayalam exceeding 99% accuracy. However, languages like Marathi and Telugu show a drop in performance, particularly in noisy conditions. This indicates that noise significantly impacts speaker identification for these languages, potentially due to their unique acoustic characteristics. Overall, the monolingual performance demonstrates the model's capability to accurately identify speakers in controlled environments, though its performance is more sensitive to noise in certain languages.

In contrast, the multilingual setting shows a slight decrease in accuracy compared to the monolingual case, which is expected due to the added complexity of handling multiple languages. Nevertheless, the model trained on the "All" languages category maintains relatively high performance across languages, demonstrating strong generalization. The Dravidian and Indo-Aryan subsets perform similarly, with the Indo-Aryan model slightly outperforming others in some cases. Notably, the multilingual models exhibit better resilience to noise compared to the monolingual models, suggesting that training with multiple languages helps the model learn more robust speaker features. However, noise remains a challenge, and further improvements in noise robustness are needed for better performance in real-world conditions.

Next, Table 2 compares the performance of our model against two baseline models, XLS-R and IndicWav2Vec, across three tasks: SID in both monolingual (SID-Mono) and multilingual (SID-Multi) settings, and Automatic Speaker Verification (ASV). For both SID-Mono and SID-Multi tasks, our model consistently outperforms the baselines in terms of accuracy, particularly in noisy conditions. In the monolingual setting, our model achieves an accuracy of 98.04% for clean and 98.51% for noisy conditions, significantly surpassing the 95.6% and 95.2% accuracy of IndicWav2Vec and the 94.2% and 92.4% accuracy of XLS-R. Similarly, in the multilingual setting, our model shows remarkable performance, achieving 97.96% in clean and 98.12% in noisy conditions, well ahead of both XLS-R and IndicWav2Vec.

However, when it comes to ASV, our model lags behind the baselines in terms of Equal Error Rate (EER). While XLS-R and IndicWav2Vec achieve

EER values ranging from 2.08 to 2.83 for clean conditions and 11.58 to 15.39 for noisy conditions, our model exhibits better EER values, particularly in unknown conditions, with the best value being 5.15 for unknown speakers in clean conditions and 5.55 for unknown speakers in noisy conditions. These results suggest that while our model excels in speaker identification tasks, further improvements in ASV, especially under known conditions, are necessary. Despite the performance gap in ASV, the results highlight the robustness of our model in SID tasks across both monolingual and multilingual settings, making it a promising candidate for practical voice recognition applications.

5 Conclusion

In this work, we presented a novel approach for multilingual speaker identification and verification using a modified IndicWav2Vec-based model. Our model integrates self-supervised learning techniques to extract rich, robust speech features, which substantially improve speaker identification performance, especially in multilingual settings. Key innovations include a weighted average pooling mechanism for better aggregation of transformer layer representations and an additional embedding layer to refine speaker-specific features. These modifications led to significant improvements, reducing the performance gap between monolingual and multilingual systems from 15% to 1%, and lowering the equal error rate for speaker verification from 15% to 5% under noisy conditions. Our experiments, conducted with the Kathbath dataset, demonstrated the model's ability to generalize effectively across multiple languages. The simplicity of the model structure, combined with its robust performance, positions it as an efficient and scalable solution for voice-based biometric recognition.

6 Limitation

Despite the promising results, our model still faces several limitations. Although it excels in multilingual speaker identification and verification, its performance is limited by the diversity of the training dataset, as it relies heavily on the Kathbath dataset. Expanding the training data to cover a wider variety of languages and acoustic conditions will be crucial for enhancing generalization. Additionally, while the model performs well under clean and moderately noisy conditions, its robustness in highly noisy environments remains a challenge. The equal error rate, though reduced in typical scenarios, may degrade in real-world applications with severe noise or poor-quality recordings. Lastly, the model's computational complexity, especially with the added pooling and embedding layers, may limit its suitability for real-time or resource-constrained applications.

Acknowledgment

We would like to express our gratitude to the National Languages Processing (NLP) Center and DataSEARCH Research Center at the University of Moratuwa for providing the GPUs required to carry out the experiments for this research.

References

Sanyuan Chen, Chengyi Wang, Zhengyang Chen, Yu Wu, Shujie Liu, Zhuo Chen, Jinyu Li, Naoyuki Kanda, Takuya Yoshioka, Xiong Xiao, et al. 2022. Wavlm: Large-scale self-supervised pre-training for full stack speech processing. *IEEE Journal of Selected Topics in Signal Processing*, 16(6):1505–1518.

Anil K Jain, Arun Ross, and Salil Prabhakar. 2004. An introduction to biometric recognition. *IEEE Transactions on circuits and systems for video technology*, 14(1):4–20.

Tahir Javed, Kaushal Bhogale, Abhigyan Raman, Pratyush Kumar, Anoop Kunchukuttan, and Mitesh M Khapra. 2023. Indicsuperb: A speech processing universal performance benchmark for indian languages. In *Proceedings of the AAAI Conference on Artificial Intelligence*, volume 37, pages 12942–12950.

Divyanshu Kakwani, Anoop Kunchukuttan, Satish Golla, Gokul N.C., Avik Bhattacharyya, Mitesh M. Khapra, and Pratyush Kumar. 2020. IndicNLPSuite: Monolingual corpora, evaluation benchmarks and pre-trained multilingual language models for Indian languages. In *Findings of the Association for Computational Linguistics: EMNLP 2020*, pages 4948–4961, Online. Association for Computational Linguistics.

BG Nagaraja and HS Jayanna. 2012. Mono and cross lingual speaker identification with the constraint of limited data. In *International Conference on Pattern Recognition, Informatics and Medical Engineering (PRIME-2012)*, pages 439–443. IEEE.

Douglas A Reynolds. 2002. An overview of automatic speaker recognition technology. In *2002 IEEE international conference on acoustics, speech, and signal processing*, volume 4, pages IV–4072. IEEE.

Yanpei Shi, Qiang Huang, and Thomas Hain. 2020. H-vectors: Utterance-level speaker embedding using a hierarchical attention model. In *ICASSP 2020-2020 IEEE international conference on acoustics, speech and signal processing (ICASSP)*, pages 7579–7583. IEEE.

Roberto Togneri and Daniel Pullella. 2011. An overview of speaker identification: Accuracy and robustness issues. *IEEE circuits and systems magazine*, 11(2):23–61.

AS Tolba, AH El-Baz, and AA El-Harby. 2006. Face recognition: A literature review. *International Journal of Signal Processing*, 2(2):88–103.

Shu wen Yang, Po-Han Chi, Yung-Sung Chuang, Cheng-I Jeff Lai, Kushal Lakhotia, Yist Y. Lin, Andy T. Liu, Jiatong Shi, Xuankai Chang, Guan-Ting Lin, Tzu-Hsien Huang, Wei-Cheng Tseng, Ko tik Lee, Da-Rong Liu, Zili Huang, Shuyan Dong, Shang-Wen Li, Shinji Watanabe, Abdelrahman Mohamed, and Hung yi Lee. 2021. Superb: Speech processing universal performance benchmark. In *Interspeech 2021*, pages 1194–1198.

Sentiment Analysis of Sinhala News Comments Using Transformers

Isuru Bandaranayake and Hakim Usoof
Department of Statistics & Computer Science
Faculty of Science, University of Peradeniya
Peradeniya, Sri Lanka
bandaranayakeisuru@gmail.com, hau@sci.pdn.ac.lk

Abstract

Sentiment analysis has witnessed significant advancements with the emergence of deep learning models such as transformer models. Transformer models adopt the mechanism of self-attention and have achieved state-of-the-art performance across various natural language processing (NLP) tasks, including sentiment analysis. However, limited studies are exploring the application of these recent advancements in sentiment analysis of Sinhala text. This study addresses this research gap by employing transformer models such as BERT, DistilBERT, RoBERTa, and XLM-RoBERTa (XLM-R) for sentiment analysis of Sinhala news comments. This study was conducted for 4 classes: positive, negative, neutral, and conflict, as well as for 3 classes: positive, negative, and neutral. It revealed that the XLM-R-large model outperformed the other four models, and the transformer models used in previous studies for the Sinhala language. The XLM-R-large model achieved an accuracy of 65.84% and a macro-F1 score of 62.04% for sentiment analysis with four classes and an accuracy of 75.90% and a macro-F1 score of 72.31% for three classes.

1 Introduction

Sentiment analysis is a fundamental task in NLP which aims to analyze and understand the sentiment expressed in textual data. While sentiment analysis has been extensively studied for major languages such as English, research on low-resource languages is relatively limited.

Sinhala, a morphologically rich Indo-Aryan language, serves as the native language of the Sinhalese people, constituting a significant portion of the population in Sri Lanka with an estimated count of 20 million speakers. However, despite its large speaker base, Sinhala is considered a low-resource language in the context of NLP research due to the scarcity of available linguistic resources for analysis and processing (de Silva, 2019).

Sentiment analysis has experienced significant progress with the advent of large-scale pre-trained language models (Mishev et al., 2020). These models have demonstrated promising results in text classification tasks for high-resource and low-resource languages. Transformer models have revolutionized NLP tasks by leveraging attention mechanisms and self-attention layers, allowing them to capture intricate linguistic patterns and dependencies (Devlin et al., 2018). Notably, transformer-based models such as BERT (Devlin et al., 2018), RoBERTa (Liu et al., 2019), and XLM-R (Conneau et al., 2019) have shown remarkable performance across various languages, making them promising candidates for sentiment analysis in Sinhala.

One of the primary advantages of employing transformer models for sentiment analysis in Sinhala is their ability to handle the language's morphological richness and syntactic complexities. Sinhala exhibits complicated morphological variations and context-dependent sentiment expressions (Medagoda, 2017), which transformer models can effectively capture.

However, applying transformer models to sentiment analysis in Sinhala also poses specific challenges. One major challenge is the scarcity of

Proceedings of the First Workshop on Natural Language Processing for Indo-Aryan and Dravidian Languages (IndoNLP2025), pages 74–82
January 20, 2025. ©2025 Association for Computational Linguistics

annotated sentiment datasets for fine-tuning transformer models. There exists a sentiment dataset of 15,059 Sinhala news comments, annotated with four classes: Positive, Negative, Neutral, and Conflict (Senevirathne et al., 2020). However, the limited size of this dataset hinders the ability of transformer models to achieve optimal performance.

To address this limitation, we expanded the existing Sinhala news comments dataset by adding 5,000 annotated comments to the dataset. While the dataset size may still be considered limited, this extension introduced more diverse examples and enabled some level of expansion for training and evaluation purposes.

In this research, we conducted two sentiment analysis experiments considering four sentiment classes and three sentiment classes respectively. The goal was to evaluate the performance of monolingual models such as BERT, DistilBERT, and RoBERTa as well as multilingual models such as XLM-R-base and XLM-R-large models in sentiment analysis for the Sinhala language. We investigated their capabilities in effectively capturing sentiment information, accommodating the morphological variations of the language, and addressing the limited availability of labeled data. These research outcomes will contribute valuable insights to the field of sentiment analysis in Sinhala and will provide a foundation for future studies and applications.

2 Related Work

Recent developments in deep learning techniques have made it possible to achieve better results in the domain of NLP. Deep learning techniques do not use language-dependent features. Therefore, deep learning techniques have outperformed traditional statistical machine learning techniques (dos Santos and Gatti, 2014). Convolutional Neural Network (CNN) and Recurrent Neural Network (RNN) were the most popular deep learning techniques used in the NLP domain until Long Short-Term Memory (LSTM) and Transformer models were introduced. Kim (2014) proposed a method using CNN with hyperparameter tuning for sentiment analysis, and it was shown that a simple CNN with one layer of convolution and little hyperparameter tuning performs remarkably well. LSTM encoders were experimented for sentiment analysis by Yang et al. (2016) and bi-directional LSTM by G. Xu et al. (2019). Both studies showed improved results compared to previous studies, which used deep learning techniques such as CNN and RNN. An attention-based Bi-LSTM with a convolutional layer scheme called AC-BiLSTM was proposed by W. Liu et al. (2017) for sentiment analysis. Word2Vec, which is one of the most popular word-embedding models, was introduced by Goldberg & Levy (2014). Word2Vec improved the efficiency of the training procedure and enhanced the training speed and accuracy. An improved version of the Word2Vec model called GloVe was introduced by Pennington et al. (2014). GloVe outperformed other models on word analogy, word similarity, and named entity recognition tasks. Transformer models were introduced by Vaswani et al. (2017). Transformers could train significantly faster than architectures based on recurrent or convolutional layers. H. Xu et al. (2019) carried out aspect-based sentiment analysis using the BERT model, producing a state-of-the-art performance for sentiment analysis. Liao et al. (2021) used RoBERTa, an improved version of BERT, to carry out aspect-category sentiment analysis and it outperformed other models for comparison in aspect-category sentiment analysis.

Since Sinhala is a low-resource language, research done on the Sinhala language is very limited. The first sentiment analysis for the Sinhala language was carried out by N. Medagoda et al. (2015) by constructing a sentiment lexicon for Sinhala with the aid of the SentiWordNet 3.0, an English sentiment lexicon. It achieved a maximum accuracy of 60% in Naïve Bayes (NB) classification. The first sentiment analysis for the Sinhala language using an artificial neural network was conducted by N. Medagoda (2016) using a simple feed-forward neural network and part of speech tags as a feature. This model achieved an accuracy of 55%. Chathuranga et al. (2019) used a rule-based technique for binary sentiment classification of Sinhala news comments. In this study, they generated a Sinhala sentiment lexicon in a semi-automated way and used it for sentiment classification of Sinhala news comments. NB, Support Vector Machines (SVM), and decision trees were used in this study and obtained accuracy between 65% - 70%. The best accuracy of 69.23% was obtained for the NB model. Ranathunga & Liyanage (2021) conducted sentiment analysis for Sinhala news comments with deep learning techniques such as LSTM and CNN+SVM. Also, this study experimented with Word2Vec and fastText word embeddings for Sinhala (Ranathunga and Liyanage, 2021). Further, statistical machine learning algorithms such as NB, logistic regression, decision trees, random forests, and SVM were experimented by training them with the same features and conducting a sentiment analysis for Sinhala news comments. This research was carried out to study the use of various models with respect to the dimensionality of the embeddings and the effect of punctuation marks (Ranathunga and Liyanage, 2021). Demotte et al. (2020) used an approach based on the S-LSTM model for sentiment analysis of Sinhala news comments. The same dataset used by Ranathunga & Liyanage (2021) was used in this study, and it was found that S-LSTM outperforms the traditional LSTM used in the study conducted by Ranathunga & Liyanage (2021). Senevirathne et al. (2020) conducted comprehensive research on the use of RNN, LSTM, and Bi-LSTM models as well as more recent models such as hierarchical attention hybrid neural networks and capsule networks for sentiment analysis. As part of this study, they released a dataset of 15059 Sinhala news comments, annotated with four classes (Positive, Negative, Neutral, and Conflict) and a corpus of 9.48 million tokens (Senevirathne et al., 2020). Dhananjaya et al. (2022) conducted experiments to explore the performance of transformer models in various linguistic tasks, including sentiment analysis, for the Sinhala language. Their study evaluated LASER, LaBSE, XLM-R-large, XLM-R-base, and three RoBERTa-based models pre-trained specifically for Sinhala: SinBERT, SinBERTo, and SinhalaBERTo.

3 Models

In this study, we used the following transformer models to carry out sentiment analysis for the Sinhala language,

- BERT: Bidirectional Encoder Representations from Transformers
- DistilBERT: Distilled version of BERT
- RoBERTa: Robustly Optimized BERT Pretraining Approach
- XLM-R: Cross-lingual Language Model – RoBERTa
    - XLM-R-base
    - XLM-R-large

BERT, which stands for Bi-directional Encoder Representations from Transformers, is a bidirectional transformer model pre-trained on Toronto Book Corpus and Wikipedia. BERT was developed by Google, and it was the state-of-the-art language model for NLP tasks at the time it was released (Devlin et al., 2018).

DistilBERT is a lighter and faster version of the BERT model, and it was developed by Huggingface. DistilBERT has the same general architecture as BERT, but the size is 40% less than that of BERT and retains 97% of the language understanding capabilities of BERT. Also, DistilBERT is 60% faster than BERT, which is another benefit of this model (Sanh et al., 2019).

RoBERTa stands for Robustly Optimized BERT Pre-training Approach. It is an improved version of the BERT model. RoBERTa has the same architecture as the BERT model but is trained with more data and has better parameter settings (Liu et al., 2019).

XLM-R is a multilingual model pre-trained on filtered Common Crawl data containing more than 100 languages, including Sinhala. This model was developed and released by Facebook AI in 2019 (Conneau et al., 2019). XLM-R model outperformed the multilingual BERT (mBERT) and achieved state-of-the-art results on multiple cross-lingual benchmarks (Conneau et al., 2019). This model can be directly fine-tuned for a downstream task without pre-training on a Sinhala corpus, as this model is already pre-trained on Sinhala. XLM-R consists of two variants: XLM-R-base and XLM-R-large. XLM-R-base is the base version with fewer parameters.

4 Dataset

This study required two datasets to carry out pre-training and fine-tuning of the models. Since the pre-training is unsupervised, it does not require a labeled dataset. However, it required two separate datasets annotated with four classes (Positive, Negative, Neutral, and Conflict) and three classes (Positive, Negative, and Neutral) to fine-tune the models.

4.1 Dataset for pre-training

We used the Sinhala corpus extracted from "Open Super-large Crawled Aggregated coRpus" (OSCAR) dataset to pre-train the models. OSCAR dataset is a multilingual corpus obtained by language classification and filtering of the Common Crawl corpus using the Ungoliant architecture. Common Crawl corpus is a huge corpus that contains petabytes of raw web page data, metadata extracts, and text extracts gathered over 12 years of web crawling (Abadji et al., 2022). The OSCAR dataset has raw text from 162 languages, including the Sinhala language. This dataset contains 108,593 documents in the Sinhala language and 113,179,741 Sinhala words. The total size of the dataset is around 2.0 GB (Abadji et al., 2022).

4.2 Dataset for fine-tuning

The dataset[1] published by Senevirathne et al. (2020) contains 15059 news comments annotated with four classes: Positive, Negative, Neutral, and Conflict. This dataset contains 9,059 news comments extracted from the Lankadeepa online newspaper[2] by Ranathunga & Liyanage (2021), along with 6,000 news comments extracted from the GossipLanka news website[3]. This annotation has been done by three annotators following the guidelines mentioned below,

- A comment is annotated as positive or negative if it expresses purely a positive or negative opinion.
- A comment is annotated as a conflict if it gives both positive and negative opinions.
- A comment is annotated as neutral if it does not give any positive or negative opinion.

In this study, we expanded this dataset by following the steps below.

Data collection: We collected 803,623 news comments from the GossipLanka news website and filtered them to include only comments written in Sinhala Unicode characters. These comments were then cleaned by removing any characters outside the Unicode range (0D80 - 0DFF). The final dataset of Sinhala news comments contained 417,332 comments.

Classes	Dataset 1 (Four Classes)	Dataset 2 (Three Classes)
Positive	3,587	4,414
Negative	10,228	11,639
Neutral	3,822	3,822
Conflict	2,238	0
Total	19,875	19,875

Table 1: Distribution of comments per class

Data annotation: Two annotators who are native Sinhala speakers carried out the annotating task following the guidelines mentioned previously. We used Cohen's Kappa measure to evaluate the inter-annotator agreement, which yielded a value of 0.794. Both annotators collectively annotated 5,037 Sinhala news comments with four classes (Positive, Negative, Neutral, and Conflict). These annotated comments were added to the existing Sinhala news comments dataset. We carefully removed duplicate entries from the combined dataset to ensure data integrity. The final dataset comprised 19,875 unique comments.

The newly generated dataset was annotated again using Positive, Negative, and Neutral to create a sentiment dataset with three classes. Comments initially labeled as Conflict were annotated as Positive or Negative based on their predominant sentiment. Table 1 shows the distribution of comments per class in the two datasets.

4.3 Model pre-training

Pre-training the XLM-R-base and XLM-R-large models for Sinhala was not required, as these models are already pre-trained on a multilingual corpus that includes Sinhala. However, we had to pre-train the other three models for the Sinhala language, and these were pre-trained using the Sinhala dataset extracted from the OSCAR dataset.

BERT	DistilBERT	RoBERTa
[PAD]	[PAD]	<s>
[UNK]	[UNK]	<pad>
[CLS]	[CLS]	</s>
[SEP]	[SEP]	<unk>
[MASK]	[MASK]	<mask>

Table 2: Special tokens included in tokenizers

Since models cannot process raw data directly, they need to be converted to a representation that the models can process. Therefore, it was necessary to train tokenizers for these models from scratch. BERT and DistilBERT tokenizers use the WordPiece method (Devlin et al., 2018; Sanh et al., 2019), while the RoBERTa tokenizer uses the Byte-

[1] https://github.com/LahiruSen/sinhala_sentiment_anlaysis_tallip
[2] https://www.lankadeepa.lk/
[3] https://www.gossiplankanews.com/

Models	Four Classes				Three Classes			
	F1	Accuracy	Precision	Recall	F1	Accuracy	Precision	Recall
BERT	46.34%	47.07%	48.12%	52.13%	59.19%	63.32%	58.22%	61.36%
DistilBERT	49.49%	51.72%	49.59%	53.69%	60.63%	65.13%	60.59%	61.66%
RoBERTa	37.50%	37.36%	41.08%	46.27%	53.17%	56.48%	53.08%	56.67%
XLM-R$_{base}$	59.16%	62.84%	59.17%	61.85%	69.52%	73.56%	68.45%	71.06%
XLM-R$_{large}$	62.04%	65.84%	61.79%	64.48%	72.31%	75.90%	72.02%	73.20%

Table 3: Results for sentiment analysis using four classes and three classes

Pair Encoding method (Liu et al., 2019). Tokenizers for the three models were trained with a vocabulary size of 52,000 and a minimum frequency of 2 using the Sinhala dataset extracted from the OSCAR dataset. The vocabulary size defines the number of tokens and alphabets included in the final vocabulary, and the minimum frequency defines the minimum frequency a pair should have to be merged. Special tokens included in BERT, DistilBERT, and RoBERTa tokenizers are listed in Table 2.

After training the tokenizers, the three models were trained for masked language modeling task using the same dataset that was used to train the tokenizers. The models were trained with a vocabulary size of 52,000, a maximum position embedding of 512, a hidden size of 768, 12 attention heads, and 12 hidden layers. During training, tokens in the input sequences were randomly masked with a probability of 0.15. This means that, for each input sequence, approximately 15% of the tokens were selected at random to be replaced with a special token: [MASK] for BERT and DistilBERT, and <mask> for RoBERTa. We used AdamW as an optimizer with a learning rate of 5×10^{-5} and a batch size of 16.

The training of both the models and tokenizers was conducted in the Google Colaboratory environment with V100 16GB GPUs. Due to the high computational cost of pre-training, the models were trained for only one epoch.

4.4 Model fine-tuning

The pre-trained models should be fine-tuned to carry out sentiment analysis. Even though XLM-R-base and XLM-R-large models are already pre-trained for the Sinhala language, it needs to be fine-tuned for sentiment analysis in the Sinhala language. Therefore, all five pre-trained models were fine-tuned for sentiment analysis. Each pre-trained model was fine-tuned twice using Dataset 1 and Dataset 2 separately. According to the original paper of BERT, the recommended number of epochs for fine-tuning a model is 2, 3 and 4 (Devlin et al., 2018). Therefore, BERT and DistilBERT models were fine-tuned for five epochs and at the end of each epoch, the trained model was saved as a checkpoint. The best performing model was selected from the saved checkpoints by considering the loss at each epoch. Similarly, the other three models were fine-tuned for five epochs, and the best performing checkpoint was chosen.

The fine-tuning process for the models involved the use of a consistent set of parameters across BERT, DistilBERT, RoBERTa, XLM-R-base, and XLM-R-large models. For all models, the batch size was set to 16, and a dropout rate of 0.1 was applied to prevent overfitting.

The learning rates were adjusted to optimize training performance, with BERT and DistilBERT using a rate of 2×10^{-5}, RoBERTa using 1×10^{-5}, and both XLM-R-base and XLM-R-large using a rate of 5×10^{-6}. Weight decay was uniformly applied at 0.01 for all models to control overfitting further. The training was conducted using the AdamW optimizer to ensure stable convergence.

5 Results and Discussion

We evaluated the performance of the fine-tuned models using accuracy, macro-F1 score, macro-precision, and macro-recall. The results obtained by Dhananjaya et al. (2022) for the sentiment task serve as the baseline for our study. Table 3 presents the results obtained for sentiment analysis for three and four classes. In this study, we conducted all model training and evaluation using the Transformers library provided by HuggingFace (Wolf et al., 2019) on the Google Colaboratory environment.

For sentiment analysis using four classes, we observe that XLM-R-large achieved the highest macro-F1 score of 62.04%, followed closely by XLM-R-base with a macro-F1 score of 59.16%. Similarly, XLM-R-large continues to display superior performance for sentiment analysis using three classes, achieving a macro F1-score of 72.31% and an accuracy of 75.90%. Dhananjaya et al. (2022) obtained a macro-F1 score of 60.45% for sentiment analysis using four classes, which serve as the baseline model. This indicates that our model outperformed the baseline model slightly. One potential reason for the improved performance of XLM-R-large is the utilization of a larger training dataset, allowing the model to learn from a more diverse set of examples and generalize better.

Our study observed that BERT and DistilBERT achieved competitive macro-F1 scores and accuracy for both sentiment analysis tasks with four and three classes. However, the macro-F1 scores of BERT, DistilBERT, and RoBERTa were relatively lower than XLM-R models. The outcome of these monolingual models achieving lower results than XLM-R models was unexpected. Monolingual models are typically trained specifically for a single language, and they would have a better understanding of linguistic patterns, leading to better performance in sentiment analysis tasks. However, the observed results highlighted that XLM-R models performed better in sentiment analysis for Sinhala despite being pre-trained on a multilingual corpus. The reason for this unexpected outcome is the difference in the pre-training process. BERT, DistilBERT, and RoBERTa models were pre-trained for only one epoch, while XLM-R models were pre-trained for a higher number of epochs. This longer pre-training process allowed XLM-R models to gain a deeper understanding of linguistic patterns and representations, making them more effective in sentiment analysis for Sinhala. However, it is important to note that these monolingual models still demonstrate promising capabilities in capturing sentiment patterns in Sinhala text. The performance of these monolingual models can be further improved by pre-training the models on a larger Sinhala corpus for a higher number of epochs.

Figure 1 displays the row-wise normalized confusion matrix for sentiment analysis conducted using the XLM-R-large model with four classes. Based on the confusion matrix, we can deduce that the XLM-R-large model performs better in predicting the majority classes (Negative, Neutral, and Positive) than the Conflict class. There is a noticeable tendency for the model to misclassify instances labeled as Conflict as Negative at a relatively higher frequency. This misclassification pattern may be influenced by the class imbalance in the dataset, where the Negative class is the majority class with over 10,000 instances. The model might have learned to favor the majority class, leading to more frequent misclassifications for the Conflict class. The class imbalance poses a challenge for the model to accurately distinguish between the classes, particularly affecting its ability to predict the minority class accurately.

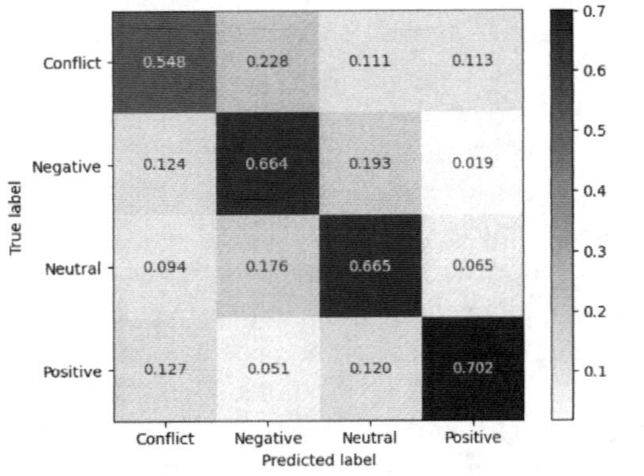

Figure 1: Normalized confusion matrix of XLM-R-large for sentiment analysis with four classes

6 Conclusion

This study evaluates the performance of various transformer models fine-tuned for sentiment analysis in the Sinhala language. This study marks the first experimentation of BERT and DistilBERT for sentiment analysis in Sinhala. The findings demonstrate that transformer models exhibit remarkable performance, even when fine-tuned using a small dataset. This outcome highlights the significant potential of transformer models in addressing challenges for languages with limited available resources. We also showed that the extensive pre-training process of the XLM-R models played a pivotal role in their superior performance compared to other models pre-trained for a single epoch.

In this study, we have made several contributions to the research community. We have made publicly available the pre-trained models of BERT, DistilBERT, and RoBERTa, along with the fine-tuned models of BERT, DistilBERT, RoBERTa, XLM-R-base, and XLM-R-large.

Additionally, three new datasets [4] have been released, which include a sentiment dataset comprising 5,037 news comments annotated with four classes, another dataset with 5,037 news comments annotated for three classes, and a large Sinhala news comments dataset containing 417,332 unannotated comments. These resources aim to foster further advancements and enable researchers to explore sentiment analysis in the Sinhala language more effectively.

These research outcomes contribute valuable insights to the field of sentiment analysis of low-resource languages and provide a foundation for future studies and applications. The utilization of transformer models, especially XLM-R-large, showcased promising results, indicating the potential for further advancements in sentiment analysis tasks for the Sinhala language.

7 Limitations

Despite the efforts to build and fine-tune transformer models for Sinhala sentiment analysis, several limitations remain.

Dataset Limitations: Although we used the OSCAR dataset for pre-training, the dataset size is limited to 2 GB, which may not fully encompass the diversity and complexity of the Sinhala language. This limited corpus may not provide sufficient exposure to a variety of linguistic expressions and dialects in Sinhala, thereby constraining the model's ability to generalize across different text types. Additionally, the fine-tuning dataset, consisting of comments from sources such as Lankadeepa online newspaper and GossipLanka news website, may introduce topic or sentiment biases that are not representative of broader Sinhala language use.

Annotation Limitations: Data annotation for sentiment analysis was conducted by two native Sinhala speakers, achieving an inter-annotator agreement score (Cohen's Kappa) of 0.794. While this indicates a good level of agreement, it also suggests some level of disagreement, which could lead to inconsistencies in sentiment labels and affect model performance. The annotations might contain subjective interpretations, especially in cases where sentiments are not explicit, and this could influence the accuracy and reliability of the final dataset.

Class Imbalance: Both datasets used in this study exhibit significant class imbalances, especially with the "Negative" class being dominant, which may bias the model towards negative predictions and reduce accuracy for underrepresented classes like "Conflict".

Limited Epochs for Pre-training: Given computational constraints, pre-training was limited to one epoch, which may not provide the models with enough iterations to fully capture the language patterns and features of Sinhala. However, the XLM-R model, which was already pre-trained for multiple epochs on a large corpus, produced better results due to its extensive pre-training process.

Limited Fine-Tuning: The models were fine-tuned using default configurations recommended in the original papers, without exploring alternative hyperparameters to identify the best setup. Although adjusting these settings could have enhanced model performance, this approach was not pursued due to limited computational resources.

These limitations indicate potential areas for future work, such as expanding the dataset, increasing annotation consistency, exploring additional model architectures, and conducting further experiments to enhance model generalizability for Sinhala language applications.

References

Julien Abadji, Pedro Ortiz Suarez, Laurent Romary, and Benoît Sagot. 2022. Towards a Cleaner Document-Oriented Multilingual Crawled Corpus.

P. D. T. Chathuranga, S. A. S. Lorensuhewa, and M. A. L. Kalyani. 2019. Sinhala Sentiment Analysis using Corpus based Sentiment Lexicon. In *2019 19th International Conference on Advances in ICT for Emerging Regions (ICTer)*, pages 1–7. IEEE.

Alexis Conneau, Kartikay Khandelwal, Naman Goyal, Vishrav Chaudhary, Guillaume Wenzek, Francisco Guzmán, Edouard Grave, Myle Ott, Luke Zettlemoyer, and Veselin Stoyanov. 2019. Unsupervised Cross-lingual Representation Learning at Scale.

Nisansa de Silva. 2019. Survey on Publicly Available Sinhala Natural Language Processing Tools and Research.

Piyumal Demotte, Lahiru Senevirathne, Binod Karunanayake, Udyogi Munasinghe, and Surangika Ranathunga. 2020. Sentiment Analysis of Sinhala

[4] `https://github.com/bandaranayake/sinhala-sentiment-analysis`

News Comments using Sentence-State LSTM Networks. In *2020 Moratuwa Engineering Research Conference (MERCon)*, pages 283–288. IEEE.

Jacob Devlin, Ming-Wei Chang, Kenton Lee, and Kristina Toutanova. 2018. BERT: Pre-training of Deep Bidirectional Transformers for Language Understanding.

Vinura Dhananjaya, Piyumal Demotte, Surangika Ranathunga, and Sanath Jayasena. 2022. BERTifying Sinhala - A Comprehensive Analysis of Pre-trained Language Models for Sinhala Text Classification. In *Proceedings of the Thirteenth Language Resources and Evaluation Conference*, pages 7377–7385, Marseille, France. European Language Resources Association.

C\'\icero dos Santos and Ma\'\ira Gatti. 2014. Deep Convolutional Neural Networks for Sentiment Analysis of Short Texts. In *Proceedings of COLING 2014, the 25th International Conference on Computational Linguistics: Technical Papers*, pages 69–78, Dublin, Ireland. Dublin City University and Association for Computational Linguistics.

Yoav Goldberg and Omer Levy. 2014. word2vec Explained: deriving Mikolov et al.'s negative-sampling word-embedding method.

Yoon Kim. 2014. Convolutional Neural Networks for Sentence Classification. In *Proceedings of the 2014 Conference on Empirical Methods in Natural Language Processing (EMNLP)*, pages 1746–1751, Stroudsburg, PA, USA. Association for Computational Linguistics.

Wenxiong Liao, Bi Zeng, Xiuwen Yin, and Pengfei Wei. 2021. An improved aspect-category sentiment analysis model for text sentiment analysis based on RoBERTa. *Applied Intelligence*, 51(6):3522–3533.

Weibo Liu, Zidong Wang, Xiaohui Liu, Nianyin Zeng, Yurong Liu, and Fuad E. Alsaadi. 2017. A survey of deep neural network architectures and their applications. *Neurocomputing*, 234:11–26.

Yinhan Liu, Myle Ott, Naman Goyal, Jingfei Du, Mandar Joshi, Danqi Chen, Omer Levy, Mike Lewis, Luke Zettlemoyer, and Veselin Stoyanov. 2019. RoBERTa: A Robustly Optimized BERT Pretraining Approach.

Nishantha Medagoda. 2016. Sentiment Analysis on Morphologically Rich Languages: An Artificial Neural Network (ANN) Approach. In pages 377–393.

Nishantha Priyanka Kumara Medagoda. 2017. *Framework for Sentiment Classification for Morphologically Rich Languages: A Case Study for Sinhala*. Ph.D. thesis, Auckland University of Technology.

Nishantha Medagoda, Subana Shanmuganathan, and Jacqueline Whalley. 2015. Sentiment lexicon construction using SentiWordNet 3.0. In *2015 11th International Conference on Natural Computation (ICNC)*, pages 802–807. IEEE.

Kostadin Mishev, Ana Gjorgjevikj, Irena Vodenska, Lubomir T. Chitkushev, and Dimitar Trajanov. 2020. Evaluation of Sentiment Analysis in Finance: From Lexicons to Transformers. *IEEE Access*, 8:131662–131682.

Jeffrey Pennington, Richard Socher, and Christopher Manning. 2014. Glove: Global Vectors for Word Representation. In *Proceedings of the 2014 Conference on Empirical Methods in Natural Language Processing (EMNLP)*, pages 1532–1543, Stroudsburg, PA, USA. Association for Computational Linguistics.

Surangika Ranathunga and Isuru Udara Liyanage. 2021. Sentiment Analysis of Sinhala News Comments. *ACM Transactions on Asian and Low-Resource Language Information Processing*, 20(4):1–23.

Victor Sanh, Lysandre Debut, Julien Chaumond, and Thomas Wolf. 2019. DistilBERT, a distilled version of BERT: smaller, faster, cheaper and lighter.

Lahiru Senevirathne, Piyumal Demotte, Binod Karunanayake, Udyogi Munasinghe, and Surangika Ranathunga. 2020. Sentiment Analysis for Sinhala Language using Deep Learning Techniques.

Ashish Vaswani, Noam Shazeer, Niki Parmar, Jakob Uszkoreit, Llion Jones, Aidan N. Gomez, Lukasz Kaiser, and Illia Polosukhin. 2017. Attention Is All You Need.

Thomas Wolf, Lysandre Debut, Victor Sanh, Julien Chaumond, Clement Delangue, Anthony Moi, Pierric Cistac, Tim Rault, Rémi Louf, Morgan Funtowicz, Joe Davison, Sam Shleifer, Patrick von Platen, Clara Ma, Yacine Jernite, Julien Plu, Canwen Xu, Teven Le Scao, Sylvain Gugger, et al. 2019. HuggingFace's Transformers: State-of-the-art Natural Language Processing.

Guixian Xu, Yueting Meng, Xiaoyu Qiu, Ziheng Yu, and Xu Wu. 2019a. Sentiment Analysis of Comment Texts Based on BiLSTM. *IEEE Access*, 7:51522–51532.

Hu Xu, Bing Liu, Lei Shu, and Philip Yu. 2019b. BERT Post-Training for Review Reading Comprehension and Aspect-based Sentiment Analysis. In *Proceedings of the 2019 Conference of the North*, pages 2324–2335, Stroudsburg, PA, USA. Association for Computational Linguistics.

Zichao Yang, Diyi Yang, Chris Dyer, Xiaodong He, Alex Smola, and Eduard Hovy. 2016. Hierarchical Attention Networks for Document Classification. In *Proceedings of the 2016 Conference of the North American Chapter of the Association for Computational Linguistics: Human Language Technologies*, pages 1480–1489, Stroudsburg, PA, USA. Association for Computational Linguistics.

ExMute: A Context-Enriched Multimodal Dataset for Hateful Memes

Riddhiman Swanan Debnath[1], Nahian Beente Firuj[1], Abdul Wadud Shakib[1], Sadia Sultana[1], Md Saiful Islam[1, 2]
[1]Computer Science and Engineering, Shahjalal University of Science and Technology, Sylhet, Bangladesh
[2]Computing Science, University of Alberta, Edmonton, Alberta, Canada

Abstract

In this paper, we introduce ExMute, an extended dataset for classifying hateful memes that incorporates critical contextual information, addressing a significant gap in existing resources. Building on a previous dataset of 4,158 memes without contextual annotations, ExMute expands the collection by adding 2,041 new memes and providing comprehensive annotations for all 6,199 memes. Each meme is systematically labeled across six defined contexts—religion, politics, celebrity, male, female, and others—with language markers indicating code-mixing, code-switching, and Bengali captions, enhancing its value for linguistic and cultural research while facilitating a nuanced understanding of meme content and intent. To evaluate ExMute, we apply state-of-the-art textual, visual, and multimodal approaches, leveraging models including BanglaBERT, Visual Geometry Group (VGG), Inception, ResNet, and Vision Transformer (ViT). Our experiments show that our custom LSTM attention-based textual model achieves an accuracy of 0.60, while VGG-based visual models reach up to 0.63. Multimodal models, which combine visual and textual features, consistently achieve accuracy scores of around 0.64, demonstrating the dataset's robustness for advancing multimodal classification tasks. ExMute establishes a valuable benchmark for future NLP research, particularly in low-resource language settings, highlighting the importance of context-aware labeling in improving classification accuracy and reducing bias.

1 Introduction

The exponential growth of social media platforms such as Facebook, TikTok, Reddit, and Instagram has paralleled the expansion of the internet, transforming them into powerful tools for expressing opinions on politics, business, entertainment, and current events (Oldenbourg, 2024). However,

Figure 1: **Category -** Hateful, **Context:** Religion

this increased connectivity has also boosted the spread of offensive content targeting individuals or groups based on race, religion, and sexual orientation. The rise of this toxic content poses significant challenges, particularly in the form of hateful memes—visual and textual media repurposed to convey cultural, social, or political views with a mask of humor (Mukhtar et al., 2024). While memes often serve as light-hearted content, they can also propagate harmful and prejudiced messages, exacerbating issues such as cyberbullying, harassment, and societal discord (Sambasivan et al., 2019; Romim et al., 2021b).

In recent years, the popularity of multimodal memes has surged as an effective means of communication in this era of digital interconnectivity (Abdullakutty and Naseem, 2024). However, identifying and mitigating the spread of such harmful content remains a significant challenge due to the sheer scale of online platforms and the complexity of multimodal content. Significant progress has been achieved in detecting hateful memes in English, with several studies and resources available (Waseem and Hovy, 2016; Davidson et al., 2017). In Bangla, however, existing work focuses primarily on text-based hate speech detection (Al Maruf et al., 2024; Romim et al., 2022; Das et al., 2021; Romim et al., 2021a), leaving hateful meme detection largely unexplored. This gap underscores the

Proceedings of the First Workshop on Natural Language Processing for Indo-Aryan and Dravidian Languages (IndoNLP2025), pages 83–89
January 20, 2025. ©2025 Association for Computational Linguistics

need for comprehensive multimodal approaches in Bangla. In addition, these advancements have yet to be equally replicated in low-resource languages, particularly Bangla, code-switch (Bangla dialects in English script), and code-mix (Bangla and English) languages. This is noteworthy given that Bangla is the fifth most spoken language worldwide, with over 230 million speakers, including approximately 100 million in Bangladesh and 85 million in India. (Karim et al., 2022).

Despite the rising use of memes in Bengali due to the increasing number of social media users in Bangladesh, there has been limited research focused on the identification and contextual analysis of hate speech in this language (Hossain et al., 2022a,b). Furthermore, existing studies often lack detailed categorization based on different contexts or target audiences (Figure 1). We introduce ExMute, an extended dataset for classifying Bangla hateful memes across various social media platforms to address this gap. Our work also includes categorizing the data into six distinct contexts: religion, politics, celebrity, male, female, and others, providing an enriched framework for nuanced hateful meme analysis. The overall contribution of our paper:

- Curated a human-annotated multimodal hateful memes dataset enriched with six contexts: religious, celebrity, political, male, female, and others.
- Annotated 6,199 memes as hateful or non-hateful, with context labels, using a detailed guideline for Bangla, code-mixed, and code-switched captions.
- Established baselines by extensively testing various textual and visual models, including a custom LSTM with attention, Vision Transformer, and Bangla BERT.
- Released code and data publicly to support further research in this area.

2 ExMute: An Extended Dataset

We extended the **Mute** Hossain et al. (2022b) which consisted of 4,158 labeled memes, and added an additional amount of 2,041 memes along with code mix, code switch, and Banglish captions. For data collection, we followed the approaches shown in these two studies Hossain et al. (2022b) and Kiela et al. (2020).

class	train	test	valid	total
hateful	540	684	925	2149
non-hateful	1943	1182	924	4050

Table 1: Number of instances in train, test, and validation sets for each class.

2.1 Data Collection

We collected memes and texts containing common slurs and terms from Facebook, Reddit, and Instagram. We searched for these using keywords like "Bangla Memes," "Bangla Troll Memes," etc., on platforms like Wittigenz and Halal Meme posting. During data collection, we exclude some irrelevant memes by considering the rules stated by Pramanick et al. (2021). The criteria for discarding data are **(i)** memes containing only unimodal data (only text or image) and **(ii)** memes whose textual or visual information is unclear. We collected 2,098 memes, and through this filtering process, 57 memes were removed from newly collected data. Afterward, we manually extracted captions from the memes, as Bengali lacks a standardized OCR system, and provided them to annotators for labeling with corresponding memes.

During data collection, memes were sourced from 15 different contexts, such as racial, misogynist, geopolitical, sports, and so on. Emphasis was placed on the frequency of instances across these contexts, with male, female, political, religious, celebrity, and other categories emerging as the most prominent.

2.2 Dataset Annotation

To establish clear annotation guidelines, we followed the approach of prior studies Kiela et al. (2020), Islam et al. (2022), and Perifanos and Goutsos (2021) and defined hateful and non-hateful in the following ways:

- **Hateful:** Targets an entity based on its gender, race, religion, caste, or organizational status and intends to vilify, denigrate, and mock.
- **Non-hateful:** Expresses positive feelings such as affection, gratitude, support, and motivation, whether openly or implicitly.

We also determined the contexts of the memes, hateful or not, by observing the captions and visual characteristics in the following way:

- **Male**: Clearly indicates a male context.

Name	context-wise	Percentage
Political	149	49.83
Religious	293	32.89
Female	677	61.15
Male	772	36.01
Celebrity	870	40.23
Others	3438	26.53

Table 2: Context-wise distribution of hate-non-hate memes and percentage of hateful memes

Characteristics	Hateful	Non-hateful
#Code-Mix Cap	588	1088
#Code-Switch Cap	58	119
#Bangla Cap	223	396
#Words	29245	50215
#Unique Words	9251	13223
Max Caption length	186	241
Avg #Words/Cap	13.6	12.3

Table 3: Distribution of data across various characteristics related to meme captions. Here, cap represents caption

- **Female**: Clearly indicates a female context.
- **Religious**: Refers to an individual or group based on religious beliefs.
- **Political**: Refers to an individual or group based on political beliefs.
- **Celebrity**: Refers to a celebrity.
- **Others**: Does not fit into any of the above categories.

Initially, we hired undergraduate students from different faculties, aged 24-26, with 50% female, and provided training using sample memes. We use five annotators for each instance, which are annotated independently. The final label was assigned based on consensus, with a linguistic expert verifying the labels. For instances with unresolved disagreements, we sought expert adjudication. Annotators were instructed to follow label definitions and guidelines closely and to document their reasoning for each annotation. This documentation helped the expert make informed decisions in cases of conflict. Compensation for annotators was provided according to the university research ethics board's standard local rate, and they were encouraged to pace their work, taking regular breaks to avoid prolonged sessions and negative mental health impacts of annotators Ybarra et al. (2006), Levin (2017).

3 Dataset Statistics

Our final dataset comprises a total of 6,199 instances. The dataset displays an imbalanced distribution, with the 'Non-Hate' class representing about 65% of the dataset, as shown in Table 1. Additionally, Table 2 provides a breakdown of instances by context. Notably, the "Others" category has a disproportionately high number of instances compared to other contexts, as annotators often placed memes here when they didn't clearly fit any other context.

From Table 2, it is evident that memes targeting females are overrepresented in gender-based contexts. Common Bangla words, such as "আমি, না, আমার, কি," appear frequently across all contexts. Words like "girl" are common in female-targeted memes, while terms like "ramadan" and "নামাজ" are primarily associated with religious memes. Figure 2 and Figure 3 further illustrate caption characteristics. Figure 2 shows the number of captions across different contexts based on caption length, providing insights into how caption length varies contextually. Figure 3 displays the distribution of caption lengths between hate and non-hate categories, highlighting any notable differences in caption length within each category. For training and evaluation, we divided the dataset into three parts: 80% for training, 10% for testing, and 10% for validation. The class distribution across these subsets is presented in Table 1.

4 Methodology

In this section, we outline the methods used to develop benchmark models for detecting hateful memes through unimodal and multimodal approaches, utilizing both visual and textual features.

4.1 Data Cleaning and Preprocessing

Initially, HTML tags and URLs were removed from the text captions, followed by the elimination of newline characters to normalize the text layout into a cohesive string. Punctuation marks and special characters were subsequently filtered out to simplify the textual data further.

For compatibility with deep learning architectures, particularly DNN and transformer-based models, the cleaned text was tokenized at the word level using the Keras tokenizer. This step involved

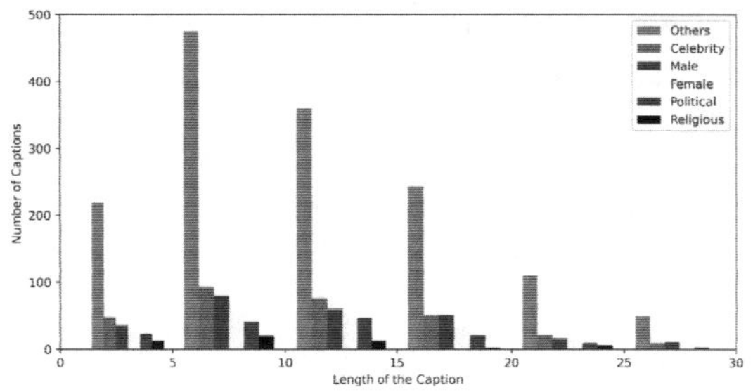

Figure 2: Number of captions according to the length of the captions in different contexts

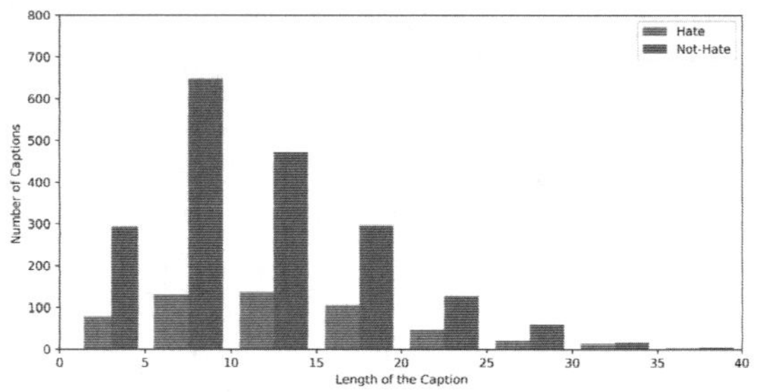

Figure 3: Number of captions according to the length of the captions of hate-nonhate

mapping each unique word to a corresponding integer index, effectively converting the text into a numerical vector representation. To ensure consistent input dimensions across samples, sequences were padded to a maximum length of 50, a necessary step for deep learning models requiring fixed-length input.

For the visual modality, the images were resized to a uniform dimension of 150×150×3, preserving their three-channel (RGB) format. Keras image preprocessing functions were employed to standardize the image data and enhance its compatibility with convolutional neural networks (CNNs). This resizing and adjustment ensured uniformity in input data and facilitated effective model training.

4.2 Textual Model

For text-based hateful memes analysis, various deep learning models are employed, including BiLSTM + CNN (Sharif et al., 2020), BiLSTM + Attention (Zhang et al., 2018), and Transformers (Vaswani, 2017). Additionally, we developed a custom LSTM model with an attention mechanism to enhance performance.

Initially, the word embedding vectors (Mikolov, 2013) are fed into a BiLSTM layer of 64 hidden units. Then a convolution layer with 32 filters with a kernel size of two is added, followed by a max-pooling layer to extract the significant contextual features. Then, a sigmoid layer is used for classification. Finally, the output of the BiLSTM network provides contextual information for the overall text.

Also, we used the additive attention mechanism introduced by Bahdanau (2014) to analyze the representations of individual words in the BiLSTM cell. The CNN is replaced with an attention layer. The attention layer prioritizes significant words to infer a specific class.

Our custom LSTM model integrates an attention mechanism to enhance performance and interpretability. The attention layer computes scores by combining features and hidden states, normalizing them using softmax. A context vector is then derived as a weighted sum of the features. The input sequence is embedded and processed through a bidirectional LSTM, capturing both forward and backward contextual information by concatenating hidden and cell states. The attention layer applies to the LSTM output, producing context vectors and attention weights. The final output layer uses a sigmoid activation function, suitable for binary classification tasks.

4.3 Visual Model

For the visual models, we used advanced architectures, including VGG19, VGG16,(Simonyan and Zisserman, 2014), ResNet50(He et al., 2016), and Vision Transformer(ViT).(Dosovitskiy, 2020). Specifically, VGG19, VGG16, and ResNet50 were fine-tuned on the MUTE dataset through transfer learning. For hate-non-hate classification, the upper layers of these models were frozen, utilizing weights pre-trained on ImageNet (Deng et al., 2009) for 1000 classes, and the top layers were replaced with a sigmoid layer to enable binary classification.

4.4 Multimodal Model

Recent studies, including Hori et al. (2017), Yang et al. (2019), and Alam et al. (2021), indicate that combining visual and textual data improves performance in complex NLP tasks. For multimodal feature representation, we applied a feature fusion approach Nojavanasghari et al. (2016), integrating both visual and textual models such as Bangla-BERT(Sarker, 2020; Bhattacharjee et al., 2022). We added a dense layer with 100 neurons to each modality, then concatenated their outputs to create a unified feature representation, followed by a dense layer with 32 neurons and a sigmoid layer for classification. We used Bangla-BERT (Sarker, 2020) for text encoding, generating input IDs and attention masks for captions with a maximum sequence length of 50. For the Vision Transformer, we employed ViT_b16 (Ghiasi et al., 2022) with pre-trained weights and resized images to 224 × 224 pixels. The ViT model processes images, and Bangla-BERT processes text, with their outputs fused into a joint feature space. A sigmoid activation at the final output provides binary classification.

5 Benchmark Evaluation and Discussion

Table 4 summarizes the performance of textual, visual, and multimodal models in terms of accuracy, precision, and F1 score. For textual models, BiLSTM + Attention performs poorly (F1 = 0.19), while LSTM + Attention achieves the best results (F1 = 0.60). BiLSTM + CNN (F1 = 0.58) improves performance by leveraging convolutional layers, and BanglaBERT performs similarly (F1 = 0.56), benefiting from pre-trained embeddings.

For the visual-only models, InceptionResNetV2, ResNet-50, and NASNet achieve moderate performance (F1 ranges from 0.34 to 0.50), suggesting room for improvement in extracting meaningful visual features. InceptionV3 and VGG16 both perform slightly better, with VGG16 showing more consistency across metrics. Similarly, among the models with PA (Positional Attention), ResNet-50 achieves slightly higher and more consistent performance compared to VGG16. ViT and InceptionResNetV2 + PA both achieve the highest accuracy of 0.63.

Interestingly, combining modalities did not improve results significantly; most multimodal models achieve similar F1 scores, showing limited gain from integrating visual and textual features. VGG19 + SBB shows the best balance across metrics, with an accuracy of 0.64 and an F1-Score of 0.49, highlighting its potential for multimodal tasks. VGG16 (Att) + SBB achieves comparable performance to other multimodal configurations (F1 = 0.49), though attention did not significantly improve results. These findings suggest that further refinement in model architecture or additional data may be necessary to leverage multimodal features effectively for hate detection in Bangla memes.

App.	Model	A	P	F1
Tex.	Bi-LSTM + Attention	0.36	0.13	0.19
	Bi-LSTM + CNN	0.57	0.59	0.58
	Bangla BERT	0.58	0.56	0.56
	LSTM + Attention	0.60	0.59	0.60
Vis.	InceptionResNetV2	0.41	0.57	0.34
	ResNet-50	0.49	0.56	0.49
	NASNet	0.49	0.56	0.50
	InceptionV3 + PA	0.49	0.54	0.49
	VGG16	0.52	0.54	0.53
	InceptionV3	0.54	0.53	0.54
	ResNet-50 + PA	0.59	0.57	0.58
	VGG16 + PA	0.59	0.55	0.55
	NASNet + PA	0.63	0.40	0.49
	InceptionResnet50V2 + PA	0.63	0.40	0.49
	VIT	0.63	0.40	0.49
MultiM.	VIT + SBB	0.63	0.40	0.49
	VGG19 + SBB	0.64	0.49	0.49
	VGG16 + SBB	0.63	0.40	0.49
	VGG16 + BBB	0.63	0.40	0.49
	VGG19 + BBB	0.63	0.40	0.49
	VGG16(Att) + SBB	0.64	0.40	0.49

Table 4: Performance of the models on the Ex-Mute dataset. Here, A, P, and F1 represent accuracy, precision, and weighted F1 scores. SBB: SagorSarker Bangla BERT, BBB: BUET Bangla BERT, Tex: Textual, Vis: Visual, MultiM: MultiModal

6 Conclusion

In this paper, we introduced ExMute, a multimodal dataset enriched with contextual information to support the detection of hateful memes in Bangla, code-switched, and code-mixed captions. Our findings indicate that textual models outperform visual-only models; however, combining visual and textual features yields the most accurate results, demonstrating the strength of multimodal analysis for identifying hateful content. We observed that model performance can be affected by class imbalance, leading to a bias toward certain classes. To address this, future work will focus on expanding the dataset and exploring advanced computational methods to reduce bias. Additionally, we plan to improve accuracy and incorporate context prediction through Generative AI, CLIP architecture, and comprehensive ablation studies, enhancing the model's interpretability and effectiveness in real-world applications.

References

Faseela Abdullakutty and Usman Naseem. 2024. Decoding memes: A comprehensive analysis of late and early fusion models for explainable meme analysis. In *Companion Proceedings of the ACM Web Conference 2024*, WWW '24, page 1681–1689, New York, NY, USA. Association for Computing Machinery.

Abdullah Al Maruf, Ahmad Jainul Abidin, Md Mahmudul Haque, Zakaria Masud Jiyad, Aditi Golder, Raaid Alubady, and Zeyar Aung. 2024. Hate speech detection in the bengali language: a comprehensive survey. *Journal of Big Data*, 11(1):97.

Firoj Alam, Stefano Cresci, Tanmoy Chakraborty, Fabrizio Silvestri, Dimiter Dimitrov, Giovanni Da San Martino, Shaden Shaar, Hamed Firooz, and Preslav Nakov. 2021. A survey on multimodal disinformation detection. *arXiv preprint arXiv:2103.12541*.

Dzmitry Bahdanau. 2014. Neural machine translation by jointly learning to align and translate. *arXiv preprint arXiv:1409.0473*.

Abhik Bhattacharjee, Tahmid Hasan, Wasi Ahmad, Kazi Samin Mubasshir, Md Saiful Islam, Anindya Iqbal, M. Sohel Rahman, and Rifat Shahriyar. 2022. BanglaBERT: Language model pretraining and benchmarks for low-resource language understanding evaluation in Bangla. In *Findings of the Association for Computational Linguistics: NAACL 2022*, pages 1318–1327, Seattle, United States. Association for Computational Linguistics.

Amit Kumar Das, Abdullah Al Asif, Anik Paul, and Md Nur Hossain. 2021. Bangla hate speech detection on social media using attention-based recurrent neural network. *Journal of Intelligent Systems*, 30(1):578–591.

Thomas Davidson, Dana Warmsley, Michael Macy, and Ingmar Weber. 2017. Automated hate speech detection and the problem of offensive language. In *Proceedings of the international AAAI conference on web and social media*, volume 11, pages 512–515.

Jia Deng, Wei Dong, Richard Socher, Li-Jia Li, Kai Li, and Li Fei-Fei. 2009. Imagenet: A large-scale hierarchical image database. In *2009 IEEE conference on computer vision and pattern recognition*, pages 248–255. Ieee.

Alexey Dosovitskiy. 2020. An image is worth 16x16 words: Transformers for image recognition at scale. *arXiv preprint arXiv:2010.11929*.

Amin Ghiasi, Hamid Kazemi, Eitan Borgnia, Steven Reich, Manli Shu, Micah Goldblum, Andrew Gordon Wilson, and Tom Goldstein. 2022. What do vision transformers learn? a visual exploration. *Preprint*, arXiv:2212.06727.

Kaiming He, Xiangyu Zhang, Shaoqing Ren, and Jian Sun. 2016. Deep residual learning for image recognition. In *Proceedings of the IEEE conference on computer vision and pattern recognition*, pages 770–778.

Chiori Hori, Takaaki Hori, Teng-Yok Lee, Ziming Zhang, Bret Harsham, John R Hershey, Tim K Marks, and Kazuhiko Sumi. 2017. Attention-based multimodal fusion for video description. In *Proceedings of the IEEE international conference on computer vision*, pages 4193–4202.

Eftekhar Hossain, Omar Sharif, and Mohammed Moshiul Hoque. 2022a. MemoSen: A multimodal dataset for sentiment analysis of memes. In *Proceedings of the Thirteenth Language Resources and Evaluation Conference*, pages 1542–1554, Marseille, France. European Language Resources Association.

Eftekhar Hossain, Omar Sharif, and Mohammed Moshiul Hoque. 2022b. MUTE: A multimodal dataset for detecting hateful memes. In *Proceedings of the 2nd Conference of the Asia-Pacific Chapter of the Association for Computational Linguistics and the 12th International Joint Conference on Natural Language Processing: Student Research Workshop*, pages 32–39, Online. Association for Computational Linguistics.

Khondoker Ittehadul Islam, Tanvir Yuvraz, Md Saiful Islam, and Enamul Hassan. 2022. EmoNoBa: A dataset for analyzing fine-grained emotions on noisy Bangla texts. In *Proceedings of the 2nd Conference of the Asia-Pacific Chapter of the Association for Computational Linguistics and the 12th International Joint Conference on Natural Language Processing (Volume 2: Short Papers)*, pages 128–134, Online only. Association for Computational Linguistics.

Md. Rezaul Karim, Sumon Kanti Dey, Tanhim Islam, Md. Shajalal, and Bharathi Raja Chakravarthi. 2022. Multimodal hate speech detection from bengali memes and texts. *Preprint*, arXiv:2204.10196.

Douwe Kiela, Hamed Firooz, Aravind Mohan, Vedanuj Goswami, Amanpreet Singh, Pratik Ringshia, and Davide Testuggine. 2020. The hateful memes challenge: Detecting hate speech in multimodal memes. *Advances in neural information processing systems*, 33:2611–2624.

Sam Levin. 2017. Moderators who had to view child abuse content sue microsoft, claiming ptsd. *The Guardian*, 12.

Tomas Mikolov. 2013. Efficient estimation of word representations in vector space. *arXiv preprint arXiv:1301.3781*.

Shahira Mukhtar, Qurat Ul Ain Ayyaz, Sadaf Khan, Atiya Muhammad Nawaz Bhopali, Muhammad Khalid Mehmood Sajid, Allah Wasaya Babbar, et al. 2024. Memes in the digital age: A sociolinguistic examination of cultural expressions and communicative practices across border. *Educational Administration: Theory and Practice*, 30(6):1443–1455.

Behnaz Nojavanasghari, Deepak Gopinath, Jayanth Koushik, Tadas Baltrušaitis, and Louis-Philippe Morency. 2016. Deep multimodal fusion for persuasiveness prediction. In *Proceedings of the 18th ACM international conference on multimodal interaction*, pages 284–288.

Andreas Oldenbourg. 2024. Digital freedom and corporate power in social media. *Critical Review of International Social and Political Philosophy*, 27(3):383–404.

Konstantinos Perifanos and Dionysis Goutsos. 2021. Multimodal hate speech detection in greek social media. *Multimodal Technologies and Interaction*, 5(7):34.

Shraman Pramanick, Dimitar Dimitrov, Rituparna Mukherjee, Shivam Sharma, Md Shad Akhtar, Preslav Nakov, and Tanmoy Chakraborty. 2021. Detecting harmful memes and their targets. *arXiv preprint arXiv:2110.00413*.

Nauros Romim, Mosahed Ahmed, Md Saiful Islam, Arnab Sen Sharma, Hriteshwar Talukder, and Mohammad Ruhul Amin. 2021a. Hs-ban: A benchmark dataset of social media comments for hate speech detection in bangla. *arXiv preprint arXiv:2112.01902*.

Nauros Romim, Mosahed Ahmed, Md Saiful Islam, Arnab Sen Sharma, Hriteshwar Talukder, and Mohammad Ruhul Amin. 2022. Bd-shs: A benchmark dataset for learning to detect online bangla hate speech in different social contexts. In *Proceedings of the Thirteenth Language Resources and Evaluation Conference*, pages 5153–5162.

Nauros Romim, Mosahed Ahmed, Hriteshwar Talukder, and Md Saiful Islam. 2021b. Hate speech detection in the bengali language: A dataset and its baseline evaluation. In *Proceedings of International Joint Conference on Advances in Computational Intelligence: IJCACI 2020*, pages 457–468. Springer.

Nithya Sambasivan, Amna Batool, Nova Ahmed, Tara Matthews, Kurt Thomas, Laura Sanely Gaytán-Lugo, David Nemer, Elie Bursztein, Elizabeth Churchill, and Sunny Consolvo. 2019. " they don't leave us alone anywhere we go" gender and digital abuse in south asia. In *proceedings of the 2019 CHI Conference on Human Factors in Computing Systems*, pages 1–14.

Sagor Sarker. 2020. Banglabert: Bengali mask language model for bengali language understanding.

Omar Sharif, Eftekhar Hossain, and Mohammed Moshiul Hoque. 2020. Techtexc: Classification of technical texts using convolution and bidirectional long short term memory network. *arXiv preprint arXiv:2012.11420*.

Karen Simonyan and Andrew Zisserman. 2014. Very deep convolutional networks for large-scale image recognition. *arXiv preprint arXiv:1409.1556*.

A Vaswani. 2017. Attention is all you need. *Advances in Neural Information Processing Systems*.

Zeerak Waseem and Dirk Hovy. 2016. Hateful symbols or hateful people? predictive features for hate speech detection on twitter. In *Proceedings of the NAACL student research workshop*, pages 88–93.

Fan Yang, Xiaochang Peng, Gargi Ghosh, Reshef Shilon, Hao Ma, Eider Moore, and Goran Predovic. 2019. Exploring deep multimodal fusion of text and photo for hate speech classification. In *Proceedings of the third workshop on abusive language online*, pages 11–18.

Michele L Ybarra, Kimberly J Mitchell, Janis Wolak, and David Finkelhor. 2006. Examining characteristics and associated distress related to internet harassment: findings from the second youth internet safety survey. *Pediatrics*, 118(4):e1169–e1177.

Ziqi Zhang, David Robinson, and Jonathan Tepper. 2018. Detecting hate speech on twitter using a convolution-gru based deep neural network. In *The Semantic Web: 15th International Conference, ESWC 2018, Heraklion, Crete, Greece, June 3–7, 2018, Proceedings 15*, pages 745–760. Springer.

Studying the capabilities of Large Language Models in solving Combinatorics Problems posed in Hindi

Yash Kumar and Subhajit Roy

Indian Institute of Technology Kanpur, India
{yashk, subhajit}@iitk.ac.in

Abstract

There are serious attempts at improving the mathematical acumen of LLMs in questions posed in English. In India, where a large fraction of students study in regional languages, there is a need to assess and improve these state-of-the-art LLMs in their reasoning abilities in regional languages as well. As Hindi is a language predominantly used in India, this study proposes a new dataset on mathematical combinatorics problems consisting of a parallel corpus of problems in English and Hindi collected from NCERT textbooks. We evaluate the "raw" single-shot capabilities of these LLMs in solving problems posed in Hindi. Then we apply a chain-of-thought approach to evaluate the improvement in the abilities of the LLMs at solving combinatorics problems posed in Hindi. Our study reveals that while smaller LLMs like LLaMA3-8B shows a significant drop in performance when questions are posed in Hindi, versus questions posed in English, larger LLMs like GPT4-turbo shows excellent capabilities at solving problems posed in Hindi, almost at par its abilities in English. We make two primary inferences from our study: (1) large models like GPT4 can be readily deployed in schools where Hindi is the primary language of study, especially in rural India; (2) there is a need to improve the multilingual capabilities of smaller models. As these smaller open-source models can be deployed on not so expensive GPUs, it is easier for schools to provide these models to the students, and hence, the latter is an important direction for future research.

1 Introduction

Large Language Models (LLMs) have revolutionized the technological landscape, with newer applications emerging each day. One of the prime benefactors of this revolution has been the education sector. While initially these models were used as a large knowledge base for facts, the recent models also excel at reasoning tasks like programming and mathematics. This has benefited a large class of students who are using these models as a "personalized tutor" to understand their course material.

These language models are essentially trained over a large corpus of text across the breadth of the internet—online books, wiki articles, blogs, code repositories—to capture the essence of human knowledge. However, most of the text available on the internet is in English. In a country like India, 68.83%(cen) of the population is rural, who predominantly communicate in Hindi and other regional languages. In fact, more than 58%(nue) of the population undergo their school education in the regional languages. Even prestigious exams like IIT-JEE is conducted in thirteen languages, namely English, Assamese, Bengali, Gujarati, Hindi, Kannada, Malayalam, Marathi, Odia, Punjabi, Tamil, Telugu, and Urdu. Hence, it raises an important question the regional language speaking population of the country is equally benefited by the LLMs as the urban, English-speaking population. Or, is the emergence of LLMs increasing the chasm between the Indian population that is being educated in English and other regional languages.

In this work, we investigate the effectiveness of large language models at solving questions presented to them in Hindi, and compare its effectiveness at handling the same problems in English. We use the NCERT textbooks (nce) for the English and Hindi to collect Mathematics questions in the area of Combinatorics. We use multiple strategies and prompting techniques to study the gap in the capabilities of the LLMs at solving mathematical problems posed in these two languages. We conduct this study on three popular models: GPT–3.5 (Radford, 2018), GPT–4(Achiam et al., 2023) and LLaMA3-8B(lla). The reason for selecting these models were that the chat interface of GPT–3.5 is now available freely, making it the most accessible

Proceedings of the First Workshop on Natural Language Processing for Indo-Aryan and Dravidian Languages (IndoNLP2025), pages 90–99
January 20, 2025. ©2025 Association for Computational Linguistics

model for students. GPT–4 is a superior model, but is available against a small monthly fees, and so, is reasonably accessible to students. LLaMA3-8B is a small "open" model that can be run on not-very-expensive GPUs; hence, we believe that soon, schools may decide to host such models within their premises for their students.

We made the following inferences from our study:

- There is a decline in the accuracy of LLMs when it comes to solving problems in Hindi versus English.
- Using different prompting strategies we showed the difference in the performance of the LLMs. "Manual Subcategory" performs better as compared to the other two strategies by upto 14 percent in overall study of Cobinatorics.
- LLaMA3 and GPT-3.5 outperformed themselves when Chain-of-thought prompt strategy is used as compared to the One-shot by a margin of 5 percent for collectively for both the languages.
- LLaMA3-8B and GPT-3.5 showed a significant increase in performance when prompted with an Chain-of-thought in subcategorical analysis by that LLM.
- The above prompt strategy outperformed the other two strategies in 3-4 subcategory cases by a factor of 0.5 to 5 for both the languages.
- GPT-4, being the latest and largest model among others in our studied, outperformed both other models.

This work makes the following contributions:

- We formulate a study to understand the gap in the mathematical abilities of popular open-source models;
- We create a dataset of parallel set of questions in English and Hindi;
- We attempt multiple prompting techniques, single-shot and chain-of-thought prompts and study the improvement in inference accuracy.
- We draw relevant inferences from our study.

In the future, we intend to broaden the scope of this study to more languages, more models and more prompting strategies.

2 Overview

In this work, we attempt to study the following research questions:

- Does posing questions in Hindi as effective as posing the same question in English with single-shot prompts?
- Can inference accuracy be improved with chain-of-thought prompting where the LLM infers the problem subcategory before solving a problem?

To conduct our analysis, we create our own dataset sourcing problems in the area of *Combinatorics* from higher secondary mathematics NCERT textbook (nce) in Hindi and English languages. The dataset contains total of 100 problems in English sourced from English version of the NCERT book and their corresponding parallel counterparts in Hindi sourced from Hindi version of the NCERT book. These problems can be categorised into five subcategories: *Fundamental principle of Counting*, *Permutation with restrictions*, *Permutation without restrictions*, *Combination with restrictions*, and *Combination without restrictions*. The distribution of problems in these subcategories are shown in Table 1.

Table 1: Number of samples in each subcategory

Sub-Category of the Problem	Number of Samples
Fundamental principle of Counting	16
Permutation with restrictions	31
Permutation without restrictions	11
Combinations with restrictions	31
Combinations without restrictions	10

Figure 1 shows an instance from our dataset, consisting of the English and Hindi versions of the problem, its subcategory being "Fundamental principle of counting" and the solution to the problem as "8".

We conducted experiments on three well known large language models: LLaMA3-8B, GPT-3.5 Turbo-175B and GPT-4 Turbo. We used the API calls for the inference of LLaMA3, and chat version of GPT-3.5 Turbo and GPT-4 Turbo for our experimentation . We conduct all experiments on NVIDIA RTX A4000 GPUs. As the responses of the LLMs are sampled from a distribution, we execute each prompt thrice: if any of the answers is

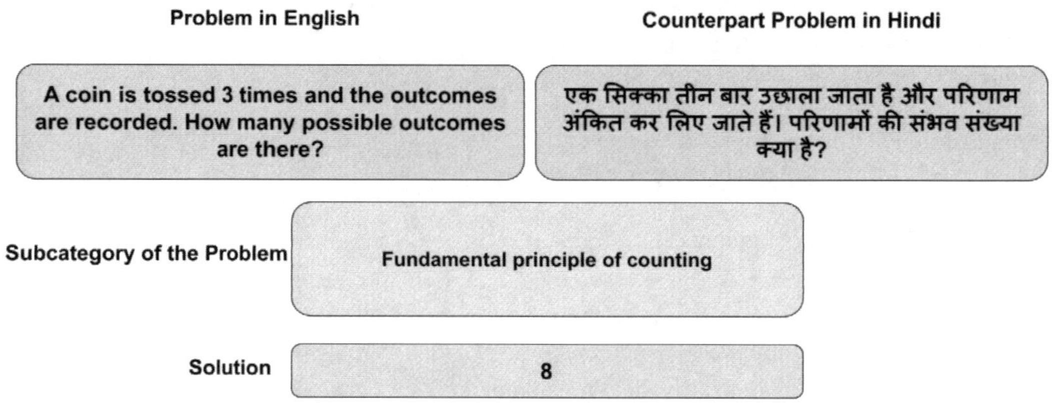

Figure 1: Sample problem from our dataset

correct, we mark the problem as solved successfully.

We prompt the LLMs via two prompting strategies: (1) a plain one-shot prompt, requesting the LLM to solve the problem, and (2) a chain-of-thought prompt that asks the LLM to infer the subcategory, and then asks it solve the problem given the subcategory. We discuss this in the subsequent section.

3 One-shot Prompting

In this set of experiments, we prompted the large language models to solve the provided problem. The prompt instructions remain the same for English and Hindi, and only the problem statement is provided in the chosen language. We show an example of the prompts used in Figure 4.

Figure 2 (without the hashed bars) shows the performance of the LLM models for English versus Hindi. There indeed seems to be a chasm between the performance of English versus Hindi, especially for the smaller LLaMA3-8B model. All the LLMs show a decline in accuracy when prompted for Hindi problems as compared to the English problems. The overall difference between the accuracy of English and Hindi problems ranges from 8 percent to 14 percent across all LLMs. The smallest variation in the accuracies if for the case of GPT-4 and highest variation is observed in GPT-3.5.

4 Chain-of-thought Prompting

In this strategy, we apply the following steps:

- We prompted the LLMs to identify the category of the problem out of the given 5 subcategories;
- We prompt the LLM, requesting it to solve the problem *while providing the subcategory.*

A sample prompt given to the LLMs in this stage is given in Figure 1.

4.1 Overall performance

The hashed stacked bars in Figure 2 shows the increase in the accuracy of inference for this prompting strategy versus the single-shot prompting (discussed in Section 3). This prompting strategy does improve the solving capabilities of the LLMs, especially for the smaller LLaMA3-8B model. The overall accuracy increase we found was in the range of 1 percent and 5 percent across all LLMs. LLaMA3-8B shows the highest jump in the accuracy: 5 percent for English problems and 3 percent for Hindi problems using the Chain-of-thought prompt. Another high variation in accuracy can be seen in GPT-3.5 case for Hindi problems where we got an increase of 4 percent.

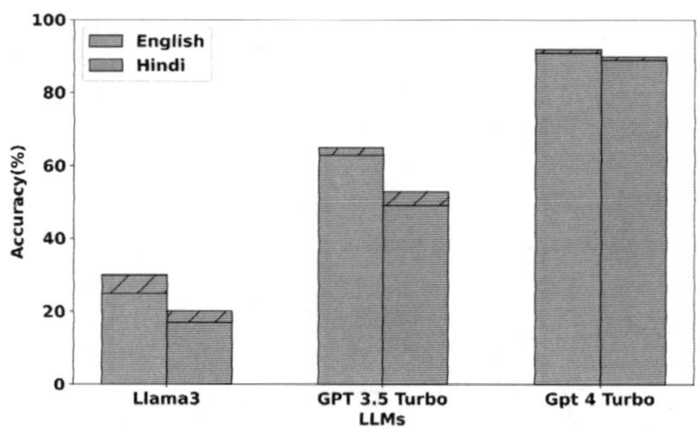

Figure 2: Comparison of One Shot and Chain-of-thought prompt strategies applied on English and Hindi problems

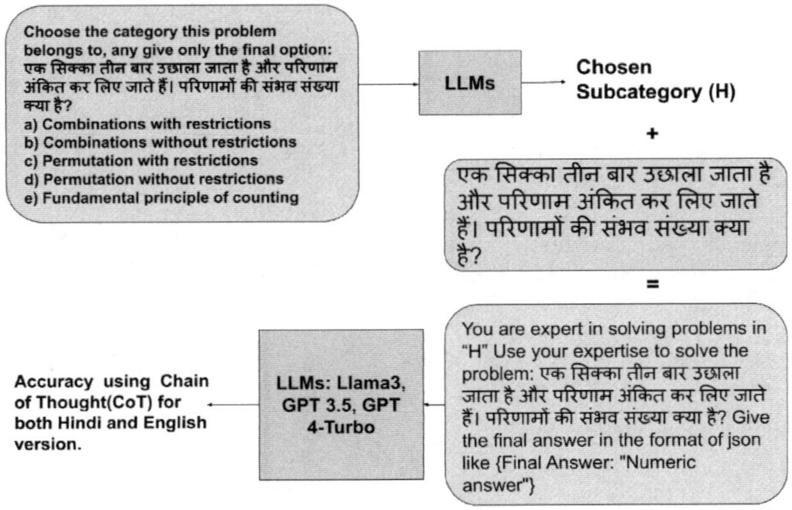

Figure 3: Inference using the Chosen Subcategory by LLM

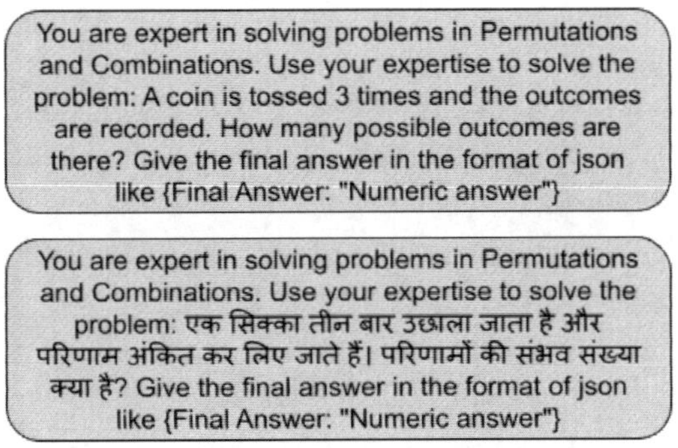

Figure 4: Prompt used in One Shot Prompt

Then, in the second stage, the LLMs were prompted to choose the subcategory that the problem belonged to given in Figure 3. Here also, we had total 100 prompts for each language. Only one trial was run acrosss all LLMs. After the successful completion of this setting we obtained the Chosen Subcategories: **E** for English version and **H** for Hindi version of the problem. We used only the this H for the overall analysis and accurately chosen subcategories for subcategorical analysis below further in our pipeline. Lastly, we experimented with the actual subcategories-Manual Subcategory. The prompts which we designed here were again used in the inference of all the three LLMs for three trails each. The bar plots mentioned in Section 4.2, show an increase in performance for 3-4 categories when using Chain-of-thought prompting strategy and Manual Subcategory also shows an increase in accuracy as compared to the One-Shot prompt strategy. The subcategorical analysis is discussed in detail in Section 4.2.

4.2 Detailed analysis by subcategories

Table 2 shows the accuracy of LLMs in choosing or assigning the correct subcategory out of the 5 choices given to them. Here, as expected GPT-4 performs better as compared to GPT-3.5 and LLaMA3 in classifying the given problem, be it in Hindi or English, with its associated subcategory. In most of the subcategories, we observed GPT-4 Turbo performing well in assigning the subcategories with an exception in Fundamental principle of Counting category in English problems and Combination without restriction in Hindi problems. LLaMA3 performed lowest among all the three LLMs in this task with an exception in case of Fundamental principle of Counting subcategory where it outperformed both GPT-versions.

Now, we discuss about the LLMs performance in each subcategory across English and Hindi problems using three prompting strategies: "One-shot", "Chain-of-thought" and "Manual Subcategory". Please refer to Table 4 for finding the full name of subcategory mentioned in the bar plots. From Figure 7, we can infer that the cases where we used Chain-of-thought prompt strategy, the performance increases by a factor starting from 0.42 to as high as 4.92 times when compared with One-

Table 2: LLMs' Accuracy for choosing Question's Sub-Category

Sub-Category	LLMs	Question in English	Question in Hindi
Fundamental principle of Counting	LLaMA3	81.25	81.25
	GPT-3.5	12.5	31.25
	GPT-4	18.75	43.75
Permutation with restrictions	LLaMA3	22.58	0
	GPT-3.5	61.29	9.27
	GPT-4	87.09	80.64
Permutation without restrictions	LLaMA3	18.18	0
	GPT-3.5	18.18	0
	GPT-4	45.45	54.54
Combination with restrictions	LLaMA3	3	6.45
	GPT-3.5	61.29	19.25
	GPT-4	83.87	74.19
Combination without restrictions	LLaMA3	10	0
	GPT-3.5	20	30
	GPT-4	20	20

shot prompt strategy when both language cases are taken collectively. There are exception cases of $\mathbf{2}$ subcategories in English version where the performance is almost the same as observed in the One-shot prompt strategy. For Hindi case, LLaMA3 couldn't solve any sample for Subcat 4 and Subcat 5. Also, in 3-4 subcategories in both the languages, we see an increase in the performance of Chain-of-thought prompt strategy when we compare with the subcategory prompt strategy by a factor of $\mathbf{1.2}$ to $\mathbf{3.2}$ times. It is worth mentioning the results we observed when using subcategory prompt strategy, where we got an increase in performance from One-shot prompt strategy by a factor of $\mathbf{1.42}$ to $\mathbf{4}$ times. There are cases where it showed similar performance as that of One-shot prompt strategy and an exception of 1 category with low performance than One-shot.

Similarly, from Figure 8, in English language we see an increase in performance while using Chain-of-thought prompt strategy over the other two strategies in 4 subcategories. For Hindi case, we see either similar or more performance in 3 subcategories for Chain-of-thought prompt strategy. The performance increase that we observed ranged from $\mathbf{1.11}$ to $\mathbf{2}$ times for English case and $\mathbf{1.06}$ to $\mathbf{2}$ times for Hindi case. If we compare the cases where we used subcategories for prompting, we got a performance increase of $\mathbf{1.14}$ to $\mathbf{1.25}$ times for English case and $\mathbf{1.33}$ to $\mathbf{1.73}$ times for Hindi problems. If we look at Figure 9, we observed almost similar performance in all three strategies. There was an exception of Subcat 1, 2 and 3 where Chain-of-thought outperformed the One-shot prompt in both the languages. The subcategory prompt strategy was also similar to the other two. Given the fact that GPT-4 is the latest and largest model in our study, the result obtained is expected.

Table 3: Accuracy of LLMs in identiying the Subcategories

Model	English	Hindi
LLaMA3	24	15
GPT-3.5	46	17
GPT-4	63	63

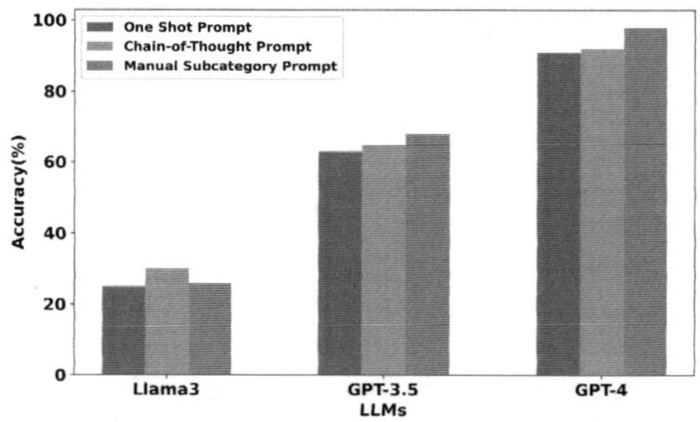

Figure 5: Results using different prompt strategies on English problems

5 Error Analysis

The performance of this scheme depends on the following factors:

Table 4: Name of abbreviations used in bar plots

Sub-Category	Name of the abbreviated Subcategory
Subcat 1	Fundamental principle of Counting
Subcat 2	Permutation with restrictions
Subcat 3	Permutation without restrictions
Subcat 4	Combinations with restrictions
Subcat 5	Combinations without restrictions

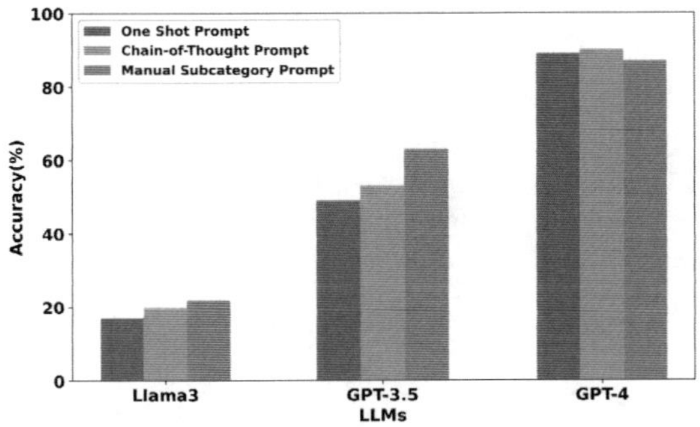

Figure 6: Results using different prompt strategies on Hindi problems

1. The *understanding of Hindi* language by the Large Language Models, i.e. how well LLaMA, GPT-3.5 and GPT-4 understand Hindi? (Task 1)

2. The accuracy of the classification into subcategories, i.e. does the LLM classify the problems into the right subcategories? (Task 2)

3. The accuracy of problem solving *once the subcategory is provided.* (Task 3)

For task 1, we utilized Hindi comprehension problems derived from NCERT textbooks (nce) to evaluate the performance of large language models (LLMs). Specifically, we curated a dataset comprising ten passages in Hindi, each accompanied by five corresponding questions. These passages and questions were directly provided as prompts to the LLMs to assess their accuracy on this task. Our results indicate that LLaMA3-8B achieved an accuracy of 50%, whereas GPT-3.5 and GPT-4 Turbo both attained 76% accuracy. These findings highlight the superior proficiency of GPT-3.5 and GPT-4 Turbo in understanding Hindi compared to the smaller LLaMA3 model. This also concludes the similar trends observed in task involving combinatorics problems framed in Hindi, further corroborating the relative strengths of GPT-based models in processing the Hindi language.

Table 3 studies the accuracy for the subcategory classification task 2. As can be seen, the accuracy of identifying the problem type is low. However, the language models are more accurate in choosing the subcategory of the problem given in English compared to the same problem in Hindi which we can conclude from the results obtained from task 1.

To further understand the impact of this on Combinatorics problems, we ran another set of experiments in task 3 where we manually provided these subcategories within the prompt. The first two bars in the plots 5 and 6 show the solving accuracy corresponding to one-shot and chain-of-thought prompting (for English and Hindi, respectively). The third bar shows the accuracy of the end-to-end pipeline for solving the mathematical problems if the subcategory is provided (*manually*) within the prompt; we refer to this as "Manual Subcategory". We highlight the inference of the performance of language models on problems posed in English with chain-of-thought prompts and manual subcategory prompts from the second and third bar of the plot 5 after the results obtained in task 2.

Interestingly, LLaMA3-8B provides a curious case: though its subcategory inference accuracy is low, the inference accuracy of the end-to-end pipeline increases with chain-of-thought prompting. Still more strangely, its accuracy drops if we manually provide the right categories for English problems. We are still trying to understand this counter-intuitive behavior from LLaMA3-8B.

6 Related Work

In this section, we will discuss about any recent works related to our LLMs solving mathematical problems in English. To the best of our knowledge, there is currently a lack of research on improving the mathematical capabilities of LLMs in regional languages.

Attempts have been made to improve the math-

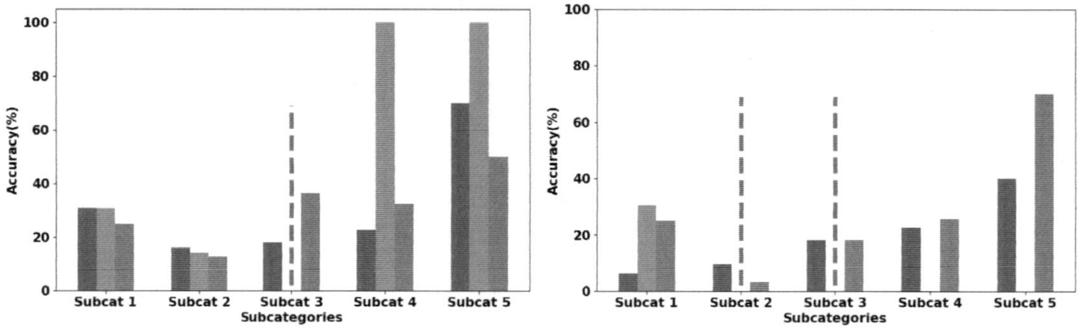

(a) (b)

Figure 7: (a) LLaMA3-8B performance in three strategies for English problems, (b) LLaMA3 performance in three strategies for Hindi problems: **Orange bars: Chain-of-thought prompt strategy**, **Green bars: Manual Subcategory Prompt Strategy** and **Blue bars: One-Shot Prompt Strategy**. **Red line** shows there are no samples/problems for which LLM chose subcategory accurately.

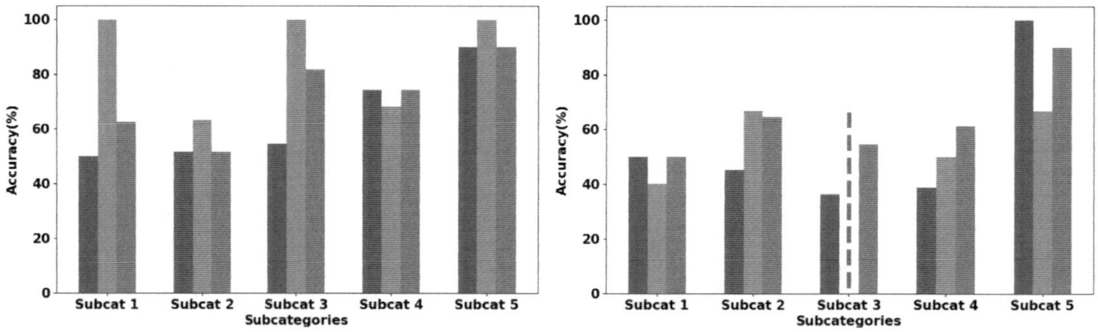

(a) (b)

Figure 8: (a) GPT-3.5 Turbo performance in three strategies for English problems (b) GPT-3.5 Turbo performance in three strategies for Hindi problems: **Orange bars: Chain-of-thought prompt strategy**, **Green bars: Manual Subcategory Prompt Strategy** and **Blue bars: One-Shot Prompt Strategy**. **Red line** shows there are no samples/problems for which LLM chose subcategory accurately.

ematical capabilities of LLMs in solving mathematical word problems in English language. Recent works highlight the performance of LLMs in English mathematical word problems. A major part of advances in the area started with the design of datasets for math word problems in English, (Frieder et al., 2024) is one such work where miniGHOSTS and GHOSTS are extracted from publicly available datasets and were used to analyse the abilities of ChatGPT-3.5 and 4. (Srivastava and Kim, 2024) proposes a strategised version of masking during pre-training stage of Encoder-Decoder models instead of random masking which significantly improved the performance of Encoder-Decoder small scale models by 2-3 times on benchmark mathematical datasets (English). A special method, MathPrompter(Imani et al., 2023), enhances arithmetic operations and reasoning capabilities of LLMs leveraging the programming capabilities of LLMs as an intermediate step in solving the problem. They worked on english word problems dataset (Roy and Roth, 2015) and showed an improved performance by almost 15%. Mathify(Anand et al., 2024), another recent study in this area, where they sourced a mathematical word problem dataset, named MathQuest, from the English NCERT textbook. Using this dataset they fine-tuned open source large language models and compared their performance. Another work (Wei et al., 2022), uses the Chain of Thoughts prompt strategy on LaMDA(Thoppilan et al., 2022) and PaLM(Chowdhery et al., 2023) and showed almost 100ing accuracy on GSM8K(Cobbe et al., 2021). (Chen et al., 2023) used Program of Thoughts strat-

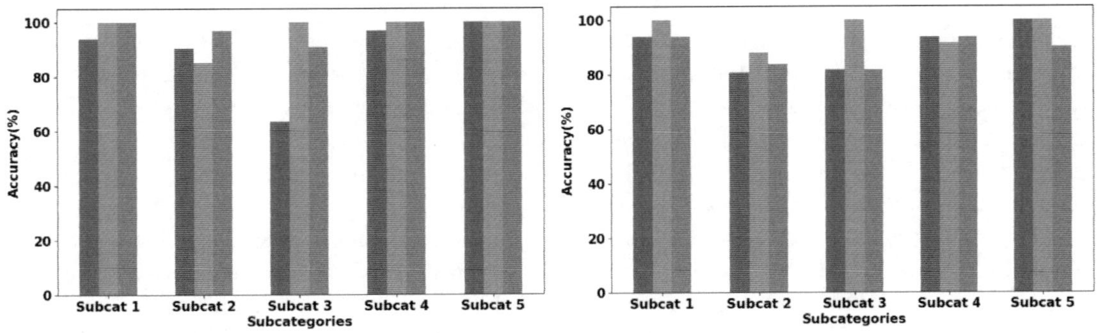

(a) (b)

Figure 9: (a) GPT-4 Turbo performance in three strategies for English problems (b) GPT-4 Turbo performance in three strategies for Hindi problems: **Orange bars: Chain-of-thought prompt strategy**, **Green bars: Manual Subcategory Prompt Strategy** and **Blue bars: One-Shot Prompt Strategy**

egy instead of Chain of Thoughts, just like Math-Prompter discussed above to improve LLMs' performance on numerical tasks. It compared the CoT methods and PoT meth- ods, resulting in the PoT method outperforming the CoT method in solving numerical problems.

Some works targeting multilingual tasks include xSTREET(Li et al., 2024), which targets to improve the reasoning capabilities including but not limited to mathematics of LLMs across non-English languages: Arabic, Spanish, Russian, Chinese, and Japanese. Here, they leveraged the reasoning capabilities of LLMs trained on code or programs, which they claim that are good reasoners from their study as compared to the LLMs trained on non-code data. ConceptMath(Wu et al., 2024), another study that targets to analyse and comprehend the LLMs in mathematical reasoning tasks in English and Chinese. They did this study on elementary and middle school level mathematical data. Their study focuses ore on the granules of mathematics like statistic, geometry, etc. instead of studying mathematical work problems as a whole. This study contributed to improvement part using an efficient fine-tuning setting where post their analysis on granular level, they used benchmark datasets like MATH(Hendrycks et al., 2021) and GSM-8K(Cobbe et al., 2021) along with their data, to fine-tune the LLM to improve it's performance in that mathematical area. (Le et al., 2024) uses chain-of-thought technique with high-quality in-context learning exemplars obtained by multilingual dense retrieval to enhance LLM's performance in mathematics.

7 Supplementary Materials

We encourage readers to review the prompts used and datasets created for this study. The access to the datasets developed and the prompts used to carry out this study is given in this github link:[1]. The supplementary materials accompanying this paper include a folder named Datasets which includes three CSV files, one for each of the language models evaluated in the study, containing problems in permutations and combinations presented in both English and Hindi. There is prompts file having the prompts used to generate the responses from LLMs. Furthermore, these prompts can be utilized to interface with the language models. These resources are provided to ensure transparency, reproducibility, and ease of future research based on our findings.

8 Conclusions and Future Work

Our main focus of study was analysing the performance of LLMs in solving combinatorics problems in Hindi so as to assess them, if they can be readily deployed in the education sector. For our study, we used GPT-3.5, a freely available LLM with a chat interface; LLaMA3-8B, a small "open" source model that can be run on an affordable GPU, and GPT-4 Turbo, one of the most powerful models available currently. In future research, we plan to significantly expand our dataset to encompass over 100 problems per subcategory, aiming to improve both its comprehensiveness and robustness. This effort will facilitate a deeper exploration of mathematical problem-solving across diverse categories,

[1] `https://github.com/yash-raj-verma/IndoNLP_COLING_2025.git`

ensuring more representative benchmarks. Furthermore, we will broaden the linguistic scope of our study by incorporating additional Indian regional languages, such as Bengali, Tamil, Assamese, and Urdu, alongside non-Indian languages, including Greek and Arabic. This expansion will enable a cross-cultural examination of mathematical reasoning and problem formulation in various linguistic contexts.
To further enhance the scope and impact of our work, we intend to evaluate the capabilities of emerging state-of-the-art language models on our enriched datasets. By incorporating models with improved architectures and training paradigms, we aim to uncover new insights into their generalization and adaptability. Additionally, we plan to use our dataset for fine-tuning smaller, efficient models, such as LLaMA3, with a focus on exploring their potential for targeted improvements in performance, particularly in resource-constrained environments. This dual approach promises to deepen our understanding of model behavior while driving innovation in both large-scale and lightweight language model applications. We believe that such studies would benefit a country like India or others (once the analysis and scope of this work expands to other regions and their regional languages), where there exists a large number of regional languages in which education is imparted, and show the way forward for LLMs effective currently for all segments of the Indian population with the intention of expanding this to other countries.

Limitations

While our research investigates the application of large language models (LLMs) to solving mathematical problems in Hindi, certain limitations persist. One significant constraint is the size and scope of our dataset, which comprises only 100 problems per subcategory. This limited sample may hinder the robustness and comprehensiveness of our evaluation. Expanding the dataset to encompass a wider range of problems, drawn from additional mathematical topics or diverse educational resources such as textbooks in other languages, would help enhance its representativeness and reliability.

Moreover, our study is centered on evaluating the performance of LLMs, but it does not explore the potential benefits of fine-tuning smaller, more resource-efficient models on the same dataset. Investigating the performance improvements achievable with such fine-tuning could provide valuable insights into balancing computational efficiency with model accuracy.

To address these limitations, future work would prioritize not only the expansion of the dataset to include a richer variety of problem types but also the exploration of smaller, fine-tuned models. This dual approach could increase the diversity of the mathematical problems handled while also improving the accessibility and scalability of our study, particularly for educational settings with limited computational resources and diverse linguistic backgrounds.

References

Census 2011. https://web.archive.org/web/20180127163347/http://planningcommission.gov.in/data/datatable/data_2312/DatabookDec2014%20307.pdf.

Meta llama team. introducing meta llama 3: The most capable openly available llm to date. (accessed on this url). https://ai.meta.com/blog/meta-llama-3/.

National council of educational research and training. https://ncert.nic.in/textbook.php.

National institute of educational planning and administration. https://niepa.org.

Josh Achiam, Steven Adler, Sandhini Agarwal, Lama Ahmad, Ilge Akkaya, Florencia Leoni Aleman, Diogo Almeida, Janko Altenschmidt, Sam Altman, Shyamal Anadkat, et al. 2023. Gpt-4 technical report. *arXiv preprint arXiv:2303.08774*.

Avinash Anand, Mohit Gupta, Kritarth Prasad, Navya Singla, Sanjana Sanjeev, Jatin Kumar, Adarsh Raj Shivam, and Rajiv Ratn Shah. 2024. Mathify: Evaluating large language models on mathematical problem solving tasks. *arXiv preprint arXiv:2404.13099*.

Wenhu Chen, Xueguang Ma, Xinyi Wang, and William W. Cohen. 2023. Program of thoughts prompting: Disentangling computation from reasoning for numerical reasoning tasks. *Transactions on Machine Learning Research*.

Aakanksha Chowdhery, Sharan Narang, Jacob Devlin, Maarten Bosma, Gaurav Mishra, Adam Roberts, Paul Barham, Hyung Won Chung, Charles Sutton, Sebastian Gehrmann, et al. 2023. Palm: Scaling language modeling with pathways. *Journal of Machine Learning Research*, 24(240):1–113.

Karl Cobbe, Vineet Kosaraju, Mohammad Bavarian, Mark Chen, Heewoo Jun, Lukasz Kaiser, Matthias

Plappert, Jerry Tworek, Jacob Hilton, Reiichiro Nakano, Christopher Hesse, and John Schulman. 2021. Training verifiers to solve math word problems. *CoRR*, abs/2110.14168.

Simon Frieder, Luca Pinchetti, Ryan-Rhys Griffiths, Tommaso Salvatori, Thomas Lukasiewicz, Philipp Petersen, and Julius Berner. 2024. Mathematical capabilities of chatgpt. *Advances in neural information processing systems*, 36.

Dan Hendrycks, Collin Burns, Saurav Kadavath, Akul Arora, Steven Basart, Eric Tang, Dawn Song, and Jacob Steinhardt. 2021. Measuring mathematical problem solving with the MATH dataset. In *Thirty-fifth Conference on Neural Information Processing Systems Datasets and Benchmarks Track (Round 2)*.

Shima Imani, Liang Du, and Harsh Shrivastava. 2023. Mathprompter: Mathematical reasoning using large language models. In *ACL (industry)*, pages 37–42. Association for Computational Linguistics.

Nguyen-Khang Le, Dieu-Hien Nguyen, Dinh-Truong Do, Chau Nguyen, and Minh Le Nguyen. 2024. Vietnamese elementary math reasoning using large language model with refined translation and dense-retrieved chain-of-thought. In *JSAI International Symposium on Artificial Intelligence*, pages 260–268. Springer.

Bryan Li, Tamer Alkhouli, Daniele Bonadiman, Nikolaos Pappas, and Saab Mansour. 2024. Eliciting better multilingual structured reasoning from LLMs through code. In *Proceedings of the 62nd Annual Meeting of the Association for Computational Linguistics (Volume 1: Long Papers)*, pages 5154–5169, Bangkok, Thailand. Association for Computational Linguistics.

Alec Radford. 2018. Openai gpt paper titled improving language understanding by generative pre-training.

Subhro Roy and Dan Roth. 2015. Solving general arithmetic word problems. In *Proceedings of the 2015 Conference on Empirical Methods in Natural Language Processing*, pages 1743–1752, Lisbon, Portugal. Association for Computational Linguistics.

Nilesh Srivastava and Seongchan Kim. 2024. Enhancing mathematical reasoning in math word problems: A numerical masking approach for encoder-decoder models. *Elsevier BV*.

Romal Thoppilan, Daniel De Freitas, Jamie Hall, Noam Shazeer, Apoorv Kulshreshtha, Heng-Tze Cheng, Alicia Jin, Taylor Bos, Leslie Baker, Yu Du, et al. 2022. Lamda: Language models for dialog applications. *arXiv preprint arXiv:2201.08239*.

Jason Wei, Xuezhi Wang, Dale Schuurmans, Maarten Bosma, Fei Xia, Ed Chi, Quoc V Le, Denny Zhou, et al. 2022. Chain-of-thought prompting elicits reasoning in large language models. *Advances in neural information processing systems*, 35:24824–24837.

Yanan Wu, Jie Liu, Xingyuan Bu, Jiaheng Liu, Zhanhui Zhou, Yuanxing Zhang, Chenchen Zhang, Zhiqi Bai, Haibin Chen, Tiezheng Ge, et al. 2024. Conceptmath: A bilingual concept-wise benchmark for measuring mathematical reasoning of large language models. *arXiv preprint arXiv:2402.14660*.

From Scarcity to Capability: Empowering Fake News Detection in Low-Resource Languages with LLMs

Hrithik Majumdar Shibu[†], **Shrestha Datta**[†], **Md. Sumon Miah, Nasrullah Sami, Mahruba Sharmin Chowdhury, Md. Saiful Islam**
Shahjalal University of Science and Technology, Sylhet, Bangladesh
{hrithik11804064, shresthadatta910, iamsumon111, samrevolutionz69}@gmail.com
{mahruba-cse, saiful-cse}@sust.edu

Abstract

The rapid spread of fake news presents a significant global challenge, particularly in low-resource languages like Bangla, which lack adequate datasets and detection tools. Although manual fact-checking is accurate, it is expensive and slow to prevent the dissemination of fake news. Addressing this gap, we introduce BanFakeNews-2.0, a robust dataset to enhance Bangla fake news detection. This version includes 11,700 additional, meticulously curated fake news articles validated from credible sources, creating a proportional dataset of 47,000 authentic and 13,000 fake news items across 13 categories. In addition, we created a manually curated independent test set of 460 fake and 540 authentic news items for rigorous evaluation. We invest efforts in collecting fake news from credible sources and manually verified while preserving the linguistic richness. We develop a benchmark system utilizing transformer-based architectures, including fine-tuned Bidirectional Encoder Representations from Transformers variants (F1-87%) and Large Language Models with Quantized Low-Rank Approximation (F1-89%), that significantly outperforms traditional methods. BanFakeNews-2.0 offers a valuable resource to advance research and application in fake news detection for low-resourced languages. We publicly release our dataset and model on Github[1] to foster research in this direction.

1 Introduction

The widespread dissemination of fake news, defined as intentionally misleading information, has become a critical issue in modern society with social consequences. Fake news and misinformation circulate across media channels—from social networks to online news portals—often aiming to mislead and manipulate public opinion. The consequences of such disinformation can range from shaping public opinion on critical matters to catalyzing large-scale societal unrest. For example, during the COVID-19 pandemic, misinformation regarding vaccine safety led to substantial vaccine reluctance (Lee et al., 2022; O'Connor and Murphy, 2020). In Bangladesh, the effects of such misinformation have been severe, including incidents of violence and communal discord spurred by false rumors online (Shirina and Prodhan, 2020; Bhikkhu, 2014). Moreover, the infodemic—defined as an overabundance of information, including false or misleading details—further complicated efforts to combat COVID-19 globally, as highlighted in studies exploring misinformation trends and mitigation strategies (Kouzy et al., 2020; Bridgman et al., 2020; Uddin et al., 2021). This challenge extends to various content forms, such as articles, images, videos, and memes, amplifying the difficulty of detection (Cao et al., 2020; Das et al., 2021; Singh and Sharma, 2022; Das et al., 2022).

Dataset Source	#FN	#TN
(SadikAlJarif, 2022)	4.5K	10K
(Al-Zaman and Noman, 2023)	2K	5k
(Hossain et al., 2020)	1.3K	48.6k
(Hussain et al., 2020)	1K	2.5K
BanFakeNews-2 (Proposed)	13K	47k

Table 1: Overview of existing Bangla fake news datasets. Here #FN represents No. of fake news and #TN represents the No. of authentic news dataset

Detecting fake news in low-resource languages like Bangla remains challenging due to limited datasets and resources. While English-language fake news detection has progressed, robust datasets for Bangla remain scarce, hindering model development. Although efforts like the BanFakeNews dataset (Hossain et al., 2020) and others (Al-Zaman and Noman, 2023) have made initial strides, existing datasets remain limited in size and coverage, and manual fact-checking is impractical at scale. To address these limitations, we present

[1] Github: https://github.com/Shibu4064/IndoNLP
† These authors have equal contributions.

Proceedings of the First Workshop on Natural Language Processing for Indo-Aryan and Dravidian Languages (IndoNLP2025), pages 100–107
January 20, 2025. ©2025 Association for Computational Linguistics

BanFakeNews-2.0, a substantially extended dataset tailored for improved Bangla fake news detection. Building upon BanFakeNews, this new dataset includes 13,000 source-verified fake news articles, forming a balanced collection of 60,000 news items (47,000 authentic, 13,000 fake) across 13 diverse categories compared to the previous largest BanFakeNews dataset. Manually curating an independent test set of 1,000 news articles further enables rigorous model evaluation. Our benchmarks incorporate transformer-based models, such as BERT, and fine-tuned large language models (LLMs) using Quantized Low-Rank Approximation (QLORA).

BLOOM is a state-of-the-art, open-access large language model that is collaboratively developed by hundreds of researchers and trained on the multilingual ROOTS corpus. It supports 46 natural and 13 programming languages, enabling broad applications and competitive performance across benchmarks (Workshop et al., 2023). We observe that our fine-tuned BLOOM 560M model achieves the highest performance, with a macro F1 score of 89. This dataset and benchmark represent a crucial step in advancing fake news detection for low-resource languages like Bangla, providing a foundation for future research and practical applications. Our main contributions include:

- We present BanFakeNews-2.0, a significant incremental version of BanFakeNews as shown in Table 1, while previous research is limited in size and highly imbalanced. We manually collected and validated 60K Bangla news articles, including 13K fake news.
- We conducted extensive experiments using traditional linguistic features, transformer-based models like BERT, and LLMs to improve the performance of detecting fake news in Bangla.
- We create an independent test set of 1,000 news articles (460 fake, 540 authentic) to ensure rigorous evaluation and cross-comparison of models.

2 Development of BanFakeNews-2.0

We focused on data preparation to ensure linguistic richness and dataset diversity with two main objectives: (1) collect verified fake news from diverse sources and domains and (2) enhance dataset variety while minimizing redundancy. Our newly curated dataset comprises approximately 13,000 fake and 47,000 authentic news articles from online news portals and mainstream media. We have collected the misleading or false context type of news mostly from `www.jaachai.com` and `www.bdfactcheck.com`. These two websites provide a logical and informative explanation of the authenticity of the news published on other sites. So, we have also collected the news mentioned on those two sites from the actual publishing sites and ensured that we avoid duplicates. We have used Python's web-scraping method for automated and accurate collection of category-based news from different online news portals, such as politics, sports, entertainment, medical, religious, etc. The initial screening has been conducted by evaluating the credibility of sources and verifying claims through fact-checking platforms, authoritative references, or collaborative verification methods. Relevant keywords such as "rumor," "hoax," "viral news," and Bangla-specific terms linked to sensational topics have helped in categorizing the articles. Employing automated web-scraping techniques alongside manual validation ensures data accuracy and quality. Additionally, maintaining a balanced representation of topics, time-frames, and domains has been ensured to create this dataset.

For authentic news, we selected the top 30 Bangladeshi news portals, recognized for their credibility and high readership. For fake news, we gathered content from six major fact-checking platforms that frequently debunk misinformation in Bangladesh, identifying and validating articles as probable fake news for inclusion. To ensure uniqueness, we filtered out duplicates and removed items with over 50% or 300 words of token overlap, aiming to expand vocabulary diversity and contextual variety. This broad range of content enhances the robustness of our classification system, supporting better generalization across various linguistic styles.

Each article was cross-checked by three annotators to confirm authenticity. Five undergraduate students, guided by detailed source verification protocols, reviewed potentially misleading sources and excluded redundant entries. Note that, we define a verified source of news when the source is at least a person or organization capable of verification of claimed news. When no specific source is available, the reporters or journalists themselves are considered the source of the news. We used majority voting to assign a final label of "fake" or "authentic," achieving a high inter-annotator agreement score of 0.93, indicating strong labelling consistency (Fleiss, 1971). During dataset analysis, we standardized categories to align with the classifications used in BanFakeNews (Hossain et al., 2020), resulting in 13 distinct categories. Categories were assigned based on the classification of the news at its source. If the source did not provide a category, the news was thoroughly read to understand its context and categorized accordingly. We focus on increasing the number of fake news articles to reduce the data imbalance, with 500 fake news articles per category. Still, we face challenges in the lifestyle, medical, and religious categories. The final dataset, comprising 60K news articles, is distributed across 13 categories in Table 2.

Category	Authentic	Fake
Politics	3141	3403
Miscellaneous	2218	1655
International	6990	1461
Lifestyle	901	308
Medical	112	448
Religious	118	359
Sports	6526	925
Educational	1115	808
Technology	843	725
National	18708	1167
Crime	1272	720
Entertainment	2636	1441
Finance	1259	573

Table 2: Statistics of the dataset.

3 Methodologies

Here, we will outline the methods to create a benchmark model for detecting fake news in Bangla. Our methodologies include traditional linguistic attributes as well as neural networks and transformer-based models.

3.1 Traditional Approaches

We extracted lexical linguistic features using TF-IDF for character n-grams (n = 3,4,5) and word n-grams (n = 1,2,3) similarly as existing works (Islam et al., 2022). We applied a Linear Support Vector Machine (SVM) (Hearst et al., 1998) to these features for classification. Recognizing the value of semantic information, we experimented with pre-trained word embeddings to represent articles. Specifically, we used Bangla 300-dimensional word vectors pre-trained with FastText on Common Crawl and Wikipedia (Hossain et al., 2020; Romim et al., 2022). Finally, we combined all the features with SVM.

3.2 Transformer-based BERT Models

Encoder-based pre-trained BERT (Devlin et al., 2018a) models are exceptional in downstream tasks due to their superior contextual understanding capabilities. We chose five pre-trained model bases: BanglaBERT (Bhattacharjee et al., 2022) and SagorBERT (Sarker, 2020), which are monolingual, XLM-RoBERTa (XRoBERTa) (Conneau et al., 2019), multilingual-BERT cased and uncased (m-BERT-c and m-BERT-unc, respectively) (Devlin et al., 2018b) which are multilingual. We shuffled the training samples and enforced gradient clipping to fine-tune these models. We utilized the outputs from the last two layers of multi-head attention, subsequently employing a linear layer for classification. We fine-tuned the model using Adam optimizer (Kingma and Ba, 2014).

3.3 Large Language Model

Large language models (LLMs) have recently demonstrated impressive linguistic analysis and reasoning abilities. In our experiments, we applied several advanced LLMs to our dataset, including BLOOM 560M (Scao et al., 2022), Phi-3 Mini 3.8B (Abdin et al., 2024), Stable LM 2 1.6B (Bellagente et al., 2024), and Llama 3.2 1B (Inan et al., 2023). To fine-tune these models, we employed QLoRA, loading them in 4-bit precision and setting the rank and alpha parameters to 8 and 32, respectively, for trainable adapters. Each model was configured in half-precision floating-point format with normalized 4-bit quantization, using the final token for classification. To manage model complexity and avoid overfitting, alpha is used as a regularization parameter. Its value is adjusted to strike a compromise between underfitting and overfitting (Moradi et al., 2020). 4-bit quantization (Pan et al., 2023) is perfect for devices with limited resources or for quicker inference because it drastically reduces model size and increases computing efficiency. Modern quantization methods provide low accuracy loss, allowing for effective deployment with respectable performance. Fine-tuning was optimized through gradient accumulation at each step with a paged Adam 8-bit optimizer(Simoulin et al., 2024).

4 Experimental Setup

4.1 Data Preprocessing and Model Validation

English words and hyperlinks were removed from the dataset. Text normalization, punctuation, and stop-words removal were performed for traditional models. We have done some pre-processing, including removing NaN values, deleting duplicate rows, etc. As punctuation is essential for capturing context in a sentence, there was no punctuation removal for our LLM experiments.

We validated the models using the holdout method. For this purpose, we split the dataset into train and test sets containing 70% and 30%, respectively, following the distribution by the authors of the BanFakeNews (Hossain et al., 2020) dataset while keeping the same class ratio. We took half of the test split as validation and the rest for testing purposes. This split strikes a practical balance, maintaining sufficient data for each phase while ensuring reliable model evaluation.

4.2 Baselines

In our experimental evaluation, we benchmark our results against two baseline approaches. Firstly, a majority baseline assigns the predominant class label (in this case, 'authentic news') to all articles. The second is a random baseline, which randomly classifies articles as authentic or fake. Table 3 presents the average precision, recall, and F1-score obtained from 10 random baseline experiments.

4.3 Experiments

For each experiment, we chose the hyperparameters based on the validation set (Andonie, 2019) and evaluated the model on the test set as well as our independent test set. For traditional models, we only trained on the content of the news. For BERTs and LLMs, we trained both on content and headlines while keeping a maximum limit of 512 input tokens. To differentiate the headline and content of each news sample, we added the string " \\ " between these.

5 Result and Analysis

Model	Authentic			Fake			Macro
	P	R	F1	P	R	F1	F1
Baselines							
Majority	79	100	88	0	0	0	78
Random	79	50	61	21	51	30	63
Linguistic Features with SVM							
Unigram(U)	92	95	93	78	70	74	84
Bigram(B)	91	95	93	78	67	72	83
Trigram(T)	91	88	90	62	69	66	78
U+B+T	92	95	94	79	70	75	85
C3-Gram(C3)	96	97	98	80	74	77	86
C4-Gram(C4)	97	98	97	79	75	77	86
C5-Gram(C5)	96	97	96	81	74	77	86
C3+C4+C5	97	98	97	79	75	77	86
Embedding	89	98	93	90	57	70	82
All Features(All)	92	96	94	85	72	78	86
BERT models							
BanglaBERT	89	99	94	97	53	69	81
SagorBERT	92	99	95	95	68	79	87
m-BERT-c	92	98	95	93	69	79	87
m-BERT-unc	92	98	95	93	70	79	87
XRoBERTa	90	98	94	89	61	72	83
LLMs							
BLOOM 560M	92	100	96	99	69	81	89
Phi 3 mini 3.8B	90	98	94	92	58	71	83
Stable LM 2 1.6B	90	98	94	89	61	71	83
Llama 3.2 1B	92	99	95	94	66	78	86

Table 3: Precision (P), Recall (R), and F1 score for each categorical class (Authentic and Fake)

Table 3, describes the performance of various models in terms of Precision (P), Recall (R), and F1 (F1-Score) for both the authentic and fake news classes. Our approach, validated using the independent holdout dataset, yields an unbiased performance measure compared to previous works in Bangla fake news detection. The results indicate high P, R, and F1 scores for the authentic class, with nearly perfect recall. For fake news detection, performance varies by model, reflecting the unique challenges of this classification task.

Among word n-grams, unigrams achieved the highest F1 score of 84%, outperforming bigrams (83%) and trigrams (78%). Combining these n-grams resulted in an F1 score of 85%, demonstrating that multi-gram approach enhances classification accuracy. Character n-grams yielded similar performance; however, combinations of character n-grams did not provide substantial gains. Across experiments, authentic news classification achieved over 90% in P, R, and F1. However, fake news classification showed greater variability. Traditional SVM models, employing linguistic features, outperformed LLMs and transformers-based models in identifying authentic news. Conversely, LLM-based models excelled in detecting fake news, yielding higher F1 scores. Notably, the transformer models multilingual BERT (m-BERT-unc) and BLOOM achieved an F1 score of 81% in the fake news class, surpassing the 77% F1-score achieved by the C3-Gram model. However, traditional models performed slightly better overall, reaching an F1 score of 98% in the authentic class, compared to the highest F1 score of 96% for transformers. This discrepancy may stem from the increased volume of fake news in the dataset, posing unique challenges for transformers in handling nuanced

Model	Train dataset	Test dataset	Mac. F1
SVM (All)	BanFakeNews	Test (internal)	74
SVM (All)	BanFakeNews-2.0	Test (internal)	86
SVM (All)	BanFakeNews	Test (external)	39
SVM (All)	BanFakeNews-2.0	Test (external)	91
BLOOM	BanFakeNews	Test (internal)	78
BLOOM	BanFakeNews-2.0	Test (internal)	89
BLOOM	BanFakeNews	Test (external)	29
BLOOM	BanFakeNews-2.0	Test (external)	67

Table 4: Ablation experiments with different train-test combinations of existing BanFakeNews and proposed BanFakeNews-2.0

distinctions within the fake class. Among the tested transformers, BLOOM and m-BERT-uncased consistently achieved top performance. However, BanglaBERT lagged, exhibiting low P and R for both classes. For linguistic features, character-based models outperformed word-based models in fake news detection. The C3-Gram model surpassed the unigram+bigram+trigram(U+B+T) feature model, showing a 1%, 4%, and 2% higher P, R, and F1, respectively, for fake news. This trend also held for authentic news detection, underscoring the effectiveness of character-level features in handling the nuanced patterns of Bangla fake news.

To assess the generalisability of our models, we evaluated them using a manually curated external test set of 1,000 samples. We tested the top-performing models—the traditional linguistic feature-based SVM and the LLM-based BLOOM—both trained on the BanFakeNews-2.0 dataset, as shown in Table 4. On this external test set, models trained with BanFakeNews-2.0 consistently outperformed those trained on the original BanFakeNews dataset, demonstrating BanFakeNews-2.0's improved diversity and balance. This enhancement, similar to expanding interview questions to address a wide range of scenarios, equips the models to handle complex and varied data, establishing BanFakeNews-2.0 as a valuable resource for Bangla fake news detection.

6 Conclusion and Future Works

The study presents BanFakeNews-2.0, a Bangla fake news dataset with 13K manually annotated articles across 13 categories aimed at improving fake news detection in Bangla. Our evaluation demonstrated that BLOOM and m-BERT-unc models outperformed other models, highlighting the importance of contextually diverse datasets over basic linguistic features for achieving high accuracy. BanFakeNews-2.0 allowed transformer models and LLMs to excel, highlighting the need for diverse datasets and robust detection tools. Future work will focus on enhancing dataset features, refining models, and exploring real-time monitoring. Testing emerging LLMs like Mistral, Minitron, and GPT 4 in zero-shot settings may provide further insights. BanFakeNews-2.0 provides a strong foundation for advancing research in Bangla fake news detection and mitigation.

7 Limitations

Generative language models are becoming more human-like, enabling them to imitate authentic news. However, the proposed dataset and pretrained models may struggle to differentiate advanced fabricated news from upcoming generative models. The low fake news count in some news categories makes it difficult to differentiate. Despite high classification capabilities, the current dataset is imbalanced due to insufficient fake news. A more balanced dataset could improve model capabilities.

References

Marah Abdin, Sam Ade Jacobs, Ammar Ahmad Awan, Jyoti Aneja, Ahmed Awadallah, Hany Awadalla, Nguyen Bach, Amit Bahree, Arash Bakhtiari, Jianmin Bao, Harkirat Behl, Alon Benhaim, Misha Bilenko, Johan Bjorck, Sébastien Bubeck, Qin Cai, Martin Cai, Caio César Teodoro Mendes, Weizhu Chen, Vishrav Chaudhary, Dong Chen, Dongdong Chen, Yen-Chun Chen, Yi-Ling Chen, Parul Chopra, Xiyang Dai, Allie Del Giorno, Gustavo de Rosa, Matthew Dixon, Ronen Eldan, Victor Fragoso, Dan Iter, Mei Gao, Min Gao, Jianfeng Gao, Amit Garg, Abhishek Goswami, Suriya Gunasekar, Emman Haider, Junheng Hao, Russell J. Hewett, Jamie Huynh, Mojan Javaheripi, Xin Jin, Piero Kauffmann, Nikos Karampatziakis, Dongwoo Kim, Mahoud Khademi, Lev Kurilenko, James R. Lee, Yin Tat Lee, Yuanzhi Li, Yunsheng Li, Chen Liang, Lars Liden, Ce Liu, Mengchen Liu, Weishung Liu, Eric Lin, Zeqi Lin, Chong Luo, Piyush Madan, Matt Mazzola, Arindam Mitra, Hardik Modi, Anh Nguyen, Brandon Norick, Barun Patra, Daniel Perez-Becker, Thomas Portet, Reid Pryzant, Heyang Qin, Marko Radmilac, Corby Rosset, Sambudha Roy, Olatunji Ruwase, Olli Saarikivi, Amin Saied, Adil Salim, Michael Santacroce, Shital Shah, Ning Shang, Hiteshi Sharma, Swadheen Shukla, Xia Song, Masahiro Tanaka, Andrea Tupini, Xin Wang, Lijuan Wang, Chunyu Wang, Yu Wang, Rachel Ward, Guanhua Wang, Philipp Witte, Haiping Wu, Michael Wyatt, Bin Xiao, Can Xu, Jiahang Xu, Weijian Xu, Sonali Yadav, Fan Yang, Jianwei Yang, Ziyi Yang, Yifan Yang, Donghan Yu, Lu Yuan, Chengruidong Zhang, Cyril Zhang, Jianwen Zhang, Li Lyna Zhang, Yi Zhang, Yue Zhang,

Yunan Zhang, and Xiren Zhou. 2024. Phi-3 technical report: A highly capable language model locally on your phone. *Preprint*, arXiv:2404.14219.

Md. Sayeed Al-Zaman and Mridha Md. Shiblee Noman. 2023. A dataset on social media users' engagement with religious misinformation. *Data in Brief*, 49:109439.

Răzvan Andonie. 2019. Hyperparameter optimization in learning systems. *Journal of Membrane Computing*, 1(4):279–291.

Marco Bellagente, Jonathan Tow, Dakota Mahan, Duy Phung, Maksym Zhuravinskyi, Reshinth Adithyan, James Baicoianu, Ben Brooks, Nathan Cooper, Ashish Datta, et al. 2024. Stable lm 2 1.6 b technical report. *arXiv preprint arXiv:2402.17834*.

Abhik Bhattacharjee, Tahmid Hasan, Wasi Ahmad, Kazi Samin Mubasshir, Md Saiful Islam, Anindya Iqbal, M. Sohel Rahman, and Rifat Shahriyar. 2022. BanglaBERT: Language model pretraining and benchmarks for low-resource language understanding evaluation in Bangla. In *Findings of the Association for Computational Linguistics: NAACL 2022*, pages 1318–1327, Seattle, United States. Association for Computational Linguistics.

Pragyananda Bhikkhu. 2014. Who will be tried for ramu destruction? Published: 30 Sep 2014, 16: 58.

Aengus Bridgman, Eric Merkley, Peter John Loewen, Taylor Owen, Derek Ruths, Lisa Teichmann, and Oleg Zhilin. 2020. The causes and consequences of covid-19 misperceptions: Understanding the role of news and social media. *Harvard Kennedy School Misinformation Review*, 1(3).

Juan Cao, Peng Qi, Qiang Sheng, Tianyun Yang, Junbo Guo, and Jintao Li. 2020. Exploring the role of visual content in fake news detection. *Disinformation, Misinformation, and Fake News in Social Media: Emerging Research Challenges and Opportunities*, pages 141–161.

Alexis Conneau, Kartikay Khandelwal, Naman Goyal, Vishrav Chaudhary, Guillaume Wenzek, Francisco Guzmán, Edouard Grave, Myle Ott, Luke Zettlemoyer, and Veselin Stoyanov. 2019. Unsupervised cross-lingual representation learning at scale. *CoRR*, abs/1911.02116.

Sowmen Das, Md. Saiful Islam, and Md. Ruhul Amin. 2022. Gca-net: Utilizing gated context attention for improving image forgery localization and detection. In *Proceedings of the IEEE/CVF Conference on Computer Vision and Pattern Recognition (CVPR) Workshops*, pages 81–90.

Sowmen Das, Selim Seferbekov, Arup Datta, Md. Saiful Islam, and Md. Ruhul Amin. 2021. Towards solving the deepfake problem: An analysis on improving deepfake detection using dynamic face augmentation. In *Proceedings of the IEEE/CVF International Conference on Computer Vision (ICCV) Workshops*, pages 3776–3785.

Jacob Devlin, Ming-Wei Chang, Kenton Lee, and Kristina Toutanova. 2018a. Bert: Pre-training of deep bidirectional transformers for language understanding. *arXiv preprint arXiv:1810.04805*.

Jacob Devlin, Ming-Wei Chang, Kenton Lee, and Kristina Toutanova. 2018b. BERT: pre-training of deep bidirectional transformers for language understanding. *CoRR*, abs/1810.04805.

Joseph L Fleiss. 1971. Measuring nominal scale agreement among many raters. *Psychological bulletin*, 76(5):378.

Marti A. Hearst, Susan T Dumais, Edgar Osuna, John Platt, and Bernhard Scholkopf. 1998. Support vector machines. *IEEE Intelligent Systems and their applications*, 13(4):18–28.

Md Zobaer Hossain, Md Ashraful Rahman, Md Saiful Islam, and Sudipta Kar. 2020. BanFakeNews: A dataset for detecting fake news in Bangla. In *Proceedings of the Twelfth Language Resources and Evaluation Conference*, pages 2862–2871, Marseille, France. European Language Resources Association.

Md Gulzar Hussain, Md Rashidul Hasan, Mahmuda Rahman, Joy Protim, and Sakib Al Hasan. 2020. Detection of bangla fake news using mnb and svm classifier. In *2020 International Conference on Computing, Electronics & Communications Engineering (iCCECE)*, pages 81–85.

Hakan Inan, Kartikeya Upasani, Jianfeng Chi, Rashi Rungta, Krithika Iyer, Yuning Mao, Michael Tontchev, Qing Hu, Brian Fuller, Davide Testuggine, and Madian Khabsa. 2023. Llama guard: Llm-based input-output safeguard for human-ai conversations. *Preprint*, arXiv:2312.06674.

Khondoker Ittehadul Islam, Tanvir Yuvraz, Md Saiful Islam, and Enamul Hassan. 2022. EmoNoBa: A dataset for analyzing fine-grained emotions on noisy Bangla texts. In *Proceedings of the 2nd Conference of the Asia-Pacific Chapter of the Association for Computational Linguistics and the 12th International Joint Conference on Natural Language Processing (Volume 2: Short Papers)*, pages 128–134, Online only. Association for Computational Linguistics.

Diederik P Kingma and Jimmy Ba. 2014. Adam: A method for stochastic optimization. *arXiv preprint arXiv:1412.6980*.

Ramez Kouzy, Joseph Abi Jaoude, Afif Kraitem, Molly B El Alam, Basil Karam, Elio Adib, Jabra Zarka, Cindy Traboulsi, Elie W Akl, and Khalil Baddour. 2020. Coronavirus goes viral: quantifying the covid-19 misinformation epidemic on twitter. *Cureus*, 12(3).

Sun Kyong Lee, Juhyung Sun, Seulki Jang, and Shane Connelly. 2022. Misinformation of covid-19 vaccines and vaccine hesitancy.

Reza Moradi, Reza Berangi, and Behrouz Minaei. 2020. A survey of regularization strategies for deep models. *Artificial Intelligence Review*, 53(6):3947–3986.

Cathal O'Connor and Michelle Murphy. 2020. Going viral: doctors must tackle fake news in the covid-19 pandemic. *Bmj*, 369(10.1136).

Jiayi Pan, Chengcan Wang, Kaifu Zheng, Yangguang Li, Zhenyu Wang, and Bin Feng. 2023. Smoothquant+: Accurate and efficient 4-bit post-training weightquantization for llm. *Preprint*, arXiv:2312.03788.

Nauros Romim, Mosahed Ahmed, Md Saiful Islam, Arnab Sen Sharma, Hriteshwar Talukder, and Mohammad Ruhul Amin. 2022. Bd-shs: A benchmark dataset for learning to detect online bangla hate speech in different social contexts. In *Proceedings of the Thirteenth Language Resources and Evaluation Conference*, pages 5153–5162.

SadikAlJarif. 2022. bangla fake news dataset. `https://www.kaggle.com/datasets/sadikaljarif/bangla-fake-news-detection-dataset?select=final_bn_data.csv`.

Sagor Sarker. 2020. Banglabert: Bengali mask language model for bengali language understanding.

Teven Le Scao, Angela Fan, Christopher Akiki, Ellie Pavlick, Suzana Ilić, Daniel Hesslow, Roman Castagné, Alexandra Sasha Luccioni, François Yvon, Matthias Gallé, et al. 2022. Bloom: A 176b-parameter open-access multilingual language model. *arXiv preprint arXiv:2211.05100*.

Sharifa Umma Shirina and Md. Tabiur Rahman Prodhan. 2020. Spreading fake news in the virtual realm in bangladesh: Assessment of impact. *Global Journal of Human-Social Science*, 20(A17):11–25.

Antoine Simoulin, Namyong Park, Xiaoyi Liu, and Grey Yang. 2024. Memory-efficient fine-tuning of transformers via token selection. In *Proceedings of the 2024 Conference on Empirical Methods in Natural Language Processing*, pages 21565–21580.

Bhuvanesh Singh and Dilip Kumar Sharma. 2022. Predicting image credibility in fake news over social media using multi-modal approach. *Neural Computing and Applications*, 34(24):21503–21517.

Borhan Uddin, Nahid Reza, Md Saiful Islam, Hasib Ahsan, and Mohammad Ruhul Amin. 2021. Fighting against fake news during pandemic era: Does providing related news help student internet users to detect covid-19 misinformation? In *Proceedings of the 13th ACM Web Science Conference 2021*, pages 178–186.

BigScience Workshop, :, Teven Le Scao, Angela Fan, Christopher Akiki, Ellie Pavlick, Suzana Ilić, Daniel Hesslow, Roman Castagné, Alexandra Sasha Luccioni, François Yvon, Matthias Gallé, Jonathan Tow, Alexander M. Rush, Stella Biderman, Albert Webson, Pawan Sasanka Ammanamanchi, Thomas Wang, Benoît Sagot, Niklas Muennighoff, Albert Villanova del Moral, Olatunji Ruwase, Rachel Bawden, Stas Bekman, Angelina McMillan-Major, Iz Beltagy, Huu Nguyen, Lucile Saulnier, Samson Tan, Pedro Ortiz Suarez, Victor Sanh, Hugo Laurençon, Yacine Jernite, Julien Launay, Margaret Mitchell, Colin Raffel, Aaron Gokaslan, Adi Simhi, Aitor Soroa, Alham Fikri Aji, Amit Alfassy, Anna Rogers, Ariel Kreisberg Nitzav, Canwen Xu, Chenghao Mou, Chris Emezue, Christopher Klamm, Colin Leong, Daniel van Strien, David Ifeoluwa Adelani, Dragomir Radev, Eduardo González Ponferrada, Efrat Levkovizh, Ethan Kim, Eyal Bar Natan, Francesco De Toni, Gérard Dupont, Germán Kruszewski, Giada Pistilli, Hady Elsahar, Hamza Benyamina, Hieu Tran, Ian Yu, Idris Abdulmumin, Isaac Johnson, Itziar Gonzalez-Dios, Javier de la Rosa, Jenny Chim, Jesse Dodge, Jian Zhu, Jonathan Chang, Jörg Frohberg, Joseph Tobing, Joydeep Bhattacharjee, Khalid Almubarak, Kimbo Chen, Kyle Lo, Leandro Von Werra, Leon Weber, Long Phan, Loubna Ben allal, Ludovic Tanguy, Manan Dey, Manuel Romero Muñoz, Maraim Masoud, María Grandury, Mario Šaško, Max Huang, Maximin Coavoux, Mayank Singh, Mike Tian-Jian Jiang, Minh Chien Vu, Mohammad A. Jauhar, Mustafa Ghaleb, Nishant Subramani, Nora Kassner, Nurulaqilla Khamis, Olivier Nguyen, Omar Espejel, Ona de Gibert, Paulo Villegas, Peter Henderson, Pierre Colombo, Priscilla Amuok, Quentin Lhoest, Rheza Harliman, Rishi Bommasani, Roberto Luis López, Rui Ribeiro, Salomey Osei, Sampo Pyysalo, Sebastian Nagel, Shamik Bose, Shamsuddeen Hassan Muhammad, Shanya Sharma, Shayne Longpre, Somaieh Nikpoor, Stanislav Silberberg, Suhas Pai, Sydney Zink, Tiago Timponi Torrent, Timo Schick, Tristan Thrush, Valentin Danchev, Vassilina Nikoulina, Veronika Laippala, Violette Lepercq, Vrinda Prabhu, Zaid Alyafeai, Zeerak Talat, Arun Raja, Benjamin Heinzerling, Chenglei Si, Davut Emre Taşar, Elizabeth Salesky, Sabrina J. Mielke, Wilson Y. Lee, Abheesht Sharma, Andrea Santilli, Antoine Chaffin, Arnaud Stiegler, Debajyoti Datta, Eliza Szczechla, Gunjan Chhablani, Han Wang, Harshit Pandey, Hendrik Strobelt, Jason Alan Fries, Jos Rozen, Leo Gao, Lintang Sutawika, M Saiful Bari, Maged S. Al-shaibani, Matteo Manica, Nihal Nayak, Ryan Teehan, Samuel Albanie, Sheng Shen, Srulik Ben-David, Stephen H. Bach, Taewoon Kim, Tali Bers, Thibault Fevry, Trishala Neeraj, Urmish Thakker, Vikas Raunak, Xiangru Tang, Zheng-Xin Yong, Zhiqing Sun, Shaked Brody, Yallow Uri, Hadar Tojarieh, Adam Roberts, Hyung Won Chung, Jaesung Tae, Jason Phang, Ofir Press, Conglong Li, Deepak Narayanan, Hatim Bourfoune, Jared Casper, Jeff Rasley, Max Ryabinin, Mayank Mishra, Minjia Zhang, Mohammad Shoeybi, Myriam Peyrounette, Nicolas Patry, Nouamane Tazi, Omar Sanseviero, Patrick von Platen, Pierre Cornette, Pierre François Lavallée, Rémi Lacroix, Samyam Rajbhandari, Sanchit Gandhi, Shaden Smith, Stéphane Requena, Suraj Patil, Tim Dettmers, Ahmed Baruwa, Amanpreet Singh, Anastasia Cheveleva, Anne-Laure Ligozat, Arjun Subramonian, Aurélie Névéol, Charles Lovering, Dan Garrette, Deepak Tunuguntla, Ehud Reiter, Ekaterina Taktasheva, Ekaterina Voloshina, Eli Bogdanov, Genta Indra Winata, Hailey Schoelkopf, Jan-Christoph Kalo, Jekaterina Novikova, Jessica Zosa Forde, Jordan Clive, Jungo Kasai, Ken Kawamura, Liam Hazan, Marine Carpuat, Miruna Clinciu, Najoung Kim, Newton Cheng, Oleg Serikov, Omer Antverg, Oskar van der Wal, Rui Zhang, Ruochen Zhang, Sebastian Gehrmann, Shachar Mirkin, Shani Pais, Tatiana Shavrina, Thomas Scialom, Tian Yun, Tomasz Limisiewicz, Verena Rieser, Vitaly Protasov, Vladislav Mikhailov, Yada Pruksachatkun, Yonatan Belinkov, Zachary Bamberger, Zdeněk Kasner, Alice Rueda, Amanda Pestana, Amir Feizpour, Ammar Khan, Amy Faranak, Ana Santos, Anthony Hevia, Antigona Unldreaj, Arash Aghagol, Arezoo Abdollahi, Aycha Tammour, Azadeh HajiHosseini, Bahareh Behroozi, Benjamin Ajibade, Bharat Saxena, Carlos Muñoz Ferrandis, Daniel McDuff, Danish Contractor, David Lansky, Davis David, Douwe Kiela, Duong A. Nguyen, Edward Tan, Emi Baylor, Ezinwanne Ozoani, Fatima Mirza, Frankline Ononiwu, Habib Rezanejad, Hessie Jones, Indrani Bhattacharya, Irene Solaiman, Irina Sedenko, Isar Nejadgholi, Jesse Passmore, Josh Seltzer, Julio Bonis Sanz, Livia Dutra, Mairon Samagaio, Maraim Elbadri, Margot Mieskes, Marissa Gerchick, Martha Akinlolu, Michael McKenna, Mike Qiu, Muhammed Ghauri, Mykola Burynok, Nafis Abrar, Nazneen Rajani, Nour Elkott, Nour Fahmy, Olanrewaju Samuel, Ran An, Rasmus Kromann, Ryan Hao, Samira Alizadeh, Sarmad Shubber, Silas Wang, Sourav Roy, Sylvain Viguier, Thanh Le, Tobi Oyebade, Trieu Le, Yoyo Yang, Zach Nguyen, Abhinav Ramesh Kashyap, Alfredo Palasciano, Alison Callahan, Anima Shukla, Antonio Miranda-Escalada, Ayush Singh, Benjamin Beilharz, Bo Wang, Caio Brito, Chenxi Zhou, Chirag Jain, Chuxin Xu, Clémentine Fourrier, Daniel León Periñán, Daniel Molano, Dian Yu, Enrique Manjavacas, Fabio Barth, Florian Fuhrimann, Gabriel Altay, Giyaseddin Bayrak, Gully Burns, Helena U. Vrabec, Imane Bello, Ishani Dash, Jihyun Kang, John Giorgi, Jonas Golde, Jose David Posada, Karthik Rangasai Sivaraman, Lokesh Bulchandani, Lu Liu, Luisa Shinzato, Madeleine Hahn de Bykhovetz, Maiko Takeuchi, Marc Pàmies, Maria A Castillo, Marianna Nezhurina, Mario Sänger, Matthias Samwald, Michael Cullan, Michael Weinberg, Michiel De Wolf, Mina Mihaljcic, Minna Liu, Moritz Freidank, Myungsun Kang, Natasha Seelam, Nathan Dahlberg, Nicholas Michio Broad, Nikolaus Muellner, Pascale Fung, Patrick Haller, Ramya Chandrasekhar, Renata Eisenberg, Robert Martin, Rodrigo Canalli, Rosaline Su, Ruisi Su, Samuel Cahyawijaya, Samuele Garda, Shlok S Deshmukh, Shubhanshu Mishra, Sid Kiblawi, Simon Ott, Sinee Sang-aroonsiri, Srishti Kumar, Stefan Schweter, Sushil Bharati, Tanmay Laud, Théo Gigant, Tomoya Kainuma, Wojciech Kusa, Yanis Labrak, Yash Shailesh Bajaj, Yash Venkatraman, Yifan Xu, Yingxin Xu, Yu Xu, Zhe Tan, Zhongli Xie, Zifan Ye, Mathilde Bras, Younes Belkada, and Thomas Wolf. 2023. Bloom: A 176b-parameter open-access multilingual language model. *Preprint*, arXiv:2211.05100.

A Appendix

Authentic News Sources

Domain	Count
www.kalerkantho.com	4491
www.jagonews24.com	4426
www.banglanews24.com	4035
www.banglatribune.com	3696
www.jugantor.com	2835
www.dhakatimes24.com	2654
www.ittefaq.com.bd	2589
www.somoynews.tv	2552
www.dailynayadiganta.com	2371
www.bangla.bdnews24.com	2365
www.prothomalo.com	2350
www.bd24live.com	2335
www.risingbd.com	2220
www.dailyjanakantha.com	1531
www.bd-pratidin.com	1421
www.channelionline.com	1401
www.samakal.com	1372
www.independent24.com	1220
www.rtnn.net	1149
www.bangla.thereport24.com	859
www.mzamin.com	785
www.bhorerkagoj.net	21

Table 5: Detailed statistics of the collected authentic news with the domain URL

Fake News Sources

Domain	Count
www.boombd.com/fake-news	321
www.anandabazar.com/topic/fake-news	192
www.jachai.org/fact-checks	345
www.bangla.hindustantimes.com/fake	272
www.earki.co	231
www.balerkontho.net/2020/03/	138
www.prothom1alu.blogspot.com	154
www.motikontho.wordpress.com	271
www.bengalbeats.com	204
www.shadhinbangla24.com.bd	291
www.bengaliviralnews.com	268
www.shawdeshbhumi.com	373
www.bdexclusivenews.blogspot.com	312
www.banglainsider.com	277
www.bd-pratidin.com	293
www.dailyinqilab.com	191
www.bangla.dhakatribune.com	267

Table 6: Detailed statistics of the collected fake news with the domain URL

Enhancing Participatory Development Research in South Asia through LLM Agents System: An Empirically-Grounded Methodological Initiative and Agenda from Field Evidence in Sri Lankan

Xinjie Zhao[1], Hao Wang[3], Shyaman Maduranga Sriwarnasinghe[1], Jiacheng Tang[4], Shiyun Wang[2], Sayaka Sugiyama[1], So Morikawa[1]

[1] The University of Tokyo, [2] University of Copenhagen,
[3] China Agricultural University, [4] Shandong Normal University

Abstract

The integration of artificial intelligence into development research methodologies offers unprecedented opportunities to address persistent challenges in participatory research, particularly in linguistically diverse regions like South Asia. Drawing on empirical implementation in Sri Lanka's Sinhala-speaking communities, this study presents a methodological framework designed to transform participatory development research in the multilingual context of Sri Lanka's flood-prone Nilwala River Basin. Moving beyond conventional translation and data collection tools, the proposed framework leverages a multi-agent system architecture to redefine how data collection, analysis, and community engagement are conducted in linguistically and culturally complex research settings. This structured, agent-based approach facilitates participatory research that is both scalable and adaptive, ensuring that community perspectives remain central to research outcomes. Field experiences underscore the immense potential of LLM-based systems in addressing long-standing issues in development research across resource-limited regions, delivering both quantitative efficiencies and qualitative improvements in inclusivity. At a broader methodological level, this research advocates for AI-driven participatory research tools that prioritize ethical considerations, cultural sensitivity, and operational efficiency. It highlights strategic pathways for deploying AI systems to reinforce community agency and equitable knowledge generation, offering insights that could inform broader research agendas across the Global South.

1 Introduction

The convergence of artificial intelligence and development research heralds a transformative paradigm shift in participatory methodologies, particularly through the emergence of Large Language Models (LLMs) and their potential to revolutionize community engagement practices (Mohamed et al., 2024; Skirgård et al., 2023). As these technologies rapidly evolve, their application to development research presents both unprecedented opportunities and complex methodological challenges that demand careful examination (Roberts et al., 2024). This intersection becomes particularly significant in linguistically diverse regions like South Asia, where traditional research approaches have long struggled to bridge communication gaps and cultural divides (Kshetri, 2024; Hassan et al., 2023).

The limitations of conventional participatory research methodologies, heavily dependent on human intermediaries and constrained by resource availability, have historically impeded the scale and effectiveness of development initiatives (Göpferich and Jääskeläinen, 2009). These constraints are particularly evident in regions characterized by complex linguistic landscapes and limited technological infrastructure (Magueresse et al., 2020; Nekoto et al., 2020). However, recent advances in LLM architectures, particularly in few-shot learning and cross-lingual transfer capabilities, offer promising solutions to these longstanding challenges (Raiaan et al., 2024; Wu et al., 2023).

The integration of LLM-based systems into participatory research frameworks raises fundamental questions about the nature of community engagement and knowledge democratization (Hadi et al., 2024; Diab Idris et al., 2024). While these technologies offer powerful tools for bridging linguistic and cultural divides, their deployment must be carefully orchestrated to enhance rather than diminish the participatory nature of development research (Rane et al., 2023; Kovač et al., 2024). This necessitates a nuanced approach that balances technological capabilities with ethical considerations and community agency (Sabarirajan et al., 2024; Ray, 2023).

In this paper, we introduces and tested a novel framework (Fig.1) for leveraging LLM-based multi-agent systems in participatory development research, drawing from empirical evidence in Sri

Proceedings of the First Workshop on Natural Language Processing for Indo-Aryan and Dravidian Languages (IndoNLP2025), pages 108–121
January 20, 2025. ©2025 Association for Computational Linguistics

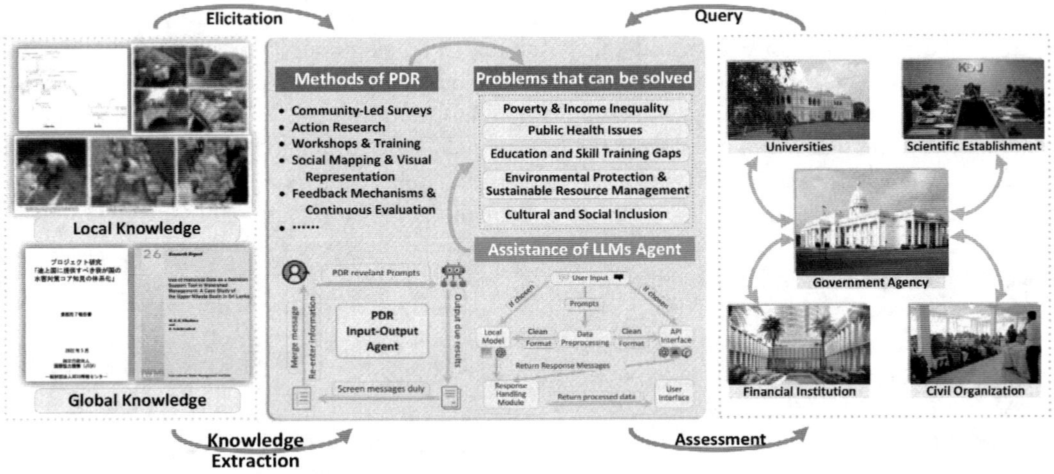

Figure 1: Proposed LLM4Participatory Research Framework

Lanka's Sinhala-speaking communities (Hashmi et al., 2024; Urwin et al., 2023). Our approach moves beyond simple technological integration to address fundamental questions of community empowerment and knowledge production in Global South contexts (Pfeffer et al., 2013). The urgency of this work is underscored by the increasing complexity of development challenges and the growing need for scalable, culturally sensitive research methodologies (van Rensburg and van der Westhuizen, 2024; Awad et al., 2016). Through critical analysis of both opportunities and challenges, we demonstrate how thoughtfully deployed NLP technologies can enhance human capabilities in development research, potentially leading to more inclusive and impactful outcomes (Ferdaus et al., 2024). Our framework provides a structured approach for implementing LLM-based multi-agent systems while maintaining core principles of participatory research, offering insights for researchers, practitioners, and policymakers working at the intersection of technology and development. We argue that these technologies, when thoughtfully deployed, can enhance rather than replace human capabilities in development research, potentially leading to more inclusive, efficient, and impactful research outcomes.

2 Why South Asia Needs This Now

South Asia stands at a nexus where rapid digitalization meets deeply ingrained linguistic and cultural heterogeneity, presenting formidable challenges but also unparalleled opportunities for participatory research (Rahman, 2024). Growing smartphone penetration, expanding internet infrastructures, and the proliferation of digital platforms have catalyzed a democratization of information (Deichmann et al., 2016). Rural communities, previously marginalized due to limited access to communication channels, now experience annual digital literacy growth rates surpassing traditional benchmarks (Kass-Hanna et al., 2022). Despite these advances, the region's linguistic complexity—home to over 650 languages—remains an enduring obstacle to effective data collection, community engagement, and knowledge co-creation (Hutson et al., 2024). The pervasive phenomenon of code-mixing, where speakers fluidly alternate between languages and dialects, further complicates meaning extraction and translation (Rodríguez Tembrás, 2024). Traditional research paradigms and even earlier-generation NLP tools struggle to handle these intricacies, leading to communication bottlenecks, inflated research costs, and a marginalization of essential local voices (Daramola et al., 2024; Björk Brämberg and Dahlberg, 2013).

Emerging LLMs and advanced NLP architectures, however, offer a pathway to transcend these limitations. State-of-the-art models, when fine-tuned and adapted through few-shot and transfer learning approaches, can now handle morphologically complex languages and capture semantic subtleties even under severe training data constraints (Tomec and Gričar, 2024; Parovic, 2024). These technological capabilities enable more equitable, scalable, and culturally sensitive research methods that respect local communication patterns and linguistic realities. Crucially, these tools do not merely solve technical challenges; they reshape the participatory research paradigm. By facilitating real-time, multilingual engagement and generating culturally resonant research activities, LLM-based systems empower communities to more actively co-produce knowledge (Kar et al., 2024), while substantially cutting resource overheads. Beyond operational efficiency, this signifies a fundamental shift toward recognizing community agency, acknowledging indigenous knowledge systems, and enhancing the overall authenticity and credibility of development research (Brown, 2024; Dutta et al., 2024). This enhanced research environment supports more sustainable interventions. Researchers can allocate fewer resources to language mediation and more to iterative engagement cycles, iterative validation, and capacity building. The outcome is a more inclusive, trusting, and impactful participatory ecosystem, where community voices shape the research agenda, and shared knowledge guides more relevant and equitable development strategies (Ullah et al., 2024; Matras et al., 2023).

3 Proposed LLM4Participatory Research Framework

Our LLM4Participatory Research Framework is designed as a modular, multi-agent ecosystem that integrates LLMs with multimodal AI capabilities to address the multifaceted challenges of participatory research in linguistically diverse settings. Each agent type is specialized for a distinct function, yet all collaborate seamlessly through well-defined interaction protocols, shared data ontologies, and unified prompt engineering guidelines. Agent interactions are orchestrated using standardized APIs, message passing interfaces, and carefully designed prompt templates, ensuring that the cognitive pipeline remains flexible, transparent, and adaptable.

3.1 Core Components

Participatory Research Design and Analytics Agents (PRDAA): These agents guide the research methodology from inception to continuous refinement. They employ LLM-driven prompt engineering to generate and adapt research instruments (e.g., surveys, interview guides) informed by precurated cultural knowledge repositories. During pre-field pilot studies, PRDAAs utilize reinforcement learning-based feedback loops to iteratively refine instruments. For instance, the prompts used may define constraints such as "Generate three culturally relevant survey questions about water usage practices, each incorporating code-mixed Sinhala-English phrases." The agents then analyze responses and community feedback, calibrating lexical and thematic complexity to ensure that instruments are both linguistically accessible and culturally resonant (Rane et al., 2024; Agathos et al., 2024).

Figure 2: LLM-agent-empowered real-time summary and translation during a participatory workshop.

Socio-Semantic Mediation Agents (SSMA): SSMAs specialize in real-time, code-mixed translation, interpretation, and semantic alignment. They combine transformer-based multilingual LLMs with domain adaptation layers and specialized tokenization schemes to handle code-mixing. The underlying algorithms utilize attention-based context retrieval and fine-grained subword embeddings for Indo-Aryan and Dravidian language families. This enables them to preserve semantic nuance across languages, dialects, and honorific forms (Mohamed et al., 2024; Sitaram et al., 2020). By continuously updating a cultural knowledge graph, SSMAs ensure fidelity to local ontologies, social hierarchies, and linguistic registers. For instance, when encountering an unexpected code-mixed utterance, the SSMA applies a disambiguation sub-module that uses few-shot prompt examples to infer the correct semantic interpretation before generating a coherent translation or summary (Dowlagar and Mamidi, 2023; Ye, 2024).

Ethnographic Intelligence Agents (EIA): EIAs integrate LLM-based natural language understanding with multimodal feature extraction to capture the richness of ethnographic data. Beyond handling textual inputs, EIAs incorporate audio and visual signals—such as speaker intonation and gesture cues—through multimodal transformers. By aligning textual embeddings with non-verbal cues and contextual metadata, these agents can infer deeper cultural subtexts. Algorithmically, EIAs utilize contrastive learning methods to align representations of linguistic and non-linguistic signals, ensuring that the ethnographic narrative remains coherent and contextually faithful (Yang, 2024; Sadia et al., 2024; Lee et al., 2024).

Community Engagement Orchestration Agents (CEOA): CEOAs manage the ethical and relational dimensions of the research. These agents are configured with ethical protocols, informed consent modules, and data sovereignty guidelines. Their internal logic includes rule-based inference systems that ensure compliance with community-established protocols. For example, CEOAs generate prompts to clarify participant consent forms in code-mixed language or to guide researchers through culturally sensitive topics. They also track and document interactions in a transparent ledger, providing stakeholders with an audit trail of engagement activities (Ninan et al., 2024; Chow and Li, 2024; Guo et al., 2023).

3.2 Integration into Participatory Methods

The integration of our LLM-driven multi-agent framework into participatory research methodologies extends far beyond basic translation or transcription. It is a holistic, context-aware process designed to meaningfully elevate the entire lifecycle of community engagement—from the earliest moments of instrument design to the final phases of data validation and policy recommendation. The guiding principle is that each agent type, while technically distinct, continuously aligns its operational parameters with the evolving socio-cultural and linguistic contours of the communities involved(Fig. 8).

To illustrate this integration, consider the workflow of a community workshop aimed at flood risk assessment in a code-mixed linguistic environment. Initially, the Participatory Research Design and Analytics Agents (PRDAAs) are responsible for selecting and tailoring research instruments—such as surveys or focus group outlines—using prompt-based generation methods that incorporate cultural knowledge repositories and previously annotated corpora. These instruments are not static; rather, they are refined in an iterative manner. For instance, PRDAAs initially produce a series of candidate questions in Sinhala-English code-mixed format, balancing linguistic accessibility with domain specificity. The questions are then tested against synthetic corpora representing likely participant responses. In this simulation step, Socio-Semantic Mediation Agents (SSMAs) perform detailed code-mixed translation and semantic alignment checks, ensuring that the initial prompts and questions maintain fidelity to cultural nuances and do not inadvertently skew participant interpretations.

Once the research instruments have passed preliminary tests, they move into the field setting. During live surveys and interviews, PRDAAs dynamically adjust question complexity and phrasing in response to real-time cues from both human researchers and Ethnographic Intelligence Agents (EIAs). If local participants exhibit confusion, fatigue, or hesitation—signaled by vocal intonation changes or subtle body language cues captured and interpreted by EIAs—PRDAAs issue refined prompt directives to SSMAs. The SSMAs then generate alternative phrasings or linguistic simplifications, ensuring that each question remains culturally resonant and accessible, without sacrificing the analytic integrity of the instrument. This tight feedback loop can occur multiple times within a single interaction, allowing the conversation to flow naturally and responsively, much like a skilled human facilitator adept at shifting linguistic registers or explanatory strategies.

Workshops and participatory group activities benefit similarly. Community Engagement Orchestration Agents (CEOA) integrate data from PRDAAs, SSMAs, and EIAs to propose culturally relevant engagement scripts. For example, if a workshop involves participatory mapping of flood hotspots, CEOAs might recommend starting with a culturally familiar narrative—such as local flood folklore or historical memory—before transitioning to spatial data collection. While participants discuss their lived experiences, EIAs track non-verbal signals indicating trust or discomfort, and SSMAs ensure that key cultural metaphors and idioms are faithfully preserved in translations and summaries. This coordination embodies a level of anthropologically informed sensitivity: it respects complex social hierarchies, local linguistic honorifics, and the dynamics of multi-generational knowledge transmission, all while operating under strict ethical guidelines that CEOAs enforce and document. The integration protocol also includes a set of formal interaction rules and metadata annotations. Each agent's output is enriched with contextual tags, which guide subsequent agent operations. These annotations form a semantic layer that human researchers can later review, providing transparency into the decision-making processes of the agents and enabling critical reflection on whether certain prompts, translations, or adjustments influenced participant responses in unintended ways.

3.3 LLM-Agents-Driven Research Workflow

The workflow orchestrated by our multi-agent system unfolds through a series of interlinked phases designed to ensure continuous adaptation, rigorous quality control, and meaningful involvement of local communities. Each phase leverages the strengths of different agent types, while also maintaining pathways for human oversight, ethical review, and methodological triangulation. The goal is a research pipeline that not only collects data efficiently but also enriches the quality, interpretability, and legitimacy of that data in the eyes of both communities and external stakeholders.

Pre-Field Preparation and Instrumentation: Before stepping into the field, the workflow begins with an extensive pre-field instrumentation phase. Here, PRDAAs generate initial drafts of research instruments—surveys, semi-structured interview guides, and community workshop outlines—based on project goals and available cultural-linguistic corpora. These initial drafts are subjected to synthetic test scenarios: code-mixed test cases are fed into SSMAs to benchmark translation accuracy and contextual fidelity, while EIAs simulate multimodal inputs (e.g., hypothetical speaker intonations, gesture-based cues) to assess whether the proposed prompts can handle complex ethnographic scenarios. Iterations are performed until a baseline set of instruments meets quality thresholds defined by the research team, including metrics for linguistic clarity, semantic accuracy, and cultural appropriateness.

Adaptive Field Deployment: With baseline instruments in hand, the team moves into the field. Surveys, interviews, and workshops commence, guided by the prepared materials but never locked into them. As participants respond, SSMAs deploy on-the-fly translation and code-switching adjustments. If a participant uses a regional idiom not encountered in pre-field training data, SSMAs rely on few-shot prompt adaptation techniques, referencing similar linguistic patterns to generate accurate, context-aware interpretations. Concurrently, EIAs capture non-verbal signals—such as prolonged pauses, changes in vocal pitch, or restless body language—to produce ethnographic annotations. These annotations are fed back into PRDAAs, which may trigger immediate modifications to the research instrument. For instance, if participants appear disengaged, PRDAAs may instruct SSMAs to simplify the phrasing or incorporate culturally salient metaphors to re-engage the community's interest.

Ethical Monitoring and Protocol Enforcement: During these field interactions, CEOAs maintain a real-time ethical interaction ledger. This ledger logs every adaptation request, every change in linguistic register, and every potential breach of community protocols. Should a line of questioning veer into sensitive territory—such as local religious traditions or gender-related norms—CEOAs issue alerts prompting the research team to reconsider the approach. If participants request anonymity or display discomfort with certain data-collection practices, CEOAs dynamically adapt the informed consent modules and ensure that new protocols are communicated in accessible, code-mixed language.

Multilingual Thematic Analysis and Iterative Refinement: After field data is collected, it passes through a multilingual thematic analysis pipeline.

PRDAAs and EIAs collaborate to identify recurring narratives, power hierarchies, and cultural themes that emerge from the data. By leveraging transformer-based topic modeling and clustering methods fine-tuned for code-mixed input, the agents reveal patterns that might be missed by single-language or monomodal approaches. This phase also includes a human-in-the-loop feedback cycle, where researchers and local experts evaluate the thematic outputs. Feedback is translated into updated prompt templates and agent-specific instructions. If local stakeholders indicate that a certain theme has been misinterpreted—perhaps a traditional narrative was wrongly associated with risk aversion instead of historical resilience—agents adjust their semantic weighting and cultural context embeddings.

Iterative Learning and Continuous Improvement: Rather than terminating after a single cycle of data collection and analysis, the workflow encourages continuous learning. New linguistic patterns, emergent cultural idioms, and shifting community priorities feed back into the system. PRDAAs update their instrument-generation models, SSMAs refine their code-switch adaptation strategies, EIAs improve their multimodal understanding, and CEOAs integrate revised ethical guidelines or local governance structures. Over time, the system becomes more attuned to community-specific realities, and its outputs become increasingly reliable, nuanced, and aligned with local perspectives.

4 Implementation in Field Work and Insights

As is shown in Fig.3 and Appendix.A, to test the feasibility of this novel system, we implemented it in our field research, which focused on enhancing the Early Warning Systems (EWS) for flood management in the Nilwala River Basin, a region prone to recurrent flooding with devastating socio-economic impacts in Sri Lanka. Sri Lanka's linguistic landscape is emblematic of South Asia's broader linguistic diversity, characterized by the prevalence of code-mixing and multilingual communication (Mandavilli, 2020). Sinhala, an Indo-Aryan language with agglutinative features and a rich system of honorifics, often intertwines with English and other local dialects in everyday discourse, which poses significant challenges for NLP, as it involves syntactic, lexical, and semantic blending that traditional language models struggle to interpret accurately. The objective was to employ the proposed system to facilitate participatory development research methods—including surveys, structured and semi-structured interviews, workshops, and other interactive engagements—with stakeholders ranging from national agencies to local communities.

4.1 Practical Experiences and Outcomes

The implementation faced several challenges, particularly in adapting the LLMs to handle Sinhala-specific linguistic features and the pervasive code-mixing in communication. The scarcity of high-quality, annotated Sinhala corpora necessitated innovative approaches, including active learning techniques and data augmentation strategies to enhance the model's proficiency(Jagosh et al., 2012).

One significant achievement was the development of a hybrid translation approach that combined statistical and neural methods, achieving a 35% improvement in translation accuracy for domain-specific terminology compared to standard multilingual models, which was critical for accurately interpreting participants' responses during interviews and ensuring that subtle nuances were not lost in translation. During workshops, they assisted in designing interactive activities that resonated with local customs and facilitated real-time feedback collection. In surveys and interviews, the agents helped generate culturally appropriate questions and dynamically adjusted to participants' inputs, enhancing the depth and authenticity of the data collected. The agents also played a crucial role in the analysis phase. They enabled cross-linguistic comparisons and facilitated the synthesis of complex data into actionable insights (Cemoge et al., 2024). For instance, they helped identify communication bottlenecks between agencies involved in the EWS, revealing that outdated communication methods and bureaucratic procedures were significant barriers to effective disaster management.

4.2 Lessons Learned and Recommendations

Community Involvement is Crucial: Active participation of local stakeholders in the development and refinement of the system was essential. Their input ensured that the agents were culturally attuned and responsive to the community's needs, enhancing acceptance and effectiveness.

Flexible Adaptation Mechanisms are Necessary: The linguistic diversity and code-mixing practices required the agents to be highly adaptable.

Figure 3: Participatory Field Research with LLM-agent-assisted tools. (Source: Authors' fieldwork)

Implementing mechanisms for continuous learning and real-time adjustment was critical for handling linguistic variations and unexpected inputs.

Human Oversight Remains Indispensable: While the agents significantly enhanced efficiency and depth, human researchers played a vital role in overseeing the process, interpreting nuanced cultural contexts, and making ethical judgments.

Addressing Technical Challenges: Overcoming the scarcity of linguistic resources demanded innovative technical solutions. Investing in the development of annotated corpora and leveraging transfer learning were effective strategies for enhancing model performance.

4.3 Implementation Considerations for Broader Deployment

The Nilwala River Basin deployment illustrates a scalable and domain-agnostic framework. To adapt it for other South Asian languages and contexts, the modular architecture allows integrating new code-mixing tokenizers, cultural knowledge bases, or domain-specific LLM fine-tunings (Finkel et al., 2022).

Technical Infrastructure: Resource-poor settings demand efficient model architectures. Lightweight LLMs combined with on-device preprocessing, federated learning, and quantization can mitigate latency and connectivity issues (Qu et al., 2024).

Data Security and Privacy: Incorporating end-to-end encryption and federated learning ensures sensitive community data remains local while still contributing to the global improvement of model quality. CEOAs enforce data usage policies, ensuring that outputs are ethically and legally compliant.

Ethical and Cultural Considerations: The framework's prompt design explicitly encodes ethical guidelines. CEOAs monitor compliance in real-time, and any deviation triggers a review workflow. Building and maintaining culturally informed knowledge graphs ensures the models reflect community values rather than imposing external biases (Suppadungsuk et al., 2023).

Capacity Building and Institutional Support: Sustained success requires local training programs and policy engagement. By equipping researchers and stakeholders with the skills to interpret, customize, and govern these systems, we foster long-term sustainability and local empowerment. Collaborations with NGOs, government agencies, and academic institutions can institutionalize best practices, streamline resource allocation, and formalize quality assurance standards.

5 Discussion and Future Agenda

The integration of LLM-based multi-agent systems into participatory development research reconfigures the conceptual space at the intersection of technology, community engagement, and anthropological inquiry (Xu et al., 2024). Far from being a mere technical enhancement, this approach prompts us to re-evaluate foundational assumptions about the production, circulation, and legitimation of knowledge in socio-culturally complex contexts. In traditional participatory frameworks, human facilitators, local knowledge brokers, and community spokespersons navigate the intricacies of language, power asymmetries, and cultural semiotics. Our LLM-driven architecture extends this negotiation field, distributing interpretive authority and methodological agency across human and non-human actors. This shift demands that we refine our criteria for epistemic robustness and ethical accountability. By introducing adaptive prompts, multimodal interpretation layers, and code-mixed language models, the research process becomes more dialogic and reflexive, simultaneously more scalable and less deterministic. While existing literature in participatory development and linguistic anthropology has long emphasized the importance of local involvement (Penuel et al., 2020), the emergence of LLM-based agents compels a reconsideration of whose voices are amplified, how biases are mitigated, and under what conditions community knowledge is validated. Methodological rigor thus transcends traditional validation protocols, calling for new evaluative paradigms where model outputs must be continually negotiated, contested, and contextualized by community stakeholders.

These technological trajectories also invoke philosophical questions about the essence of community agency and the nature of equitable development. In harnessing LLMs to broker dialogues between disparate linguistic and cultural systems, we challenge the modernist assumption that technology is a neutral mediator. Instead, AI becomes an evolving participant in a dense socio-technical network—one that can enrich cultural representation, but also requires vigilant governance to prevent the re-inscription of power imbalances. Future research must thus address the deeper normative concerns: how can we ensure that AI-enabled participatory practices bolster rather than diminish local epistemologies and life-worlds? How do we integrate metrics of cultural resilience, trust-building, and vernacular knowledge sustainability into development assessments (Falcone, 2023)? In charting this future agenda, interdisciplinary collaboration is paramount. Technologists, anthropologists, linguists, and development practitioners must co-design systems that are both contextually resonant and theoretically informed. The promise of these LLM-based frameworks lies not simply in improved data collection or analytical sophistication, but in ushering in a more philosophically coherent paradigm of research—one that values uncertainty, pluralism, and continuous ethical reflection as integral components of knowledge production.

6 Conclusion

The introduction of LLM-based multi-agent architectures into participatory research settings in South Asia signals a profound transformation, offering new avenues for bridging linguistic divides and socio-cultural complexities without reducing communities to passive data sources. Rather than replacing traditional methods, these technologies complement and extend established participatory principles: human facilitators remain indispensable ethical and interpretive anchors, while LLM-based agents broaden the scope, adaptability, and depth of engagements. The real significance of this paradigm lies in how it reconfigures the relational field of development research. By treating language models as interlocutors that adapt to local idioms, cultural protocols, and conceptual frames, the process moves closer to what humanistic inquiry has always sought: a genuine dialogic co-production of meaning. This approach transcends conventional efficiency metrics, orienting research toward a deeper, ethically engaged form of knowledge-making.

The path forward necessitates sustained reflection and critical praxis. Cross-sectoral alliances and supportive institutional frameworks are required to ensure that technology-enhanced participatory models do not inadvertently replicate existing inequalities or impose external epistemologies. Ultimately, the convergence of advanced NLP, anthropological rigor, and participatory ethos challenges the prevailing boundaries of development research. It opens the door to an epistemically plural and ethically attentive mode of inquiry, one that holds promise for more inclusive, contextually authentic, and transformative engagements with communities worldwide.

References

Leonidas Agathos, Andreas Avgoustis, Xristiana Kryelesi, Aikaterini Makridou, Ilias Tzanis, Despoina Mouratidis, Katia Lida Kermanidis, and Andreas Kanavos. 2024. Bridging linguistic gaps: Developing a greek text simplification dataset. *Information*, 15(8):500.

Germine H Awad, Erika A Patall, Kadie R Rackley, and Erin D Reilly. 2016. Recommendations for culturally sensitive research methods. *Journal of Educational and Psychological Consultation*, 26(3):283–303.

Elisabeth Björk Brämberg and Karin Dahlberg. 2013. Interpreters in cross-cultural interviews: a three-way coconstruction of data. *Qualitative health research*, 23(2):241–247.

Nik Bear Brown. 2024. Enhancing trust in llms: Algorithms for comparing and interpreting llms.

Tapumih Cemoge, Alexei Ivanov, and Isaiah Moreno. 2024. A two-stage fine-tuning approach for democratizing multilingual large language models in automated literature review tasks.

James CL Chow and Kay Li. 2024. Ethical considerations in human-centered ai: Advancing oncology chatbots through large language models. *JMIR Bioinformatics and Biotechnology*, 5:e64406.

Gideon Oluseyi Daramola, Adetomi Adewumi, Boma Sonimiteim Jacks, and Olakunle Abayomi Ajala. 2024. Navigating complexities: a review of communication barriers in multinational energy projects. *International Journal of Applied Research in Social Sciences*, 6(4):685–697.

Uwe Deichmann, Aparajita Goyal, and Deepak Mishra. 2016. Will digital technologies transform agriculture in developing countries? *Agricultural Economics*, 47(S1):21–33.

Mohamed Diab Idris, Xiaohua Feng, and Vladimir Dyo. 2024. Revolutionizing higher education: Unleashing the potential of large language models for strategic transformation. *IEEE Access*, 12:67738–67757.

Suman Dowlagar and Radhika Mamidi. 2023. A code-mixed task-oriented dialog dataset for medical domain. *Computer Speech & Language*, 78:101449.

Manaswita Dutta, Tina MD Mello, Yesi Cheng, Niladri Sekhar Dash, Ranita Nandi, Aparna Dutt, and Arpita Bose. 2024. Universal and language-specific connected speech characteristics of bilingual speakers with alzheimer's disease: Insights from case studies of structurally distinct languages. *Journal of Speech, Language, and Hearing Research*, 67(4):1143–1164.

Pasquale Marcello Falcone. 2023. Sustainable energy policies in developing countries: a review of challenges and opportunities. *Energies*, 16(18):6682.

Md Meftahul Ferdaus, Mahdi Abdelguerfi, Elias Ioup, Kendall N. Niles, Ken Pathak, and Steven Sloan. 2024. Towards trustworthy ai: A review of ethical and robust large language models.

Raphael Finkel, Daniel Kaufman, and Ahmed Shamim. 2022. Analyzing code-mixing in linguistic corpora using kratylos. *J. Comput. Cult. Herit.*, 15(1).

Susanne Göpferich and Riitta Jääskeläinen. 2009. Process research into the development of translation competence: Where are we, and where do we need to go? *Across languages and cultures*, 10(2):169–191.

Zishan Guo, Renren Jin, Chuang Liu, Yufei Huang, Dan Shi, Supryadi, Linhao Yu, Yan Liu, Jiaxuan Li, Bojian Xiong, and Deyi Xiong. 2023. Evaluating large language models: A comprehensive survey.

Muhammad Usman Hadi, Qasem Al Tashi, Abbas Shah, Rizwan Qureshi, Amgad Muneer, Muhammad Irfan, Anas Zafar, Muhammad Bilal Shaikh, Naveed Akhtar, Jia Wu, et al. 2024. Large language models: a comprehensive survey of its applications, challenges, limitations, and future prospects. *Authorea Preprints*.

Ehtesham Hashmi, Sule Yildirim Yayilgan, Ibrahim A. Hameed, Muhammad Mudassar Yamin, Mohib Ullah, and Mohamed Abomhara. 2024. Enhancing multilingual hate speech detection: From language-specific insights to cross-linguistic integration. *IEEE Access*, 12:121507–121537.

Mohammad Hassan, Prakash Rai, and Sabin Maharjan. 2023. Empowering south asian agricultural communities: A comprehensive approach to iot-driven agriculture through awareness, training, and collaboration. *Quarterly Journal of Emerging Technologies and Innovations*, 8(3):18–32.

James Hutson, Pace Ellsworth, and Matt Ellsworth. 2024. Preserving linguistic diversity in the digital age: a scalable model for cultural heritage continuity. *Journal of Contemporary Language Research*, 3(1).

Justin Jagosh, Ann C Macaulay, Pierre Pluye, JON Salsberg, Paula L Bush, JIM Henderson, Erin Sirett, Geoff Wong, Margaret Cargo, Carol P Herbert, et al. 2012. Uncovering the benefits of participatory research: implications of a realist review for health research and practice. *The Milbank Quarterly*, 90(2):311–346.

Indrajit Kar, Zonunfeli Ralte, Maheshakumara Shivakumara, Rana Roy, and Arti Kumari. 2024. Agents are all you need: Elevating trading dynamics with advanced generative ai-driven conversational llm agents and tools. In *2024 IEEE 9th International Conference for Convergence in Technology (I2CT)*, pages 1–6. IEEE.

Josephine Kass-Hanna, Angela C Lyons, and Fan Liu. 2022. Building financial resilience through financial and digital literacy in south asia and sub-saharan africa. *Emerging Markets Review*, 51:100846.

Grgur Kovač, Rémy Portelas, Peter Ford Dominey, and Pierre-Yves Oudeyer. 2024. The socialai school: a framework leveraging developmental psychology toward artificial socio-cultural agents. *Frontiers in Neurorobotics*, 18:1396359.

Nir Kshetri. 2024. Linguistic challenges in generative artificial intelligence: Implications for low-resource languages in the developing world.

Sangmin Lee, Minzhi Li, Bolin Lai, Wenqi Jia, Fiona Ryan, Xu Cao, Ozgur Kara, Bikram Boote, Weiyan Shi, Diyi Yang, and James M. Rehg. 2024. Towards social ai: A survey on understanding social interactions.

Alexandre Magueresse, Vincent Carles, and Evan Heetderks. 2020. Low-resource languages: A review of past work and future challenges.

Sujay Rao Mandavilli. 2020. Towards a comprehensive compendium of factors impacting language dynamics in post-globalized scenarios: Presenting principles, paradigms and frameworks for use in the emerging science of language dynamics. *ELK Asia Pacific Journal of Social Sciences*, 6(3).

Yaron Matras, Rebecca Tipton, and Leonie Gaiser. 2023. Agency and multilingualism in public health care: how practitioners draw on local experiences and encounters. In *Understanding the Dynamics of Language and Multilingualism in Professional Contexts*, pages 46–60. Edward Elgar Publishing.

Yasir Abdelgadir Mohamed, Akbar Khanan, Mohamed Bashir, Abdul Hakim H. M. Mohamed, Mousab A. E. Adiel, and Muawia A. Elsadig. 2024. The impact of artificial intelligence on language translation: A review. *IEEE Access*, 12:25553–25579.

Wilhelmina Nekoto, Vukosi Marivate, Tshinondiwa Matsila, Timi Fasubaa, Tajudeen Kolawole, Taiwo Fagbohungbe, Solomon Oluwole Akinola, Shamsuddeen Hassan Muhammad, Salomon Kabongo, Salomey Osei, Sackey Freshia, Rubungo Andre Niyongabo, Ricky Macharm, Perez Ogayo, Orevaoghene Ahia, Musie Meressa, Mofe Adeyemi, Masabata Mokgesi-Selinga, Lawrence Okegbemi, Laura Jane Martinus, Kolawole Tajudeen, Kevin Degila, Kelechi Ogueji, Kathleen Siminyu, Julia Kreutzer, Jason Webster, Jamiil Toure Ali, Jade Abbott, Iroro Orife, Ignatius Ezeani, Idris Abdulkabir Dangana, Herman Kamper, Hady Elsahar, Goodness Duru, Ghollah Kioko, Espoir Murhabazi, Elan van Biljon, Daniel Whitenack, Christopher Onyefuluchi, Chris Emezue, Bonaventure Dossou, Blessing Sibanda, Blessing Itoro Bassey, Ayodele Olabiyi, Arshath Ramkilowan, Alp Öktem, Adewale Akinfaderin, and Abdallah Bashir. 2020. Participatory research for low-resourced machine translation: A case study in african languages.

Johan Ninan, Stewart Clegg, Ashwin Mahalingam, and Shankar Sankaran. 2024. Governance through trust: Community engagement in an australian city rebuilding precinct. *Project Management Journal*, 55(1):16–30.

Marinela Parovic. 2024. *Improving Parameter-Efficient Cross-Lingual Transfer for Low-Resource Languages*. Ph.D. thesis.

William R Penuel, Robbin Riedy, Michael S Barber, Donald J Peurach, Whitney A LeBouef, and Tiffany Clark. 2020. Principles of collaborative education research with stakeholders: Toward requirements for a new research and development infrastructure. *Review of Educational Research*, 90(5):627–674.

Karin Pfeffer, Isa Baud, Eric Denis, Dianne Scott, and John Sydenstricker-Neto. 2013. Participatory spatial knowledge management tools: empowerment and upscaling or exclusion? *Information, Communication & Society*, 16(2):258–285.

Guanqiao Qu, Qiyuan Chen, Wei Wei, Zheng Lin, Xianhao Chen, and Kaibin Huang. 2024. Mobile edge intelligence for large language models: A contemporary survey.

Qazi Arka Rahman. 2024. Reconceptualizing south asia: Bangladeshi literature and the politics of representation.

Mohaimenul Azam Khan Raiaan, Md. Saddam Hossain Mukta, Kaniz Fatema, Nur Mohammad Fahad, Sadman Sakib, Most Marufatul Jannat Mim, Jubaer Ahmad, Mohammed Eunus Ali, and Sami Azam. 2024. A review on large language models: Architectures, applications, taxonomies, open issues and challenges. *IEEE Access*, 12:26839–26874.

Nitin Liladhar Rane, Mallikarjuna Paramesha, Saurabh P Choudhary, and Jayesh Rane. 2024. Artificial intelligence, machine learning, and deep learning for advanced business strategies: a review. *Partners Universal International Innovation Journal*, 2(3):147–171.

Nitin Liladhar Rane, Abhijeet Tawde, Saurabh P Choudhary, and Jayesh Rane. 2023. Contribution and performance of chatgpt and other large language models (llm) for scientific and research advancements: a double-edged sword. *International Research Journal of Modernization in Engineering Technology and Science*, 5(10):875–899.

Partha Pratim Ray. 2023. Chatgpt: A comprehensive review on background, applications, key challenges, bias, ethics, limitations and future scope. *Internet of Things and Cyber-Physical Systems*, 3:121–154.

John Roberts, Max Baker, and Jane Andrew. 2024. Artificial intelligence and qualitative research: The promise and perils of large language model (llm)'assistance'. *Critical Perspectives on Accounting*, 99:102722.

Vanesa Rodríguez Tembrás. 2024. *Code-Switching in Bilingual Medical Consultations (Galician-Spanish)*. Ph.D. thesis.

A Sabarirajan, Latha Thamma Reddi, Sandeep Rangineni, R Regin, S Suman Rajest, and P Paramasivan. 2024. Leveraging mis technologies for preserving india's cultural heritage on digitization, accessibility, and sustainability. In *Data-Driven Intelligent Business Sustainability*, pages 122–135. IGI Global.

Bareera Sadia, Farah Adeeba, Sana Shams, and Kashif Javed. 2024. Meeting the challenge: A benchmark corpus for automated urdu meeting summarization. *Information Processing & Management*, 61(4):103734.

Sunayana Sitaram, Khyathi Raghavi Chandu, Sai Krishna Rallabandi, and Alan W Black. 2020. A survey of code-switched speech and language processing.

Hedvig Skirgård, Hannah J Haynie, Damián E Blasi, Harald Hammarström, Jeremy Collins, Jay J Latarche, Jakob Lesage, Tobias Weber, Alena Witzlack-Makarevich, Sam Passmore, et al. 2023. Grambank reveals the importance of genealogical constraints on linguistic diversity and highlights the impact of language loss. *Science Advances*, 9(16):eadg6175.

S Suppadungsuk, C Thongprayoon, J Miao, S Tangpanithandee, I Craici, W Cheungpasitporn, et al. 2023. Ethical implications of chatbot utilization in nephrology. *Journal of Personalized Medicine*, 13(9).

Tina Tomec and Sergej Gričar. 2024. Risk language barriers in a globalized world: insights from female managers from slovenia. *Strategic Management-International Journal of Strategic Management and Decision Support Systems in Strategic Management*, 29(2).

Ehsan Ullah, Anil Parwani, Mirza Mansoor Baig, and Rajendra Singh. 2024. Challenges and barriers of using large language models (llm) such as chatgpt for diagnostic medicine with a focus on digital pathology–a recent scoping review. *Diagnostic pathology*, 19(1):43.

Eliza Urwin, Aisalkyn Botoeva, Rosario Arias, Oscar Vargas, and Pamina Firchow. 2023. Flipping the power dynamics in measurement and evaluation: International aid and the potential for a grounded accountability model. *Negotiation Journal*, 39(4):401–426.

Zander Janse van Rensburg and Sonja van der Westhuizen. 2024. Ethical ai integration in academia: Developing a literacy-driven framework for llms in south african higher education. In *AI Approaches to Literacy in Higher Education*, pages 23–48. IGI Global.

Qingyun Wu, Gagan Bansal, Jieyu Zhang, Yiran Wu, Beibin Li, Erkang Zhu, Li Jiang, Xiaoyun Zhang, Shaokun Zhang, Jiale Liu, Ahmed Hassan Awadallah, Ryen W White, Doug Burger, and Chi Wang. 2023. Autogen: Enabling next-gen llm applications via multi-agent conversation.

Haowen Xu, Jinghui Yuan, Anye Zhou, Guanhao Xu, Wan Li, Xuegang Ban, and Xinyue Ye. 2024. Genai-powered multi-agent paradigm for smart urban mobility: Opportunities and challenges for integrating large language models (llms) and retrieval-augmented generation (rag) with intelligent transportation systems.

Qian Yang. 2024. *Scottish-Chinese students' language use in Chinese complementary school classroom: a translanguaging perspective*. Ph.D. thesis, University of Glasgow.

Zixi Ye. 2024. Language barriers in intercultural communication and their translation strategies. In *International Conference on Finance and Economics*, volume 6.

A Authors' Field Works Assisted by LLM agents system

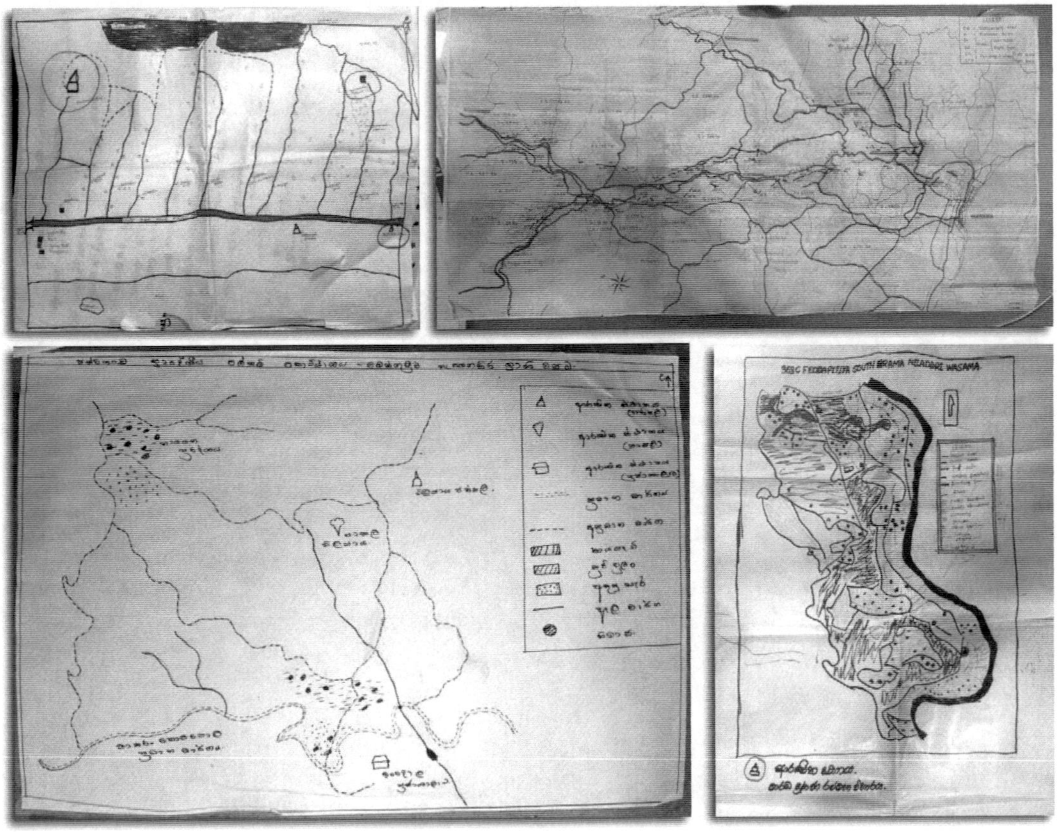

Figure 4: Collected participatory workshop results.

Figure 5: Participatory interview with local DMC (Disaster Management Centre)

Figure 6: Flood sites in Nilwala River Basin Area

Figure 7: Participatory interview with local government office and Hydrology Department

Figure 8: Participatory interview with local Irrigation Department

Identifying Aggression and Offensive Language in Code-Mixed Tweets: A Multi-Task Transfer Learning Approach

Bharath Kancharla
k_bharath@cs.iitr.ac.in

Prabhjot Singh
prabhjot_s@cs.iitr.ac.in

Lohith Bhagavan Kancharla
k_lbhagavan@cs.iitr.ac.in

Yashita Chama
c_yashita@cs.iitr.ac.in

Raksha Sharma
raksha.sharma@cs.iitr.ac.in

Abstract

The widespread use of social media has contributed to the increase in hate speech and offensive language, impacting people of all ages. This issue is particularly difficult to address when the text is in a code-mixed language. Twitter is commonly used to express opinions in code-mixed language. In this paper, we introduce a novel Multi-Task Transfer Learning (MTTL) framework to detect aggression and offensive language. By focusing on the dual facets of cyberbullying, *viz.*, aggressiveness and offensiveness, our model leverages the MTTL approach to enhance the performance of the model on the aggression and offensive language detection. Results show that our Multi-Task Transfer Learning (MTTL) setup significantly enhances the performance of state-of-the-art pretrained language models, *viz.*, BERT, RoBERTa, and Hing-RoBERTa for Hindi-English code-mixed data from Twitter.

1 Introduction

Social media encompasses a variety of internet-based applications that enable people to connect globally and share user-generated content. Platforms like Twitter and Facebook are among the most popular applications on the internet today. However, there has been a significant rise in bullying behavior on these platforms, including snide remarks, abusive language, personal attacks, and even threats of rape and violence, impacting children, individuals, and communities. This situation underscores the need for technological advancements to automatically detect offensive content and create safer environments. Machine learning models, leveraging recent techniques in natural language processing, can be utilized to effectively identify such harmful behaviors.

In countries where English is not the native language, such as India, most social media users communicate using at least two languages, predominantly English and Hindi. These texts are classified as bilingual. In a bilingual context, an entire post may be written in the script of one language while incorporating words from both languages, a phenomenon known as code-mixed (or mixed-code) text.

In this paper, we introduce a pioneering Multi-Task Transfer Learning (MTTL) framework aimed at identifying aggression and offensive language in Hindi-English code-mixed tweets. Our method delves into the correlation between aggression and offensive language. As illustrated in Figure 1, it reveals that offensive language frequently accompanies expressions of aggression, suggesting an inherent connection between the two. We validate our MTTL framework using the dataset provided for the seventh Workshop on Online Abuse and Harms (WOAH) (Nafis et al., 2023). Derived from Twitter, this dataset classifies tweets based on two primary dimensions of cyberbullying: aggressiveness and offensiveness. Each tweet is annotated with the following labels.

- **Aggression** has been defined as any behavior enacted with the intention of harming another person who is motivated to avoid that harm. This label consists of 3 sub classes:
  1. (**OAG**) - overtly aggressive
  2. (**CAG**) - covertly aggressive
  3. (**NAG**) - not-aggressive
- **Offensiveness** has been described as any word or string of words which has or can have a negative impact on the sense of self or well-being of those who encounter it– that is, it makes or can make them feel mildly or extremely discomfited, insulted, hurt or frightened. This label consists of 2 sub classes:
  1. (**OFF**) - offensive
  2. (**NOT**) - not-offensive

Proceedings of the First Workshop on Natural Language Processing for Indo-Aryan and Dravidian Languages (IndoNLP2025), pages 122–128
January 20, 2025. ©2025 Association for Computational Linguistics

- **Codemixed:** this label specifies weather the tweet is codemixed or monolingual.

The **key contributions** of this work are the following:

- We have proposed a novel MTTL framework for aggression and offensive language detection tasks. We deploy state-of-the-art pre-trained language models *viz.*, Hing-RoBERTa (Nayak and Joshi, 2022), BERT (Devlin et al., 2018), RoBERTa (Liu et al., 2019), and XLM-RoBERTa (Conneau et al., 2019) using Multi-Task Transfer Learning (MTTL) with the aim of optimizing the model's performance in detecting aggression and offensive language within the dataset.

- Extensive experiments were conducted on each sub-task independently, using monolingual, code-mixed, and combined texts. The results highlight significant improvements in detecting both tasks with the MTTL approach. Notably, MTTL-Hing-RoBERTa, MTTL-BERT, and MTTL-RoBERTa demonstrate superior performance across various categories, as depicted in the table 2.

The rest of the paper is organized as follows. Section 2 presents the associated literature. Section 4 describes the proposed MTTL approach and associated loss function. Section 3 describes the dataset. Section 5 presents the experimental setup. Section 6 elaborates the results and Section 7 concludes the paper.

2 Related work

Previous research on aggression/hate speech detection has explored various approaches. These include a unified multi-modal deep learning architecture that integrates Deep Pyramid CNN, Pooled BiLSTM, and Disconnected RNN (Khandelwal and Kumar, 2020). Additionally, studies have investigated the utilization of word-level semantic information and sub-word knowledge to counter character-level adversarial attacks (Mou et al., 2020). Another approach involves a Tabnet classifier-based model trained on features extracted by MuRIL from transliterated code-mixed data, which has demonstrated efficacy even with Devanagari text (Chopra et al., 2023). Moreover, techniques such as data balancing using Generative Pretrained Transformer (GPT-2) have been explored due to its contextual understanding and capability for more realistic data generation (Shrivastava et al., 2021).

Recent studies on offensive language detection have explored different machine learning algorithms and n-gram feature sets to identify offensiveness in social media messages (Pathak et al., 2021). Additionally, researchers have combined various multilingual transformer-based embedding models with machine learning classifiers to detect hate speech and offensive language in code-mixed text in Dravidian languages (Sreelakshmi et al., 2024). Furthermore, leveraging LSTM architecture, Zypherand, openchat-3.5, along with prompt engineering and QLoRA, has shown promising potential in addressing the challenges of hate and offensive comment classification (Shaik et al., 2024).

Research on Multi-Task Learning and Transfer Learning has explored various methodologies. These include proposing an unsupervised multi-task learning network that estimates bullying likelihood using a Gaussian Mixture Model (Cheng et al., 2020), utilizing cross-lingual contextual word embeddings and transfer learning for predictions in low-resource languages (Ranasinghe and Zampieri, 2021), enhancing AraBERT with Multi-task learning to effectively learn from limited Arabic data (Djandji et al., 2020), employing Multinomial Naive Bayes for textual data and ResNet50 for pictorial data, and integrating the results from both to identify misogynistic memes (H et al., 2024). Additionally, combining AdapterFusion with language adapters on a multilingual Large Language Model (LLM) has been explored for classifying code-mixed and code-switched social media text (Rathnayake et al., 2024). Moreover, a multi-task model based on the shared-private scheme has been proposed to capture both shared and task-specific features (Kapil and Ekbal, 2020).

In this paper, we also introduce a multi-task transfer learning approach, leveraging the intrinsic relationship between aggression and offensive language.

3 Dataset and Preprocessing

The dataset (Nafis et al., 2023) consists of 10000 tweet IDs, each labeled with offensiveness labels (OFF or NOT) and aggressiveness labels (OAG,CAG,or NAG) in addition with codemixed labels (codemixed or monolingual). We were able to retrieve text from 8281 tweets from the tweet

IDs provided in the dataset,the remaining tweets were most probably deleted. We partitioned this data randomly into an 80% training set, 10% validation set, and 10% evaluation set. Table 1 shows the distribution of the different labels across each data split.

Split	Class	OAG	CAG	NAG	OFF	NOT
Train	Codemixed	757	882	1400	1136	1903
	Monolingual	729	1137	1719	850	2735
	Combined	1486	2019	3119	1986	4638
Validation	Codemixed	83	118	197	142	256
	Monolingual	90	123	217	98	332
	Combined	173	241	414	240	588
Evaluation	Codemixed	93	118	177	140	248
	Monolingual	94	144	203	108	333
	Combined	187	262	380	248	581

Table 1: Dataset distribution

Among the 8281 instances, 4368 instances are labelled as aggressive(OAG + CAG) and 2474 instances are labelled as offensive (OFF). Of the 2474 offensive instances, 2150 overlap with the aggressive instances, as shown in Figure 1. The Venn diagram indicates that generally offensive language is used when people are aggressive(i.e., most of the offensive tweets are aggressive), highlighting a strong relationship between aggression and offensive language in the dataset.

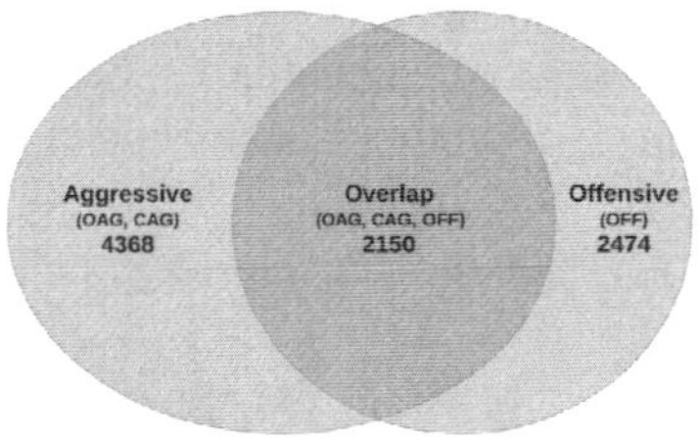

Figure 1: Overlap in aggressive and offensive instances

3.1 Preprocessing

In the preprocessing phase, we masked all the user mentions and retweet mentions with the token '@user' (e.g., `@narendramodi` $\rightarrow$ `@user`) to ensure the model does not learn features based on user-IDs. We further tokenized this data using the tokenizer corresponding to the selected pretrained language model to make sure the input would be compatible with the common layers input. We precisely applied all these preprocessing steps to each experiment conducted for both the sub tasks.

4 Proposed Model

We based our approach on the multi-task model based on the shared-private scheme that captures the shared-features and task-specific features (Kapil and Ekbal, 2020) and leverage the pretrained language models that have achieved a state-of-the-art performance in multiple Hindi-English NLP tasks. Our best model is based on augmenting the pretrained language model with task-specific layers and sharing the knowledge between them through transfer learning to achieve multi-task learning. We chose this approach to explore the relationship between aggressiveness and offensiveness of the text, and the results are more impressive than the models that achieved state-of-the-art performance in detecting aggression and offensive language from the text. [1]

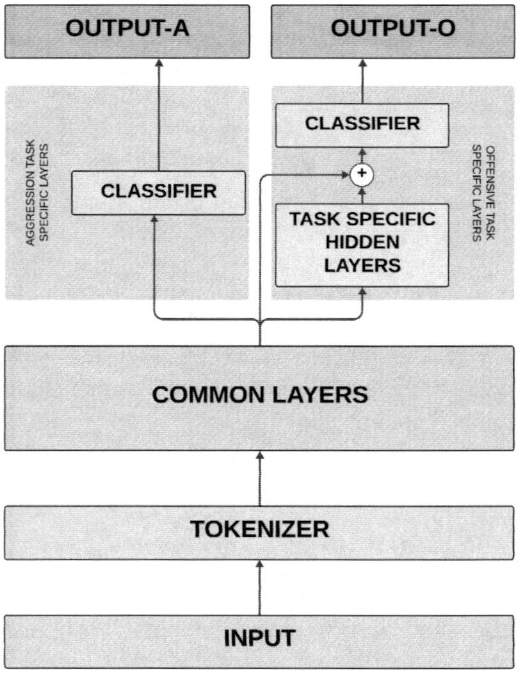

Figure 2: Model architecture

4.1 Multi-Task Transfer Learning (MTTL)

Multi-Task learning (MTL) is an approach in machine learning where a model is trained simultaneously on multiple tasks. By sharing representations between related tasks, the model can often improve performance on individual tasks compared to training separate models for each task. The core

[1] https://github.com/opius005/Aggression-and-Offensive-Language-Detection

idea is that learning to perform multiple related tasks can help a model generalize better because it captures commonalities and differences among the tasks. Transfer Learning (TL) is a technique where a model developed for a particular task is reused as the starting point for a model on a second task. It leverages the knowledge gained while solving one problem and applies it to a different but related problem. The key idea behind Multi-Task Transfer Learning (MTTL) is to combine the ideas of multi-task learning and transfer learning. This approach transfers the knowledge learned from multiple source tasks to improve learning for one or more target tasks. The aim is to leverage the shared information between the tasks to enhance the learning efficiency and performance of the target tasks. In our case, we have two sub-tasks, Aggressiveness and Offensiveness of the text; we employ the MTTL approach to augment the pretrained language model such that it can learn both tasks simultaneously, and we mainly focus on optimizing the performance of the model on both tasks by sharing the task-specific knowledge. Our MTTL model architecture consists of two components, as can be seen in Figure 2.

1. Common Layers: These layers include the pretrained language model, which is fine-tuned based on the combined weighted loss of both tasks to extract general features representing shared information between the tasks.

2. Task-Specific Layers: These layers consist of task-specific hidden layers and classification heads, designed to capture unique features for each task. They are fine-tuned based on the individual loss associated with each specific task.

From Figure 1, we can see that the number of aggression instances is almost the same as the combined task instances, while the number of offensive instances is nearly half of the combined task instances. This explains why adding task-specific hidden layers to the offensive task model helps capture task-specific features effectively, whereas adding such layers to the aggression task model leads to overfitting.

4.2 Loss Function

We need two different loss functions to efficiently tune the task specific layers and common layers to capture task specific features and common features respectively.

4.2.1 Individual Loss Function:

Cross-entropy loss is useful in classification tasks, weighted cross-entropy loss is an extension of the standard cross-entropy loss that applies different weights to different classes. This is particularly useful in scenarios where the class distribution is imbalanced, allowing the model to pay more attention to underrepresented classes. The mathematical formulation of weighted cross-entropy loss of a class i with weight W_i is given in Equation 1, the weight vector W_i is given in Equation 2.

$$L_{task}(x_i) = -W_i log\left(\frac{exp(x_i)}{\sum_j exp(x_i)}\right) \quad (1)$$

$$W_i = \frac{N^\circ samples}{N^\circ classes \times Count_i} \quad (2)$$

4.2.2 Overall Loss Function:

After deriving the individual losses of each task, we defined a custom loss function to compute the overall loss as weighted sum of the individual losses L_{agg}(loss of aggression task) and L_{off}(loss of offensive task) with parameter $w_l \in (0, 1)$.

$$Loss(x_i) = [w_l \times L_{agg}(x_i)] + [(1 - w_l) \times L_{off}(x_i)] \quad (3)$$

By adjusting the parameter w_l, we can direct the model to prioritize learning a specific task. Since our primary focus is on optimizing the model to detect offensiveness in the text, we will set the value of w_l accordingly.

5 Experimental Setup

We fine-tune the two tasks using the following pretrained language models: BERT (Devlin et al., 2018), RoBERTa (Liu et al., 2019) which are trained on English data, XLM-RoBERTa (Conneau et al., 2019) which is trained over multilingual data, Hing-RoBERTa (Nayak and Joshi, 2022) a multilingual language model specifically built for Hindi-English code-mixed language as seen in the Indian context. These are the state-of-the-art models chosen by the authors of the dataset to evaluate their dataset.

We perform the experiments using the Huggingface Transformers library (Wolf et al., 2020). We monitor the validation set's macro-F1 scores to find the best hyper-parameter values, using the following range of values for selecting the best hyperparameter:

MODEL	Offensive Language Detection			Aggression Detection		
	Combined	Codemixed	Monolingual	Combined	Codemixed	Monolingual
$BERT_{base}$	75.63	75.77	71.61	57.95	52.29	50.36
MTTL-$BERT_{base}$	79.03(+3.40)	80.78(+5.01)	**79.29(+7.68)**	64.10(+6.15)	63.32(+11.03)	61.48(+11.12)
$RoBERTa_{base}$	76.31	77.66	67.30	60.70	62.44	60.65
MTTL-$RoBERTa_{base}$	79.08(+2.77)	79.15(+1.49)	76.63(+9.33)	63.76(+3.06)	64.60(+2.16)	**64.68(+4.03)**
XLM-R_{base}	76.38	77.91	74.21	60.58	61.25	47.51
MTTL-XLM-R_{base}	76.45(+0.07)	73.61(-4.30)	74.91(+0.70)	64.29(+3.71)	62.07(+0.82)	60.44(+12.93)
Hing-RoBERTa	78.61	77.45	70.92	64.85	61.88	57.77
MTTL-Hing-RoBERTa	**82.03(+3.42)**	**81.61(+4.16)**	76.02(+5.10)	**67.01(+2.16)**	**69.10(+7.22)**	63.99(+6.22)

Table 2: Macro F1-scores obtained from pretrained language models on the dataset and the models augmented with MTTL approach are represented with 'MTTL' as the prefix. The values inside (.) represent the change in Macro-F1 score and the values in **bold** highlight represent the best-performing language model on each category of the dataset.

- w_l: [0.3, 0.4, 0.5, 0.6, 0.7, 0.8]
- No. of task specific hidden layers: [1, 2, 3, 4]
- Batch size: [4, 8, 16, 32]
- Learning rate: [1e-6, 2e-5, 2e-6, 5e-5, 5e-6]
- Number of training epochs: [2, 3, 4]

6 Results

The individual performance of these models on the two tasks, corresponding with codemixed (Hindi+English), monolingual (only English), and combined data (codemixed+monolingual) as input is shown in Table 2 with Macro-F1 as the metric. The performance of the pretrained language models fine-tuned with the MTTL approach is represented with 'MTTL' as the prefix is also shown in Table 2. We only show the results of our best MTTL model on the evaluation set in Table 2. We observed that the MTTL approach shows consistent improvement in almost all cases with MTTL-Hing-RoBERTa outperforming other models with Macro-F1 scores of 82.03%, 81.61% and 76.02% with an improvement of 3.42%, 4.16% and 5.10% respectively on combined, codemixed and monolingual data on offensive language detection and 67.01%, 69.10% and 63.99% with an improvement of 2.16%, 7.22% and 6.22% respectively on combined, codemixed and monolingual data on aggression detection. The results show that not only Hing-RoBERTa but also BERT-base, RoBERTa-base, and XLM-RoBERTa-base models show significant improvements in their performance with the MTTL approach.

6.1 Parameter Analysis

The parameter w_l plays a significant role in the model's performance on each task. The optimal performance of the MTTL model on the aggression task is observed when $0.5 < w_l < 1$, and on the offensive task, is observed when $0 < w_l < 0.5$ because the value of the w_l is indirectly the proportion of importance given to specific task. Note when the value of w_l is not optimal at the extreme value (i.e, 0 and 1) because the model completely learns only one task, nullifying the MTTL effect. We have only shown the results of our best MTTL model on each task with w_l tuned for that specific task in the given range. We explored the use of different numbers of task-specific hidden layers for each independent task to enhance the learning of task-specific features. However, we found that adding these layers to the aggression task led to overfitting on this dataset. Note that we are proposing to not to add any aggression task-specific layers to mitigate the overfitting issues for the given dataset. The model may perform better with task-specific layers for each task on other datasets depending on the dataset's class distribution.

7 Conclusion

Cyberbullying on social media platforms is a significant issue affecting many individuals, with the diverse languages and dialects in India posing a substantial challenge for automated offensive language detection systems. In this paper, we propose a Multi-Task Transfer Learning (MTTL) framework enhanced with pretrained language models like Hing-RoBERTa to efficiently learn multiple tasks and improve performance in detecting aggression and offensive language in Hindi-English code-mixed text. We explored the use of individual weighted loss functions for training task-specific layers and a custom overall loss function for training common layers. Our results demonstrate significant improvements with the MTTL approach over single-task learning across various pretrained language models, including Hing-RoBERTa, BERT, RoBERTa, and XLM-RoBERTa. Notably, MTTL-Hing-RoBERTa outperformed other models on non-monolingual data, while MTTL-BERT and MTTL-RoBERTa showed the best performance on monolingual data.

Limitations

The dataset primarily focuses on Hindi-English code-mixed tweets. While this is appropriate for the specific application, it limits the generalizability of the findings to other code-mixed languages or purely monolingual datasets. The proposed framework relies on pretrained language models such as BERT, RoBERTa, XLM-RoBERTa, and Hing-RoBERTa. These models may carry inherent biases or limitations from their original training data, which could influence their ability to accurately classify aggression and offensive language in a diverse range of contexts.

References

Lu Cheng, Kai Shu, Siqi Wu, Yasin N. Silva, Deborah L. Hall, and Huan Liu. 2020. Unsupervised cyberbullying detection via time-informed gaussian mixture model. In *Proceedings of the 29th ACM International Conference on Information & Knowledge Management*, CIKM '20, page 185–194, New York, NY, USA. Association for Computing Machinery.

Abhishek Chopra, Deepak Kumar Sharma, Aashna Jha, and Uttam Ghosh. 2023. A framework for online hate speech detection on code-mixed hindi-english text and hindi text in devanagari. *ACM Trans. Asian Low-Resour. Lang. Inf. Process.*, 22(5).

Alexis Conneau, Kartikay Khandelwal, Naman Goyal, Vishrav Chaudhary, Guillaume Wenzek, Francisco Guzmán, Edouard Grave, Myle Ott, Luke Zettlemoyer, and Veselin Stoyanov. 2019. Unsupervised cross-lingual representation learning at scale. *CoRR*, abs/1911.02116.

Jacob Devlin, Ming-Wei Chang, Kenton Lee, and Kristina Toutanova. 2018. BERT: pre-training of deep bidirectional transformers for language understanding. *CoRR*, abs/1810.04805.

Marc Djandji, Fady Baly, Wissam Antoun, and Hazem Hajj. 2020. Multi-task learning using AraBert for offensive language detection. In *Proceedings of the 4th Workshop on Open-Source Arabic Corpora and Processing Tools, with a Shared Task on Offensive Language Detection*, pages 97–101, Marseille, France. European Language Resource Association.

Shaun H, Samyuktaa Sivakumar, Rohan R, Nikilesh Jayaguptha, and Durairaj Thenmozhi. 2024. Quartet@LT-EDI 2024: A SVM-ResNet50 approach for multitask meme classification - unraveling misogynistic and trolls in online memes. In *Proceedings of the Fourth Workshop on Language Technology for Equality, Diversity, Inclusion*, pages 221–226, St. Julian's, Malta. Association for Computational Linguistics.

Prashant Kapil and Asif Ekbal. 2020. A deep neural network based multi-task learning approach to hate speech detection. *Knowledge-Based Systems*, 210:106458.

Anant Khandelwal and Niraj Kumar. 2020. A unified system for aggression identification in english code-mixed and uni-lingual texts. In *Proceedings of the 7th ACM IKDD CoDS and 25th COMAD*, CoDS COMAD 2020, page 55–64, New York, NY, USA. Association for Computing Machinery.

Yinhan Liu, Myle Ott, Naman Goyal, Jingfei Du, Mandar Joshi, Danqi Chen, Omer Levy, Mike Lewis, Luke Zettlemoyer, and Veselin Stoyanov. 2019. Roberta: A robustly optimized BERT pretraining approach. *CoRR*, abs/1907.11692.

Guanyi Mou, Pengyi Ye, and Kyumin Lee. 2020. Swe2: Subword enriched and significant word emphasized framework for hate speech detection. In *Proceedings of the 29th ACM International Conference on Information & Knowledge Management*, CIKM '20, page 1145–1154, New York, NY, USA. Association for Computing Machinery.

Nazia Nafis, Diptesh Kanojia, Naveen Saini, and Rudra Murthy. 2023. Towards safer communities: Detecting aggression and offensive language in code-mixed tweets to combat cyberbullying. In *The 7th Workshop on Online Abuse and Harms (WOAH)*, pages 29–41, Toronto, Canada. Association for Computational Linguistics.

Ravindra Nayak and Raviraj Joshi. 2022. L3Cube-HingCorpus and HingBERT: A code mixed Hindi-English dataset and BERT language models. In *Proceedings of the WILDRE-6 Workshop within the 13th Language Resources and Evaluation Conference*, pages 7–12, Marseille, France. European Language Resources Association.

Varsha Pathak, Manish Joshi, Prasad Joshi, Monica Mundada, and Tanmay Joshi. 2021. Kbcnmujal@hasoc-dravidian-codemix-fire2020: Using machine learning for detection of hate speech and offensive code-mixed social media text. *Preprint*, arXiv:2102.09866.

Tharindu Ranasinghe and Marcos Zampieri. 2021. Multilingual offensive language identification for low-resource languages. *ACM Trans. Asian Low-Resour. Lang. Inf. Process.*, 21(1).

Himashi Rathnayake, Janani Sumanapala, Raveesha Rukshani, and Surangika Ranathunga. 2024.

Adapterfusion-based multi-task learning for code-mixed and code-switched text classification. *Engineering Applications of Artificial Intelligence*, 127:107239.

Zuhair Shaik, Sai Kartheek Reddy Kasu, Sunil Saumya, and Shankar Biradar. 2024. IIITDWD-zk@DravidianLangTech-2024: Leveraging the power of language models for hate speech detection in Telugu-English code-mixed text. In *Proceedings of the Fourth Workshop on Speech, Vision, and Language Technologies for Dravidian Languages*, pages 134–139, St. Julian's, Malta. Association for Computational Linguistics.

Adarsh Shrivastava, Rushikesh Pupale, and Pradeep Singh. 2021. Enhancing aggression detection using gpt-2 based data balancing technique. In *2021 5th International Conference on Intelligent Computing and Control Systems (ICICCS)*, pages 1345–1350.

K. Sreelakshmi, B. Premjith, Bharathi Raja Chakravarthi, and K. P. Soman. 2024. Detection of hate speech and offensive language codemix text in dravidian languages using cost-sensitive learning approach. *IEEE Access*, 12:20064–20090.

Thomas Wolf, Lysandre Debut, Victor Sanh, Julien Chaumond, Clement Delangue, Anthony Moi, Pierric Cistac, Tim Rault, Remi Louf, Morgan Funtowicz, Joe Davison, Sam Shleifer, Patrick von Platen, Clara Ma, Yacine Jernite, Julien Plu, Canwen Xu, Teven Le Scao, Sylvain Gugger, Mariama Drame, Quentin Lhoest, and Alexander Rush. 2020. Transformers: State-of-the-art natural language processing. In *Proceedings of the 2020 Conference on Empirical Methods in Natural Language Processing: System Demonstrations*, pages 38–45, Online. Association for Computational Linguistics.

Team IndiDataMiner at IndoNLP 2025: Hindi Back Transliteration - Roman to Devanagari using LLaMa

Saurabh Kumar, Dhruvkumar Babubhai Kakadiya, and Sanasam Ranbir Singh
Department of Computer Science and Engineering
Indian Institute of Technology Guwahati
{saurabh1003, d.kakadiya, ranbir}@iitg.ac.in

Abstract

The increasing use of Romanized typing for Indo-Aryan languages on social media poses challenges due to its lack of standardization and loss of linguistic richness. To address this, we propose a sentence-level back-transliteration approach using the LLaMa 3.1 model for Hindi. Leveraging fine-tuning with the Dakshina dataset, our approach effectively resolves ambiguities in Romanized Hindi text, offering a robust solution for converting it into the native Devanagari script.

1 Introduction

The widespread use of social media platforms and the prevalence of English keyboards have led to a significant rise in the use of Romanized typing for Indo-Aryan languages, primarily for quick and informal communication. However, Romanized text on social media often lacks consistency, with variations in spelling, phonetic representation, and vowel omission. This lack of standardization introduces ambiguity, as the same word can be written in multiple ways, such as नमस्ते (*Namaste*) appearing as *Namste*, *Nmst*, or *Namastey*. Romanized text also involves one-to-many mappings based on context, such as Romanized text *sir* can correspond to सिर (English: head) or सर (English: Sir) based on the context. Such inconsistencies lead to misunderstandings in human communication and errors in NLP applications like machine translation.

In addition to standardization issues, Romanized scripts fail to preserve the linguistic richness and phonetic nuances of native scripts, often losing cultural and linguistic expression. Certain sounds in Hindi and other Indo-Aryan languages lack precise representation in Roman script, resulting in phonetic ambiguities. For example, the Hindi letters ट (retroflex T) and त (dental T) are both commonly written as *T* or *Ta* in Romanized text, ignoring the critical distinction between retroflex and dental sounds in native pronunciation. Similarly, English sounds do not always map neatly to Hindi phonetics. For instance, the English sounds *v* and *w* are often transliterated as व (v), which can be confused with *b*-like sounds such as ब or भ. Such limitations underscore the challenges of relying solely on Romanized text for meaningful communication and accurate linguistic representation.

These challenges emphasize the need for robust back-transliteration systems to convert Romanized Indo-Aryan text into native scripts. Back-transliteration maps Romanized text to its native script based on phonetic representation, addressing the absence of standardization and variability in typing habits. Accurate back-transliteration enhances digital communication by promoting cultural preservation, improving readability, and reducing miscommunication. Furthermore, it facilitates the integration of Romanized content into automated systems such as machine translation, text-to-speech, and text mining, significantly boosting their effectiveness and utility.

Transliteration can be approached at both the word level and the sentence level. Word-level transliteration models often fall short due to their inability to account for contextual information, which is essential for accurately resolving ambiguities in Romanized text. This study explores sentence-level transliteration for Hindi, leveraging the LLaMa 3.1(8B) (Dubey et al., 2024) model. The experiments include both zero-shot learning and fine-tuning approaches. For fine-tuning, the Dakshina dataset (Roark et al., 2020a) is employed.

The fine-tuned LLaMa 3.1 model achieves significant improvements in transliteration accuracy, as demonstrated by the BLEU scores on the Hindi Test dataset . On Test Set 1, the model achieves a BLEU score of 0.8866 for character overlap and 0.6288 for word overlap. On Test Set 2, the BLEU

Proceedings of the First Workshop on Natural Language Processing for Indo-Aryan and Dravidian Languages (IndoNLP2025), pages 129–134
January 20, 2025. ©2025 Association for Computational Linguistics

scores are 0.8176 for character overlap and 0.5105 for word overlap. These results underscore the effectiveness of fine-tuning in improving transliteration performance, providing a robust solution for the challenges associated with Romanized Hindi text conversion.

2 Related Works

In recent years, significant progress has been made in transliteration for Indo-Aryan languages. Notable contributions include Kunchukuttan et al. (2015), who introduced Brahmi-Net, a statistical transliteration system capable of handling script conversion across 18 Indo-Aryan languages, resulting in 306 language pairs, including Hindi. Similarly, Roark et al. (2020b) developed the Dakshina dataset, supporting transliteration and language modeling tasks for 12 South Asian languages written in Roman script, providing a foundational resource for this domain.

Building on these efforts, Kunchukuttan et al. (2021) explored multilingual neural machine transliteration for English and 10 Indian languages, demonstrating the potential of multilingual systems. Another significant milestone is the Aksharantar dataset presented by Madhani et al. (2023), which covers 21 Indian languages and achieved state-of-the-art results using the IndicXlit model. Additionally, Ruder et al. (2023) evaluated sentence-level transliteration across 13 languages, including 12 from the Dakshina dataset and Amharic, using transfer learning models like mT5-Base, ByT5-Base, and FlanPaLM-62B.

Transliteration for informal and social media text has also been addressed in shared tasks organized by the Forum for Information Retrieval (FIRE). For instance, FIRE 2013 and FIRE 2014 (Roy et al., 2013; Choudhury et al., 2014) focused on transliterating Hindi song lyrics written in Roman script, shedding light on the challenges of informal text processing. Transliteration of Romanized Assamese text on social media environment is explored in the study (Baruah et al., 2024b) and recently back transliteration of Romanized Assamese social media text is explored by Baruah et al. (2024a) using BiLSTM, Neural Transformer Model, mT5, and ByT5.

Despite these advancements, existing research does not specifically address the transliteration challenges posed by Romanized social media datasets, characterized by inconsistencies, non-standard typing patterns, and ad-hoc transliterations. This highlights the need for further research tailored to the complexities of social media communication.

Split	Script	#Data	#Word	#Char
Train	Roman	10041	17.50	102.08
	Native	10041	17.50	92.42
Test Set1	Roman	9998	15.30	89.09
	Native	9998	15.30	80.63
Test Set2	Roman	4998	15.29	80.11
	Native	4998	15.28	80.46

Table 1: Statistics of the Training and Testing Dataset. Here **#Data** represents the number of text samples, **#Word** denotes the average number of words per text sample, and **#Char** indicates the average number of characters per text sample.

3 Approach

In this experiment, we focus on training a back-transliteration model to convert Romanized Hindi text into Devanagari script using a sentence-level model. The architecture used is the LLaMa 3.1 model, which is fine-tuned using a pre-defined set of instructions and inputs. The model training process includes both zero-shot and fine-tuning techniques to enhance the model's transliteration capabilities. The code for training is available at this GitHub repo[1].

3.1 Dataset

For training our model, we use the Dakshina dataset(Roark et al., 2020a), which provides a transliteration parallel corpus of 12 Indian languages, including Hindi. All the samples whose lengths are greater than 100 words are manually broken into smaller sentences. For the testing, we have used the two sets of the dataset provided in the shared task[2]. The statistics of the Hindi dataset used for our training are tabulated in Table 1. The romanized text in Test Set 2 has most of the sample with the vowel omission. The same is reflected in Table 1 as well. The average character count for romanized text in Test Set 2 is less than that of Test Set 1. The word distribution of each dataset is shown in Fig. 1. It is observed that most of

[1] https://github.com/saurabhdbz/LlaMa_Translit

[2] IndoNLP Workshop 2025: https://indonlp-workshop.github.io/IndoNLP-Workshop/

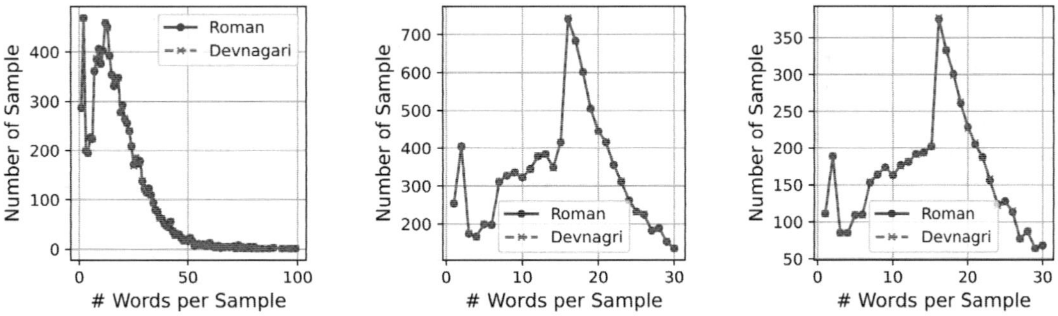

(a) Train Set (b) Test Set-1 (c) Test Set-2

Figure 1: Word distribution of the Training and the Testing dataset

the samples in training data fall under the sample length of 50 words, and for the testing data, the sample length is limited to 30 words.

The dataset is formatted to fit the Alpaca prompt structure, where the instruction is to transliterate the Romanized Hindi input back into Devanagari script. The dataset is processed by creating training examples that combine instructions, inputs, and outputs, with the end-of-sequence token (EOS) added to each instance to guide the model in generating complete sequences. The fixed instruction, *"Transliterate the given Romanized Hindi text back to Devanagari script."* is consistently used across both the training and testing phases.

3.2 Model Architecture

The foundation of our system is the LLaMA 3.1 8B model (Dubey et al., 2024), a large-scale transformer-based architecture with 8 billion parameters. This model is multilingual and supports a significantly extended context length of 128K, making it suitable for advanced use cases such as long-form text summarization, multilingual conversational agents, and coding assistants. The fine-tuned variant of LLaMA employed in this work is optimized for causal language modeling and enhanced with Low-Rank Adaptation (LoRA) and 4-bit quantization. LoRA is applied with a rank of 16, enabling efficient adaptation by training lightweight low-rank matrices while freezing the original model weights, significantly reducing the number of trainable parameters. The model consists of 32 decoder layers, each comprising self-attention and feedforward modules. All projections (query, key, value, and output) within the self-attention mechanism leverage low-rank matrices, with rotary embeddings incorporated for positional encoding. The use of 4-bit quantization further minimizes memory and computational overhead, making the model highly efficient for resource-constrained environments while maintaining its performance quality.

3.3 Training Method

The training process utilizes the `SFTTrainer` class from the `trl` library, designed explicitly for supervised fine-tuning of language models. To improve memory efficiency, we integrated the Unsloth[3] framework, which supports 4-bit quantization by loading the pre-trained model in a compressed format. This approach accelerates training and inference while significantly reducing the memory footprint.

The model is fine-tuned for one epoch with a batch size of 2, using gradient accumulation steps set to 4 to manage the training of the large model size. The learning rate was configured to 2×10^{-4}, and the AdamW optimizer was employed with 8-bit precision to further reduce memory usage. Additionally, the training process incorporated a warm-up phase followed by linear learning rate decay to ensure stable convergence.

3.4 Back-transliteration

We employ both the pre-trained LLaMa model and the fine-tuned model to perform back-transliteration of Romanized Hindi text. In both cases, the same prompt, i.e. *"Transliterate the given Romanized Hindi text back to Devanagari script."* is used. During text generation in both cases, the default temperature value of 1.0 is used, which strikes a balance between randomness and

[3]Unsloth: https://github.com/unslothai/unsloth

Model	Test Set 1				Test Set 2			
	WER	CER	BLUE$_C$	BLUE$_W$	WER	CER	BLUE$_C$	BLUE$_W$
IndicXlit	0.4552	0.1785	0.7319	0.2505	0.5320	0.2313	0.6567	0.1689
LLaMa3.1	0.2154	0.0881	0.8675	0.5996	0.2851	0.1339	0.8029	0.4879
Proposed	**0.1892**	**0.0684**	**0.8866**	**0.6288**	**0.2640**	**0.1183**	**0.8176**	**0.5105**

Table 2: Model performance on both test sets, evaluated using Word Error Rate (WER), Character Error Rate (CER), BLEU score for character overlap (BLEU$_C$), and BLEU score for word overlap (BLEU$_W$). The proposed model is the fine-tuned version of LLaMa 3.1.

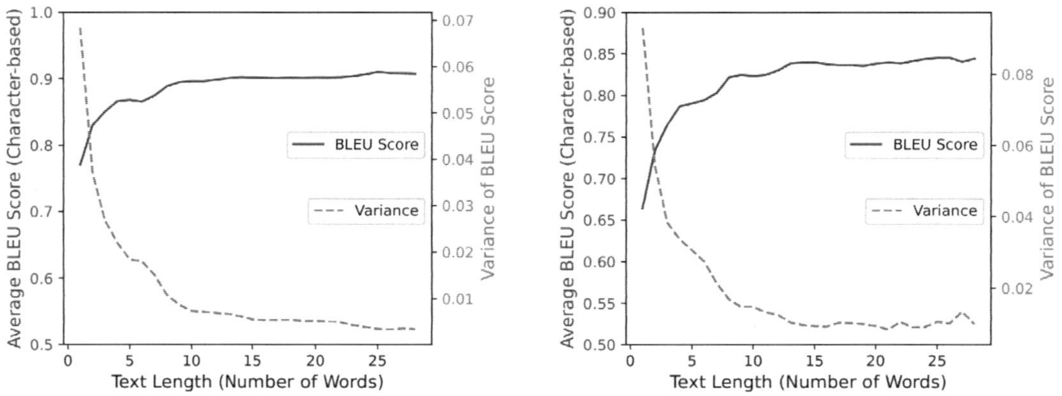

(a)Performance on Test Set-1 (b)Performance on Test Set-2

Figure 2: Average BLEU score and the variance of the BLUE score across different text lengths of the sample from both Test Set 1 and Test Set 2.

determinism, ensuring natural and coherent output.

4 Results and Discussion

We evaluate the model's performance in two scenarios: a zero-shot setting, where responses are generated directly from the pre-trained model using prompts, and after the model fine-tuning, by analyzing its responses on two test datasets: Test Set 1 and Test Set 2. The performance metrics include Word Error Rate (WER), Character Error Rate (CER), and BLEU score.

For the BLEU score, we compute two distinct types of overlap: Character-Level Overlap and Word-Level (or Token-Level) Overlap. The BLEU score for Character-Level Overlap evaluates the precision of individual characters in the generated output compared to the reference, making it particularly useful for fine-grained tasks such as transliteration. On the other hand, the BLEU score for Word-Level Overlap measures the precision of word-level tokens in the generated output, which is more suited for tasks emphasizing semantic accuracy and fluency. The BLEU score is calculated by assigning equal weight to unigrams, bigrams, trigrams, and fourgrams to ensure a balanced evaluation across different n-gram levels.

We compare our model against IndicXlit (Madhani et al., 2023), considering it as baseline. It is a transformer-based state-of-the-art multilingual transliteration model with 11 million parameters, supporting 21 Indian languages for Roman-to-native and native-to-Roman script conversions. Using IndicXlit, the Romanized Hindi text was converted into Devanagari and compared with the outputs of our trained models.

Table 2 summarizes the performance of the models on Test Set 1 and Test Set 2. The pre-trained LLaMa model outperforms the baseline IndicXlit model on both test sets, achieving significant reductions in WER and CER. On Test Set 1, the WER and CER are reduced by 24% and 9%, respectively, while on Test Set 2, the reductions are 25% and 10%, respectively. Additionally, the Character-Level BLEU score shows a gain of 13%, and the Word-Level BLEU score improves by 34% on Test Set 1, with similar improvements observed on Test Set 2.

The fine-tuned model demonstrates the best performance overall. On Test Set 1, it achieves a WER of 18.92% and a CER of 6.84%. For BLEU scores, the fine-tuned model achieves 88.66% for Character-Level Overlap and 62.88% for Word-Level Overlap, representing gains of 15.47% and 37.83%, respectively. Similarly, on Test Set 2, the model significantly reduces the WER and CER by 41.37% and 11.3%, respectively, compared to the IndicXlit baseline. Furthermore, it achieves a BLEU score of 81.76% on Character-Level Overlap for Test Set 2, underscoring its effectiveness in transliteration tasks.

Additionally, we analyze the relationship between text length and model performance by plotting line graphs of the average BLEU score and its variance against text length for both Test Set 1 and Test Set 2, as shown in Fig. 2. From the graphs, we observe that the model's performance remains relatively consistent for texts longer than 8 words across both test sets. However, a slightly higher variance in BLEU scores for smaller text indicates that the model's performance is less stable on text of smaller length.

5 Conclusion and Future Work

This paper addresses the challenges of back-transliteration of Romanized Hindi text, which often suffers from inconsistencies in spelling, phonetic representation, and the omission of vowels. We explore the use of the LLaMa 3.1 (8B) model for back-transliteration, employing both prompting and fine-tuning methods. For fine-tuning, the Dakshina dataset was utilized. Our results demonstrate significant improvements in transliteration accuracy, as measured by Word Error Rate (WER), Character Error Rate (CER), and BLEU score, providing an effective solution for handling the variability in Romanized text and enhancing the performance of NLP applications such as machine translation and text mining.

In future work, we plan to extend our approach to other Indo-Aryan languages, incorporating larger and more diverse datasets. We also aim to refine the model to handle even greater text variability and improve transliteration accuracy further. Additionally, exploring domain-specific adaptations and integrating the model into real-time applications will be key directions for advancing back-transliteration systems in the future.

Limitations

This work is primarily limited to the Hindi language and focuses on more structured text. The training data used for model development lacks the nuances of social media text, such as abbreviations, short forms, and vowel omissions. As a result, the model's performance declines for shorter sentences and on datasets like Test Set 2, which include texts with vowel omissions.

Additionally, the study is restricted to transformer-based models, specifically the encoder-decoder architecture and the LLaMa model. While large language models (LLMs) like LLaMa demonstrate superior performance, their significant size makes them less suitable for deployment on resource-constrained devices, such as mobile phones, for real-time transliteration. To address this, future work should explore model compression techniques to reduce the computational footprint and enhance applicability in such environments.

References

Hemanta Baruah, Sanasam Ranbir Singh, and Priyankoo Sarmah. 2024a. AssameseBackTranslit: Back transliteration of Romanized Assamese social media text. In *Proceedings of the 2024 Joint International Conference on Computational Linguistics, Language Resources and Evaluation (LREC-COLING 2024)*, pages 1627–1637, Torino, Italia. ELRA and ICCL.

Hemanta Baruah, Sanasam Ranbir Singh, and Priyankoo Sarmah. 2024b. Transliteration characteristics in romanized assamese language social media text and machine transliteration. *ACM Trans. Asian Low-Resour. Lang. Inf. Process.*, 23(2).

Monojit Choudhury, Gokul Chittaranjan, Parth Gupta, and Amitava Das. 2014. Overview of fire 2014 track on transliterated search. *Proceedings of FIRE*, pages 68–89.

Abhimanyu Dubey, Abhinav Jauhri, Abhinav Pandey, Abhishek Kadian, Ahmad Al-Dahle, Aiesha Letman, Akhil Mathur, Alan Schelten, Amy Yang, Angela Fan, et al. 2024. The llama 3 herd of models. *arXiv preprint arXiv:2407.21783*.

Anoop Kunchukuttan, Siddharth Jain, and Rahul Kejriwal. 2021. A large-scale evaluation of neural machine transliteration for Indic languages. In *Proceedings of the 16th Conference of the European Chapter of the Association for Computational Linguistics:*

Main Volume, pages 3469–3475, Online. Association for Computational Linguistics.

Anoop Kunchukuttan, Ratish Puduppully, and Pushpak Bhattacharyya. 2015. Brahmi-net: A transliteration and script conversion system for languages of the indian subcontinent. In *Proceedings of the 2015 conference of the North American chapter of the association for computational linguistics: demonstrations*, pages 81–85.

Yash Madhani, Sushane Parthan, Priyanka Bedekar, Gokul Nc, Ruchi Khapra, Anoop Kunchukuttan, Pratyush Kumar, and Mitesh Khapra. 2023. Aksharantar: Open Indic-language transliteration datasets and models for the next billion users. In *Findings of the Association for Computational Linguistics: EMNLP 2023*, pages 40–57, Singapore. Association for Computational Linguistics.

Brian Roark, Lawrence Wolf-Sonkin, Christo Kirov, Sabrina J Mielke, Cibu Johny, Isin Demirsahin, and Keith Hall. 2020a. Processing south asian languages written in the latin script: the dakshina dataset. *arXiv preprint arXiv:2007.01176*.

Brian Roark, Lawrence Wolf-Sonkin, Christo Kirov, Sabrina J. Mielke, Cibu Johny, Isin Demirsahin, and Keith Hall. 2020b. Processing South Asian languages written in the Latin script: the Dakshina dataset. In *Proceedings of the Twelfth Language Resources and Evaluation Conference*, pages 2413–2423, Marseille, France. European Language Resources Association.

Rishiraj Saha Roy, Monojit Choudhury, Prasenjit Majumder, and Komal Agarwal. 2013. Overview of the fire 2013 track on transliterated search. In *Proceedings of the 4th and 5th Annual Meetings of the Forum for Information Retrieval Evaluation*, FIRE '12 & '13, New York, NY, USA. Association for Computing Machinery.

Sebastian Ruder, Jonathan Clark, Alexander Gutkin, Mihir Kale, Min Ma, Massimo Nicosia, Shruti Rijhwani, Parker Riley, Jean-Michel Sarr, Xinyi Wang, John Wieting, Nitish Gupta, Anna Katanova, Christo Kirov, Dana Dickinson, Brian Roark, Bidisha Samanta, Connie Tao, David Adelani, Vera Axelrod, Isaac Caswell, Colin Cherry, Dan Garrette, Reeve Ingle, Melvin Johnson, Dmitry Panteleev, and Partha Talukdar. 2023. XTREME-UP: A user-centric scarce-data benchmark for under-represented languages. In *Findings of the Association for Computational Linguistics: EMNLP 2023*, pages 1856–1884, Singapore. Association for Computational Linguistics.

IndoNLP 2025 Shared Task: Romanized Sinhala to Sinhala Reverse Transliteration Using BERT

Sameera Perera[1], Lahiru Prabhath[2], T.G.D.K. Sumanathilaka[3], Isuri Anuradha[4]

[1]Informatics Institute of Technology, Colombo 006, Sri Lanka
[2]Techlabs Global (PVT) LTD, 9-B Horton Place, Colombo 007, Sri Lanka
[3]Swansea University, Wales, UK
[4]Lancaster University, UK
Correspondence: sameeraperera827@gmail.com

Abstract

The Romanized text has become popular with the growth of digital communication platforms, largely due to the familiarity with English keyboards. In Sri Lanka, Romanized Sinhala, commonly referred to as "Singlish" is widely used in digital communications. This paper introduces a novel context-aware back-transliteration system designed to address the ad-hoc typing patterns and lexical ambiguity inherent in Singlish. The proposed system combines dictionary-based mapping for Singlish words, a rule-based transliteration for out-of-vocabulary words and a BERT-based language model for addressing lexical ambiguities. Evaluation results demonstrate the robustness of the proposed approach, achieving high BLEU scores along with low Word Error Rate (WER) and Character Error Rate (CER) across test datasets. This study provides an effective solution for Romanized Sinhala back-transliteration and establishes the foundation for improving NLP tools for similar low-resourced languages.

1 Introduction

The rapid growth of digital communication platforms such as social media and messaging platforms has revolutionized communication with the use of informal, Romanized representations of native scripts. Sinhala is a morphologically rich language where approximately 17 million Sri Lankans (around 87% of the total population) use it as their main language for communication(De Silva, 2019). Many Sinhala speakers use Romanized Sinhala, often referred to as "Singlish", instead of the native script on digital communication platforms due to the convenience of using English keyboards. However, Singlish is non-standardized, leading to variations in spelling and structure, which pose challenges for back-transliteration. The process of back-transliteration into native script has become crucial for NLP applications such as machine translation, information retrieval and sentiment analysis. However, the following challenges make this task complex:

- Ad-hoc Nature: Singlish text often follows informal typing patterns such as vowel omissions, further complicating back-transliteration. For an instance the word "තාත්තා" can be represented as "*Thaaththaa, Thaththa, Thattha, Thatta, Tatta*".
- Lexical Ambiguity: A single Romanized form may correspond to multiple words in the native Sinhala script, depending on the context. The word *"Adaraya"* can be back transliterated to "ආදරය, ආධාරය".

A system capable of handling the typing variations, ambiguity, and contextual dependencies inherent in Singlish is required to address these challenges. Back-transliteration is a greater challenge than forward-transliteration because it requires context awareness (Nanayakkara et al., 2022). This paper introduces a novel context-aware back-transliteration system for Romanized Sinhala leveraging a hybrid approach that combines:

1. Dictionary-Based Mapping: To handle common and ambiguous words using an ad-hoc transliteration dictionary.
2. Rule-Based Techniques: For out-of-vocabulary words based on Sinhala phonetic patterns.
3. Contextual Disambiguation: Using a BERT model to resolve ambiguities by analyzing sentence-level context.

The proposed approach enables the system to handle various typing patterns in Romanized Sinhala. Experimental results demonstrate the system's effectiveness in achieving high BLEU scores,

Proceedings of the First Workshop on Natural Language Processing for Indo-Aryan and Dravidian Languages (IndoNLP2025), pages 135–140
January 20, 2025. ©2025 Association for Computational Linguistics

low Word Error Rates (WER) and low Character Error Rates (WER) on benchmark datasets. This work significantly contributes to the field of backward transliteration in NLP by addressing the existing challenges in back transliteration.

The following sections provide a comprehensive overview of the related works and the system's methodology, evaluate its performance on real-world datasets, and discuss its limitations.

2 Related Works

Back-transliteration of Romanized Sinhala has been the focus of several studies exploring various approaches including rule-based, statistical, and neural approaches. Below are some recent studies on Singlish backward transliteration. In 2018, the Sinhala Language Decoder by Vidanaralage et al. (2018) introduced a rule-based transliteration method as part of their work where Romanized input text is processed using transliteration and phoneme rule bases. However, the system struggles with handling lexical ambiguity and some English proper nouns because of the static nature of its rule base. These limitations have restricted its ability to handle the informal typing patterns of Romanized Sinhala. In 2019, Priyadarshani et al. (2019) proposed a statistical machine translation (SMT) approach to transliterate personal names across Sinhala, Tamil, and English. Since the personal name transliteration depends on the ethnicity of the name, they employed ethnicity-specific models, achieving BLEU scores of more than 89% for all language pairs. This was implemented with a classification followed by the Naive Bayes algorithm. The reason for selecting the SMT approach instead of a neural approach is that NMT lacks robustness in translating rare words, and it requires a large amount of parallel data to train the model to achieve better results than SMT.

In 2020, a combination of Trigram and Rule-based Models was proposed by Liwera and Ranathunga (2020). This hybrid approach integrated trigram models with rule-based methods to transliterate Romanized Sinhala. The trigram model was trained on Singlish YouTube comments and their corresponding Sinhala transliteration. A rule-based approach was used to handle situations where the tri-gram model could not predict the Sinhala transliteration of Singlish words. However, the system occasionally fails to deliver the correct transliteration of a word due to ambiguities. Silva and Ahangama (2021) proposed another rule-based approach for Romanized Sinhala backward transliteration in 2021. The accuracy of the rule-based approach was further improved by using an error correction module which compares a news corpus from popular news sites. In 2022, a context-aware back-transliteration for Romanized Sinhala presented a neural machine translation approach (an encoder-decoder model) based on Bidirectional LSTM and LSTM architectures (Nanayakkara et al., 2022). The study presented a transliteration unit approach considering the context of characters in a word. This system also failed to handle sentence-level word disambiguation as it focuses on the context of the characters present in a word.

A back transliteration system which can handle informal shorthand Romanized Sinhala was proposed by Sumanathilaka et al. (2023). A statistical trigram model combined with a rule-based approach for back transliteration and a knowledge base with Trie data structure for word suggestions was used in the work. The proposed system achieved 0.84 word-level accuracy. This proposed architecture has been further extended for Tamil by (Mudiyanselage and Sumanathilaka, 2024), showing the generalizability of the proposed model. However, lexical ambiguity correction (word sense disambiguation) and code-mixed Romanized Sinhala remain a persistent issue in these approaches. Athukorala and Sumanathilaka (2024) proposed a novel approach which combines rule-based methods and fuzzy logic to transliterate Romanized Sinhala to native script even when vowels are omitted. It introduced a new numeric coding system to use with the Singlish letters by matching the identified typing patterns. For the mapping process, they have developed a fuzzy logic-based implementation. However, the system performs at the word level and does not handle lexical ambiguities. In 2024, Dharmasiri and Sumanathilaka (2024) proposed a GRU-based NMT model for Singlish backward transliteration. This system combined rule-based techniques with neural machine translation to address the complexities of Romanized Sinhala. A suggestion algorithm has eliminated word selection ambiguity by choosing word suggestions from a pool of predicted words. BLEU scores reaching 0.8 indicate the high word-level transliteration accuracy of the proposed model. Though many Romonized Sinhala to Sinhala transliterators have been introduced, there still exists a gap in the availability of an effective reverse transliterator, which

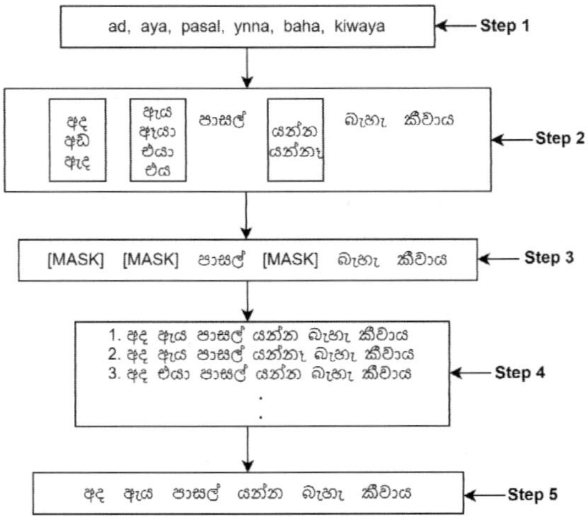

Figure 1: Transliteration Flow

needs context awareness to handle ambiguity.

3 Methodology

The proposed context-aware transliteration system is developed through a series of systematic steps to transliterate Romanized Sinhala text into native Sinhala script, ensuring accurate and contextually appropriate output even while dealing with lexical ambiguity and ad hoc typing patterns. The methodology consists of five key steps, as described below.

3.1 Word Separation

The first step involves breaking down the input Singlish sentence into individual words, enabling a word-level transliteration. This step facilitates word-level mapping and processing in subsequent steps.

3.2 Word-Level Mapping with Ad-hoc Transliteration Dictionary

After the input text is broken down into words, each Singlish word is mapped to its corresponding Sinhala words using an ad-hoc transliteration dictionary[1]. This dictionary includes ad-hoc Singlish words along with their corresponding Sinhala words. Because of the informal nature of Romanized Sinhala, a single Singlish word can often represent multiple Sinhala words (Sumanathilaka et al., 2024). Therefore, the dictionary provides multiple mappings for ambiguous words, retaining all possibilities to handle lexical ambiguity in the next step. If a Singlish word is not found in the transliteration dictionary, the system uses a rule-based approach to convert it into Sinhala script. This rule-based transliteration leverages predefined mappings between Romanized inputs and corresponding Sinhala characters, considering Sinhala phonetic patterns, consonant-vowel combinations, and special cases for modifiers.

3.3 Initial Sentence Assembly with Masked Tokens

After the word level translation using the dictionary and rule-based approach, the corresponding Sinhala sentence is formed by combining those transliterated Sinhala words. If any Singlish word is ambiguous (meaning it maps to multiple Sinhala words), it is replaced by a "[MASK]" token in the sentence. "[MASK]" token denotes that the correct Sinhala word is yet to be selected based on context. For each masked position, a list of candidate Sinhala words is stored, maintaining all possible interpretations of the ambiguous Romanized word. This intermediate step allows for context-aware word selection in the next step.

3.4 Context-Aware Lexical Disambiguation Using BERT

This step resolves lexical ambiguity by replacing the "[MASK]" tokens from the previous step with the most contextually appropriate words. This process involves two main sub-steps: candidate sentence generation and sentence scoring using BERT.In the first phase of this step, all possible sentences are generated by filling each "[MASK]" with different combinations of candidate words stored from the previous step. Then ,each generated sentence is scored using a BERT model configured for Masked Language Modeling (MLM). The goal of this scoring is to determine the most contextually appropriate sentence. Given the context, the score is calculated based on the probability of each candidate word appearing in the masked positions. To illustrate this process, let's walk through the score calculation for an example sentence in Figure 1.

sentence: "අද ඇය පාසල් යන්න බැහැ කීවාය"

Score(sentence) = P("අද"| context) × P ("ඇය"| context) × P ("යන්න"| context)

Each probability P (w | context) represents the likelihood of a candidate word appearing in its respective masked position, given the context provided by the rest of the sentence. The example of

[1] https://www.kaggle.com/datasets/tgdeshank/wsd-romanized-sinhala-dataset?select=WSD+Romanized-Sinhala+-+Sinhala+.txt

calculation for P (“අද” | context) is done as below:

- Mask the Target Word: Replace “අද” in the sentence with a [MASK] token to create a partially masked sentence: “[MASK] ඇය පාසල් යන්න බැහැ කීවාය”

- Pass the Sentence to BERT: Feed the masked sentence into the BERT model and get the generated logits for mask position. These logits represent the model’s unnormalized confidence levels for each vocabulary word in the masked slot based on the sentence context.

- Apply Softmax Activation: Convert the logits into probabilities by applying the softmax activation function. Softmax normalizes the logits to create a probability distribution over all possible words for the [MASK] position.

- Retrieve the Probability for “අද”: From the probability distribution, get the probability assigned to the word “අද” in the context of the sentence.

- Repeat for Remaining Masked Words: follow a similar process for “ඇය” and “යන්න” by masking each respective word in the sentence and calculating its probability in context.

3.5 Output Generation

Finally, the sentence representing the highest score from step 4 is returned as the transliterated Sinhala text. Following the example discussed above for the romanized Sinhala sentence *"ad aya pasal ynna baha kiwaya"* is transliterated to “අද ඇය පාසල් යන්න බැහැ කීවාය” as the output following the above approach.

4 Challenges and Solutions

The primary challenge of the proposed transliteration approach was the time consumption for processing long sentences containing highly ambiguous words. In the proposed transliteration approach, the major factor contributing to time consumption is the number of model inferences required for disambiguation. Two key aspects that influence the number of model inferences:

- High ambiguity words: Singlish words with high lexical ambiguity may represent multiple Sinhala words. This increases the number of candidate words for each ambiguous Singlish word. Consequently, the number of possible sentences generated in step 4 also increases, leading to an increase in the required model inferences.

- Number of ambiguous words: An increase in the number of ambiguous words in the input text also influences the number of model inferences as it directly increases the number of possible sentences generated in Step 4.

Two strategies were developed to reduce the processing time while maintaining accuracy, as described in section 4.1 and 4.2.

4.1 Reducing the Number of Candidate Words for Ambiguous Words Using a Filtering Mechanism

As the initial step of the reverse transliteration process, the candidate word generation occurs as illustrated in step 2 of Figure 1. This step used the Swa-bhasha dictionary, which contains the possible interpretation of the Sinhala word in Ad hoc Romanized Sinhala format. For highly ambiguous Singlish words, the dictionary often provides many Sinhala candidates. To reduce the candidate list size, the vocabulary associated with the model tokenizer is considered so that any candidate words extracted from the dictionary that are not present in the tokenizer’s vocabulary are removed from the candidate list.

4.2 Chunking Sentences Based on the Number of BERT Calls

A chunking mechanism is applied to sentences which contain at least three ambiguous words (masks) to reduce the number of model inferences (BERT calls). Chunking is performed while ensuring that each chunk contains at least three mask tokens. The process involves the following steps:

- Starting from the beginning of the sentence, it calculates the required number of model inferences for the first three ambiguous words (or “masks”).

- If the BERT call count for the first three masks is under 20 (as our analysis showed that 20 BERT calls take approximately 1 second), the next ambiguous word is added to the chunk (adding a fourth mask) and recalculate the BERT call count for the first four masks.

Figure 2: Transliteration Flow

- This process continues, adding one mask at a time and recalculating until the BERT call count exceeds 20.
- When the number of BERT calls exceeds 20, the words processed so far and the words up to the next mask are taken as a chunk.
- The next chunk starts with a two-mask overlap, including the last two ambiguous words (masks) from the previous chunk, and also includes the words after the third mask from the end of the previous chunk. This ensures the retention of unambiguous words in the new chunk to maintain the context.

Figure 2 illustrates the chunking process with an example: Assume the number of BERT calls required for processing the first three ambiguous words (MASK1, MASK2 and MASK3) is 15, which is below 20 (as 20 BERT calls take approximately 1 second). Therefore, the system includes the next ambiguous word, "MASK4", and recalculates the number of BERT calls for the first four masks (MASK1, MASK2, MASK3 and MASK4). Suppose the number of BERT calls for the first four masks is 30, which is higher than 20. As a result, the system creates the first chunk, which includes all words up to "MASK5" but excludes "MASK5" itself. The second chunk begins from the word "ගෙදර" which follows the third mask ("MASK2") from the end of the previous chunk. Then, the number of BERT calls for the first three masks (MASK3, MASK4, MASK5) of this new chunk is calculated. Assume the number of BERT calls for the first three masks of this chunk is 25, which is higher than 20. As a result, this second chunk spans from "ගෙදර" to "සනීප". Then, the third chunk starts from the word "බැහැ" which follows the third mask ("MASK3") from the end of the second chunk.

5 Result Evaluation and Discussion

For the baseline evaluation, a BERT model trained on Sinhala data sources for mask language modelling from Hugging Face (model 1[2]) was used to develop the proposed back transliteration system. Then, it was further fine-tuned using native Sinhala script data in the Dakshina dataset (Roark et al., 2020). The training hyperparameters were used during fine tuning (model 2[3]): learning-rate: 5e-05, train-batch-size: 64, eval-batch-size=16, num-epochs: 12.

Metric	Test Set 1	Test Set 2
Model 1: Sinhala BERT		
WER	0.0886	0.0914
CER	0.0200	0.0212
BLEU-1	0.9115	0.9088
BLEU-2	0.8718	0.8686
BLEU-3	0.8488	0.8452
BLEU-4	0.7963	0.7917
Model 2: Fine-tuned BERT		
WER	0.0850	0.0895
CER	0.0194	0.0210
BLEU-1	0.9151	0.9107
BLEU-2	0.8760	0.8699
BLEU-3	0.8526	0.8459
BLEU-4	0.8001	0.7916

Table 1: Evaluation Results

The evaluation was based on the validation test sets[4] provided by the INDONLP 2025 shared task organizers [5]. The test sets 1 and 2 contained 10000 and 5000 data records, respectively. Test set 2 mainly consists of Romanized Sinhala samples in ad hoc format where vowels were omitted in its Romanized presentation. The proposed system was evaluated using Word Error Rate (WER), Character Error Rate (CER) and BLEU scores. WER and CER measure the percentage of word-level errors and character-level errors, respectively. BLEU scores assess the similarity between the output of the system and the reference text, considering both precision and fluency across n-grams. Higher BLEU scores and Lower WER and CER values indicate better performance. The obtained results were compared between the two BERT models (Model 1 and Model 2) as shown in Table 1. According to the results, the fine-tuned model showed bet-

[2] https://huggingface.co/Ransaka/sinhala-bert-medium-v2

[3] https://huggingface.co/Sameera827/Sinhala-BERT-MLM

[4] https://github.com/IndoNLP-Workshop/IndoNLP-2025-Shared-Task

[5] https://indonlp-workshop.github.io/IndoNLP-Workshop/sharedTask/

ter results overall, but Model 1 was only 0.0001 higher in the BLEU-4 score. Overall, the results demonstrate that the model performs well in handling both ad-hoc transliteration scenarios (without vowels) and normal scenarios (with vowels) for the back-transliteration of Romanized Sinhala.

6 Conclusion

The proposed context-aware back-transliteration approach effectively converts Romanized Sinhala text into native Sinhala script, addressing the challenges of ad-hoc typing patterns and lexical ambiguity inherent in Romanized Sinhala back-transliteration. Evaluation results demonstrate the robustness of the proposed approach, achieving high BLEU scores along with low Word Error Rate (WER) and Character Error Rate (CER) across test datasets. The codebase can be accessed through the link below for further research in this area. GitHub link: https://github.com/Sameera2001Perera/Singlish-Transliterator

Limitations

While the proposed back-transliteration approach demonstrates significant accuracy, it has several limitations. As described earlier, the system can take time to transliterate long sentences containing highly ambiguous words. Although candidate word reduction and chunking mechanisms somewhat mitigate this issue, real-time applications may still face challenges in maintaining efficiency. The word-level transliteration relies on an ad-hoc Romanized Sinhala–Sinhala dictionary. If a Singlish word is not found in the transliteration dictionary, those words are handled using a rule-based approach. However, this rule-based method is not designed to handle ad-hoc typing patterns.

References

Maneesha U. Athukorala and Deshan K. Sumanathilaka. 2024. Swa Bhasha: Message-Based Singlish to Sinhala Transliteration. *arXiv preprint*. Version Number: 1.

Nisansa De Silva. 2019. Survey on publicly available sinhala natural language processing tools and research. *arXiv preprint arXiv:1906.02358*.

Sachithya Dharmasiri and T.G.D.K. Sumanathilaka. 2024. Swa Bhasha 2.0: Addressing Ambiguities in Romanized Sinhala to Native Sinhala Transliteration Using Neural Machine Translation. In *2024 4th International Conference on Advanced Research in Computing (ICARC)*, pages 241–246, Belihuloya, Sri Lanka. IEEE.

W.M.P. Liwera and L. Ranathunga. 2020. Combination of Trigram and Rule-based Model for Singlish to Sinhala Transliteration by Focusing Social Media Text. In *2020 From Innovation to Impact (FITI)*, pages 1–5, Colombo, Sri Lanka. IEEE.

Anuja Dilrukshi Herath Herath Mudiyanselage and TG Deshan K Sumanathilaka. 2024. Tam□□: Shorthand romanized tamil to tamil reverse transliteration using novel hybrid approach. *The International Journal on Advances in ICT for Emerging Regions*, 17(1).

Rushan Nanayakkara, Thilini Nadungodage, and Randil Pushpananda. 2022. Context Aware Back-Transliteration from English to Sinhala. In *2022 22nd International Conference on Advances in ICT for Emerging Regions (ICTer)*, pages 051–056, Colombo, Sri Lanka. IEEE.

H.S. Priyadarshani, M.D.W. Rajapaksha, M.M.S.P. Ranasinghe, K. Sarveswaran, and G.V. Dias. 2019. Statistical Machine Learning for Transliteration: Transliterating names between Sinhala, Tamil and English. In *2019 International Conference on Asian Language Processing (IALP)*, pages 244–249.

Brian Roark, Lawrence Wolf-Sonkin, Christo Kirov, Sabrina J. Mielke, Cibu Johny, Isin Demirsahin, and Keith Hall. 2020. Processing South Asian Languages Written in the Latin Script: the Dakshina Dataset. *arXiv preprint*. Version Number: 1.

Lahiru de Silva and Supunmali Ahangama. 2021. Singlish to Sinhala Transliteration using Rule-based Approach. In *2021 IEEE 16th International Conference on Industrial and Information Systems (ICIIS)*, pages 162–167, Kandy, Sri Lanka. IEEE.

Deshan Sumanathilaka, Nicholas Micallef, and Ruvan Weerasinghe. 2024. Swa-Bhasha Dataset: Romanized Sinhala to Sinhala Adhoc Transliteration Corpus. In *2024 4th International Conference on Advanced Research in Computing (ICARC)*, pages 189–194, Belihuloya, Sri Lanka. IEEE.

T.G.D.K. Sumanathilaka, Ruvan Weerasinghe, and Y.H.P.P. Priyadarshana. 2023. Swa-Bhasha: Romanized Sinhala to Sinhala Reverse Transliteration using a Hybrid Approach. In *2023 3rd International Conference on Advanced Research in Computing (ICARC)*, pages 136–141, Belihuloya, Sri Lanka. IEEE.

A.J. Vidanaralage, A.U. Illangakoon, S.Y. Sumanaweera, C. Pavithra, and S. Thelijjagoda. 2018. Sinhala Language Decoder. In *2018 National Information Technology Conference (NITC)*, pages 1–5, Colombo. IEEE.

Author Index

Association for Computational Linguistics
209 N. Eighth Street
Stroudsburg, Pennsylvania 18360

ISBN 979-8-3313-1369-2

9 798331 313692

CURRAN ASSOCIATES INC.
proceedings.com